TEACH YOURSELF BOOKS

SERBO-CROAT

A COMPLETE COURSE FOR BEGINNERS

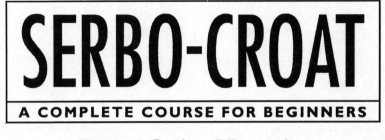

SERBO-CROAT

A COMPLETE COURSE FOR BEGINNERS

David A. Norris

TEACH YOURSELF BOOKS

For UK orders: please contact Bookpoint Ltd, 130 Milton Park, Abingdon, Oxon OX14 4SB. Telephone: (44) 01235 827720. Fax: (44) 01235 400454. Lines are open from 09.00–18.00, Monday to Saturday, with a 24 hour message answering service. Email address: *orders@bookpoint.co.uk*

For U.S.A. orders: please contact McGraw-Hill Customer Services, P.O. Box 545, Blacklick, OH 43004-0545, U.S.A. Telephone: 1-800-722-4726. Fax: 1-614-755-5645.

For Canada order enquiries: please contact McGraw-Hill Ryerson Ltd., 300 Water St, Whitby, Ontario L1N 9B6, Canada. Telephone: 905 430 5000. Fax: 905 430 5020.

Long-renowned as the authoritative source for self-guided learning – with more than 30 million copies sold worldwide – the *Teach Yourself* series includes over 300 titles in the fields of languages, crafts, hobbies, business and education.

British Library Cataloguing in Publication Data
Norris, David
   Serbo-Croat. – (Teach Yourself Series)
   I. Title II. Series
   491.8

Library of Congress Catalog Card Number: 93-83159

First published in UK 1993 by Hodder Headline Plc, 338 Euston Road, London NW1 3BH.

First published in US 1997 by Contemporary Books, A Division of The McGraw-Hill Companies, 4255 West Touhy Avenue, Lincolnwood (Chicago), Illinois 60712-1975 U.S.A.

The 'Teach Yourself' name and logo are registered trade marks of Hodder & Stoughton Ltd.

Typeset by Transet Limited, Coventry, England.
Printed in Great Britain for Hodder & Stoughton Educational, a division of Hodder Headline Plc, 338 Euston Road, London NW1 3BH by Cox & Wyman Ltd, Reading, Berkshire.

Impression number   21   20   19   18   17
Year   2004   2003   2002   2001

CONTENTS

Acknowledgements

I would like to thank Vladislava Ribnikar and Marija Marušić for their help. Their comments and suggestions as native speakers greatly contributed to the writing of this book. I also acknowledge a debt to many others, too numerous to mention here, who were my teachers and stimulated my own interest in the study of Serbo-Croat.

Note to first edition

The present situation in the region where Serbo-Croat is spoken may make some of the situations and dialogues in this book appear improbable. However, my concern throughout has been to provide you with a book which will maintain its usefulness over the years as an effective and practical course in the language.

Dr David A. Norris
Department of Slavonic Studies
University of Nottingham

— INTRODUCTION —

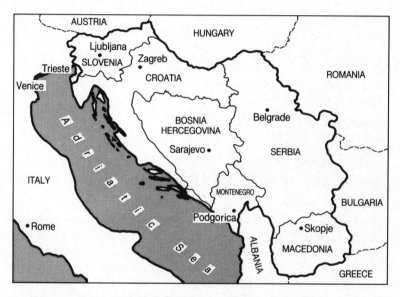

The republics of former Yugoslavia gradually being recognised as independent states since the beginning of 1992

About Serbo-Croat

Serbo-Croat is spoken on the territories of Bosnia-Hercegovina, Croatia, Montenegro and Serbia. You can see their geographical positions on the map (p. 1) at the beginning of 1992 when they were parts of former Yugoslavia. The standard literary form of the language is called **štokavski** and it can be classified in two variants. One variant of the language is called the eastern variant and is spoken largely in Serbia, while the other is called the western variant and is spoken in Croatia and most of Bosnia-Hercegovina. However, it is not an easy task to describe exactly where the border runs between them. Serbo-Croat, as spoken in Montenegro, for example, contains features of both variants. This book concentrates on the western variant of Serbo-Croat as most visitors to the region are holiday-makers on the Dalmatian coast.

The two variants of the language are so close that a thorough knowledge of the western variant will enable you to understand and communicate with a speaker of the eastern variant. Some of the standard differences between them are studied in the latter stages of this book. However, it is not the purpose of this book to examine these complex linguistic issues in detail, but to teach you effective ways to communicate with people in the region. Native speakers tend to avoid the lengthy title Serbo-Croat (**srpskohrvatski**) in favour of the shorter titles Croatian (**hrvatski**) and Serbian (**srpski**). The shorter titles which they choose reflect their national identity.

About the book

The book is intended for absolute beginners. By following each section in each unit, you will gradually build up a stock of words and phrases to be used in everyday, practical situations. The central purpose of the book is to teach you how to make your way around on your own, order meals and drinks, buy travel tickets, read notices and write messages, in short to explain what you want and how to get it.

The emphasis throughout is on functional explanations using straightforward grammatical examples. You will begin with individual words and phrases, and gradually you will be introduced to the patterns of the language which govern their usage. This is, after all, what we mean by grammar. These patterns are given as demonstrations of how you can build your own sentences to use in other situations in which you might find yourself. Do not worry if you have not studied a language before or for some time or if you feel that your last attempt was not as successful as you had hoped it would be. This book offers you units containing graded dialogues and exercises accompanied by a cassette to take you through the stages of listening, speaking, reading and writing Serbo-Croat.

———— How to use the book ————

You will find that each unit is organised in the same way. Each has seven sections:

Dialogue: this is a dialogue which shows you the langugage in operation in an everyday context and which is followed by a list of the new words and expressions used in the dialogue.

Commentary: this has notes which explain points about everyday life relevant to the dialogue.

True or false?: this gives statements about the dialogue which are either true or false for you to check that you have understood it.

Key phrases: this is a summary of the most important words and expressions used in the dialogue.

Language patterns: this section is full of notes which explain why phrases mean what they do and which show you how to create your own sentences.

Exercises: these are for you to practise the new information about the language and new words as you acquire them.

Comprehension: this is either another dialogue, or a dialogue and a text, with questions, designed to extend your comprehension of the language.

The last two units are slightly different as they give you exercises to revise phrases and language patterns studied earlier.

Teach Yourself Serbo-Croat follows the story of an English couple, Mark and Sandra Bryant, who come to Zagreb. Mark is working for a company wanting to expand its business contacts in the region. Mark and Sandra become friends with Mark's business contact, Rudolf Šimunić, and his girlfriend, Jasna Kušan. You will trace their outings together, their conversations and their holiday together, and see them in different practical situations: in restaurants, shopping, arranging accommodation, changing money, contacting a doctor, conducting business, and so on. You will also find other situations and characters in the **Comprehension** section of each unit.

There is no one way of learning a language. We all have our favourite techniques. As you progress through the book you will discover which methods suit you best. Exploit these as your strengths.

The first steps in learning a language are always important. They provide essential and basic information which you will continue to need. It is also better to look at the book every day rather than try to cram all your study in to one day at the weekend.

Go through each section of each unit in turn. Read the dialogue, and if you have the cassette which accompanies this course listen to the dialogue on the tape and repeat each phrase until you feel that you have mastered the pronunciation. Study the *Commentary* (**Objašnjenja i komentari**) and then test your knowledge of the *Dialogue* (**Dijalog**) by attempting the *True or false?* (**Istina ili neistina?**) questions. Once you have understood the passage learn the *Key phrases* (**Ključne fraze**) and the *Language patterns* (**Jezični obrasci**) before moving to the *Exercises* (**Vježbe**). The *Comprehension* (**Dopunsko štivo**) at the end of each unit develops the vocabulary and phrases which you have learnt in the unit to help reinforce you knowledge of them and to extend your stock of words and expressions.

Give yourself time for revision, and don't give up at the first sign of difficulty. What may seem complicated the first time you see it will become second nature to you by the end of the course.

—— **Pronunciation and reading** ——

Serbo-Croat is an easy language to spell and pronounce. Each letter is pronounced separately, and each word is spelt as it is pronounced. The alphabet has 30 letters. Here the capital letters are listed and their lower case letters are in brackets.

A	(a)	G	(g)	O	(o)
B	(b)	H	(h)	P	(p)
C	(c)	I	(i)	R	(r)
Č	(č)	J	(j)	S	(s)
Ć	(ć)	K	(k)	Š	(š)
D	(d)	L	(l)	T	(t)
Dž	(dž)	Lj	(lj)	U	(u)
Đ	(đ)	M	(m)	V	(v)
E	(e)	N	(n)	Z	(z)
F	(f)	Nj	(nj)	Ž	(ž)

Dž, **lj** and **nj** are combinations of other letters but are regarded as single letters for pronunciation and dictionary purposes. Some letters are formed with the help of accents and other markings. These are č, ć, đ, š and ž. As you will see this gives Serbo-Croat the advantage of having each letter represent one sound:

č like the '**ch**' in *church* but raise your tongue towards the roof of your mouth.

ć like the '**ch**' in *church* but put your tongue behind your top front teeth.

dž like the '**j**' in *judge* but raise your tongue towards the roof of your mouth.

đ like the '**j**' in *judge* but put your tongue behind your top front teeth.

š like the '**sh**' in *shoe*.

ž like the '**s**' in *pleasure*.

Others to watch for are:

c always pronounced like '**ts**' in *cats* (never as '**k**' or '**s**').

g always pronounced like '**g**' in *goat*.

h pronounced in the throat like the '**ch**' in Scottish *loch*.

j always pronounced like '**y**' in *you*.

lj sounds like '**ll**' in the middle of *million*.

nj sounds like '**ni**' in the middle of *onion*.

r is always trilled as is sometimes found in Scotland and commonly in other languages such as German or Spanish, it is never pronounced in the throat as in French. The letter '**r**' is sometimes sandwiched between two consonants and used as a vowel, e.g. **hrv**atski (*Croatian*).

The pronunciation of the remaining consonants is similar to their

English equivalents: **b d f k l m n p s t v z**

Vowel sounds are pure and tend to be shorter than in English:

a   as in *hat* but shorter.

e   as in *bell*.

i   like the '**ea**' in *meat* but shorter.

o   as in northern English *not* but with rounder lips.

u   like the '**oo**' in English *moon* but shorter and with rounder lips.

Finally, take care with the following combinations:

aj   as the vowel sound in *night*

ej   as the vowel sound in *late*

oj   as the vowel sound in *boy*

Other letters: you meet foreign letters such as **x** and **y** in the spelling of foreign names, placenames and so on.

For the cyrillic alphabet and its use see pages 212 and 220.

—————— Stress in Serbo-Croat ——————

In Serbo-Croat, as in English, one part of a longer word is pronounced more heavily than the others. This part is called the stressed syllable. So you say *lighting* and *concern* where the underlined syllable is pronounced more forcefully than the rest. Also, as in English, there are no rules to govern which part of a word is stressed, except that it is never the last syllable. So, in a word of two syllables, the first one is always stressed. The stressed syllable is not usually marked in Serbo-Croat, but by listening carefully to the cassette which accompanies this course you will be able to acquire a good pronunciation. Remember that each part of a word is pronounced without reducing or contracting sounds which often happens at the ends of words in English.

Stress in Serbo-Croat is also accompanied by tonal lengths. There are four tones in all, two rising and two falling. However, few speakers these days distinguish between all four tones. There are some instances where a tone difference indicates a different meaning of the word. These are rare occasions. You will master the tones by imitating the sounds as you hear them on the tape. Also, vowels are sometimes pronounced longer than usual. They are not necessarily the stressed syllable, but you will be able to hear them on the tape.

—— **Abbreviations and symbols** ——

☐ = This indicates material included on the cassette.

☐ = This indicates dialogue.

☐ = This indicates exercises – places where you can practice using the language.

☐ = This indicates key words or phrases.

☐ = This indicates grammar or explanations – the nuts and bolts of the language.

masc.	masculine	gen.	genitive case
fem.	feminine	e.g.	for example
neut.	neuter	nom.	nominative case
acc.	accusative case	sing.	singular
dat.	dative case	ins.	instrumental case
Lit.	literally (for a	voc.	vocative case
	literal translation)	*pron.*	pronounced

1

U HOTELU
In the hotel

In this unit you will learn how to

- form basic statements and questions
- introduce yourself and others
- identify yourself and ask others their identity
- say which languages you speak
- use words and expressions in greeting

Dijalog (*Dialogue*)

Rudolf Šimunić is looking for Mark Bryant and his wife Sandra in their hotel in Zagreb. The Bryants have just arrived. Rudolf is Mark's business contact but they have not met before.

Rudolf	Oprostite, jeste li vi gospodin Bryant?
Mark	Da, jesam. A tko ste vi, gospodine?
Rudolf	Ja sam Rudolf Šimunić. Drago mi je.
Mark	Drago mi je. Ja sam Mark Bryant.
Rudolf	Jeste li vi Englez?
Mark	Jesam.
Rudolf	Dobro govorite hrvatski.
Mark	Hvala. Jeste li vi Hrvat?
Rudolf	Jesam.

IN THE HOTEL

Mark	Govorite li engleski?
Rudolf	Govorim malo. Učim engleski.
Mark	Da vas upoznam. Ovo je moja žena, Sandra.
Rudolf	Drago mi je. Ja sam Rudolf Šimunić.
Sandra	Drago mi je. Ja sam Sandra.
Rudolf	I vi govorite hrvatski?
Sandra	Govorim malo. Učim jezik.

oprostite *excuse me* (attracting attention)
Jeste li vi..? *Are you..?*
gospodin Bryant *Mr Bryant*
da *yes*
jesam *I am*
A tko ste vi, gospodine? *And who are you, sir?*
a *and, but*
drago mi je *pleased to meet you*
ja sam... *I am...*
Englez/Hrvat *Englishman/Croat*
Dobro govorite hrvatski. *You speak Croatian well.*

hvala *thank you*
Govorite li engleski/hrvatski? *Do you speak English/Croatian?*
Govorim malo. *I speak a little.*
Učim engleski. *I am learning English.*
Da vas upoznam. *Let me introduce you.*
Ovo je moja žena. *This is my wife.*
i *and*
I vi govorite hrvatski? *And you speak Croatian (too)?*
Učim jezik. *I am studying the language.*

Rudolf arranges to meet Mark and Sandra that evening and he brings along his friend, Jasna.

Mark	Dobar večer, Rudolf. Kako ste?
Rudolf	Dobar večer. Ja sam dobro, hvala. A kako ste vi?
Sandra	Dobro, hvala.
Rudolf	Da vas upoznam. Ovo je moja prijateljica, Jasna.
Sandra	Drago mi je. Ja sam Sandra Bryant. Ovo je moj muž, Mark.
Jasna	Drago mi je. Ja sam Jasna Kušan.
Mark	Drago mi je, gospođice.
Jasna	Sandra, jeste li vi Engleskinja?
Sandra	Jesam. A vi ste Hrvatica?
Jasna	Jesam. Razumijete li hrvatski?
Sandra	Razumijem dosta, ali slabo govorim.

Dobar večer. *Good evening.*	**A vi ste Hrvatica?** *And you're a*
Kako ste? *How are you?*	*Croat*(ian woman)?
Dobro. *Fine.*	**Razumijete li..?** *Do you*
Ovo je moja prijateljica. *This is*	*understand..?*
my (female) *friend.*	**Razumijem dosta.** *I understand a*
Ovo je moj muž. *This is my*	*lot.*
husband.	**ali** *but*
gospođice *Miss*	**slabo** *not much* (Lit. *weakly*)
Jeste li vi Engleskinja? *Are you*	
(an) *English*(woman)?	

Istina ili neistina? (*True or false?*)

(*a*) Mark speaks Croatian well.
(*b*) Rudolf is studying English.
(*c*) Jasna is Rudolf's wife.

Objašnjenja i komentari (*Commentary*)

Meeting people

When meeting people for the first time it is customary to shake hands and repeat the formula as in the dialogue – **drago mi je** – and say your name. This manner avoids the old English necessity of your host repeating your name to each new person you meet.

Mr Bryant

The word **gospodin** (*Mr*) is spelt with a small letter except at the beginning of a sentence. Other common titles are **gospođa** (*Mrs*) and **gospođica** (*Miss*). They are abbreviated in writing to **g., gđa.** and **gđica.** In the dialogue when **gospodin** and **gospođica** are used to address someone directly they change slightly at the end of the word, and you have the forms **gospodine** and **gospođice**. There are a number of patterns which affect the ends of words.

In these early stages be aware that you will come across a few examples where a word will appear with a slight variation. You will gradually learn the rules which govern these changes.

Greeting people

When greeting people the following formulas are used, depending on the time of day:

dobro jutro (*good morning*) until about 10 am
dobar dan (*good day*) until late afternoon
dobar večer (*good evening*)

The word **večer** is used to refer to the time until midnight. The phrases used when parting are:

do viđenja (*goodbye*)   laku noć (*good night*)

These are somewhat formal and polite expressions. In more colloquial circumstances people use **zdravo** when both greeting and parting from people. In Zagreb, **bog** is said as a very colloquial expression meaning '*bye* or *cheerio*.

Ključne fraze (*Key phrases*)

How to:

- ask who people are.

  Tko ste vi?
  Jeste li vi ...?

- say who you are.

  Ja sam ...

- ask how someone is.

  Kako ste?

- reply that you are fine.

  Ja sam dobro.

- ask what language people speak, or understand.

  Govorite li ...
  Razumijete li ...

- say what languages you speak, or understand.

  Govorim ...
  Razumijem ...

- respond when being introduced.   **Drago mi je. Ja sam ...**

- introduce others.   **Da vas upoznam. Ove je ...**

- respond when meeting people –

  ... in the morning.   **Dobro jutro.**
  ... in the afternoon.   **Dobar dan.**
  ... in the evening.   **Dobar večer.**

- say goodbye.   **do viđenja/laku noć.**

▣ –Jezični obrasci (*Language patterns*)–

1 'The', 'a' or 'an'

Serbo-Croat does not have separate words for *the* and *a*. So, the title of the dialogue **U hotelu** may mean either *In the hotel* or *In a hotel* depending on the context. The lack of such words strikes the English ear as odd at first, but you soon get used to speaking without them.

2 'I' and 'you'

The words **ja** (*I*) and **vi** (*you*) are rarely used. They tend to be omitted unless asking a direct, personal question or if emphasis is required.

3 'I am' and 'you are'

In Serbo-Croat there are two forms for saying *I am* and *you are*:

ja sam ja jesam	*I am*
vi ste vi jeste	*you are*

The first one in both examples is called the 'short form', and the other is called the 'long form'. The main difference is that the short form (**sam, ste**) is never used as the first word of a sentence or phrase. The long form is used for:

(*a*) emphasis;
(*b*) for giving one word answers to questions;
(*c*) to ask questions.

Compare the following:

Ja sam Mark Bryant.	*I am Mark Bryant.*
Ja sam Englez.	*I am English.*
Jeste li vi Mark Bryant?	*Are you Mark Bryant?*
Jesam.	*I am.*

When **ja** or **vi** are omitted word order is affected. Compare the following:

Kako ste?	*How are you?*
Ja sam dobro, hvala.	*I am well, thank you.*
or	
Dobro sam, hvala.	*I am well, thank you.*

4 I speak / you speak

Ja and **vi** are largely unnecessary because the end of each verb (verbs are words which express actions) tells you who is performing the action. These verbs form regular patterns. Note the difference at the ends of the verbs:

govori**m**	*I speak*
govori**te**	*you speak*

You can see and hear the same differences at the ends of the other verbs used in the dialogue:

razumije**m**	*I understand*
razumije**te**	*you understand*

uči**m**	*I study*
uči**te**	*you study*

There is only one form of each verb in the present tense, so that **govorim** means *I speak*, *I am speaking* and *I do speak*.

5 Statements and questions

Compare the following constructions to see the difference between a statement and a question:

Statement

Govorim hrvatski.	*I speak Croatian.*
Razumijem engleski.	*I understand English.*

Question

Govorite li hrvatski?	*Do you speak Croatian?*
Razumijete li engleski?	*Do you understand English?*

If you include the word **vi** in the question, then the word order is as follows:

Govorite li **vi** hrvatski?
Razumijete li **vi** engleski?

A question is made by putting **li** after the verb and before **vi**. A question can also be made by putting **da li** in front of the verb:

Da li govorite hrvatski?   *Do you speak Croatian?*
Da li razumijete engleski?   *Do you understand English?*

Another type of question involves the use of an interrogative word, for example:

Tko ste vi?   *Who are you?*

6 Categories of nouns (gender)

All nouns (words which name things) in Serbo-Croat belong to one of three categories called genders: masculine, feminine and neuter. The gender of a noun can usually be recognised by its ending.

Masculine nouns end in consonants:

Engle**z**   *Englishman*
jezi**k**   *language*
mu**ž**   *husband*

Feminine nouns end in **-a**:

Engleskinj**a**   *Englishwoman*
žen**a**   *wife*
prijateljic**a**   *friend* (female)

Neuter nouns end in **-o** or **-e**:

per**o**   *pen*
mor**e**   *sea*

There are some smaller groups which do not conform to these patterns. The names of the categories are not always associated with biological gender (what is masculine about a language?) but where they are you will usually find that words are paired: e.g. **prijateljica** (female friend, feminine category), **prijatelj** (male friend, masculine category).

There are two other words to mean husband and wife which are more formal terms than the ones used in the dialogue. These are: **suprug** (*husband*, masc. category); **supruga** (*wife*, fem. category).

7 'My' and 'your'

My and *your* are called possessive adjectives because they describe the possession of an object. In common with all adjectives (words which describe objects) in Serbo-Croat and in many other languages their ending changes according to the gender of the noun. We say that the adjective agrees with the noun. Masculine adjectives end in a consonant, and feminine adjectives add **-a**:

Ovo je **moj** muž.	*This is my husband.*
Ovo je **moja** žena.	*This is my wife.*

The corresponding word for *your* is **vaš**:

Ovo je **vaš** hotel.	*This is your hotel.*
Ovo je **vaša** sekretarica.	*This is your secretary.*

8 Languages and nationalities

Languages are spelt with a small letter: **hrvatski** (*Croatian language*).

Nationalities and inhabitants of countries take a capital letter: **Hrvat** (*Croatian man*), **Hrvatica** (*Croatian woman*).

There are two different forms to denote a person by their nationality, one for men and one for women. Other examples of language and nationality are:

Language		**Nationality**
srpski	*Serbian*	Srbin/Srpkinja
slovenski	*Slovenian*	Slovenac/Slovenka
makedonski	*Macedonian*	Makedonac/Makedonka
engleski	*English*	Englez/Engleskinja
francuski	*French*	Francuz/Francuskinja
njemački	*German*	Nijemac/Njemica
ruski	*Russian*	Rus/Ruskinja

Vježbe (*Exercises*)

1 Unscramble the following letters to form words:

(a) etajipricalj
(b) bardo reveč
(c) stroopite

2 Look at the information that Mark gives about himself below.

Ja sam Mark Bryant.   Ja sam Englez.   Govorim engleski.

Make up similar sentences for:

(a) Jasna
(b) Rudolf
(c) Sandra
(d) yourself

3 Look at the following dialogue.

Jasna   Tko ste vi?
Metka   Ja sam Metka. Ja sam Slovenka.
Jasna   Govorite li slovenski?
Metka   Da, govorim slovenski.

Repeat the dialogue using the following names (say what you think their likely nationalities and languages are):

(a) Hans
(b) Pierre
(c) Ivan

4 You are introduced to someone, ask them if they speak:

(a) English
(b) French
(c) Croatian
(d) Serbian

5 What would you say to greet someone ...

(a) in the early part of the morning?
(b) in the afternoon?
(c) in the evening?
(d) How would you say goodbye?

6 Fill in the missing part of the following dialogue:

Dobar večer.
(*Good evening. How are you?*)
Dobro, hvala. Da vas upoznam. Ovo je moj muž.
(*Pleased to meet you. I am ...*)
Drago mi je. Ja sam Velimir.
(*Good night.*)
Laku noć.

7 Rudolf introduces Jasna:

Da vas upoznam.   Ovo je Jasna.   Jasna je moja prijateljica.

Make up introductions such as:

(*a*)   Sandra introduces Mark.
(*b*)   Mark introduces Sandra.

— Dopunsko štivo (*Comprehension*) —

Earlier that day Jasna went to work. She met her boss, g. Kovač, in the corridor as she arrived. She met him again later in the day as he was showing a friend of his from another company around the office. Jasna works as a secretary (**sekretarica**).

	Ujutro (*In the morning*)
G. Kovač	Dobro jutro. Kako ste godpođice Kušan?
Jasna	Dobro sam, hvala gospodine. A kako ste vi?
G. Kovač	I ja sam dobro, hvala. Do viđenja.
Jasna	Do viđenja, gospodine Kovaču.
	Kasnije poslije podne (*Later that afternoon*)
G. Kovač	Ah, ovo je Jasna Kušan, moja sekretarica. Dobar dan Jasna. Da vas upoznam. Ovo je moj prijatelj, gospodin Marinković.
Jasna	Drago mi je, gospodine Marinkoviću. Ja sam Jasna Kušan.
G. Marinković	Drago mi je.

Istina ili neistina? (*True or false?*)

(*a*) Jasna does not feel well in the morning.
(*b*) Jasna is Mr Kovač's secretary.
(*c*) Mr Kovač introduces Jasna to his friend.

NOTE that the surnames of Mr Kovač and Mr Marinković change when they are addressed directly as does the word **gospodin** (see *Mr Bryant* p. 10).

2

U KAVANI

In the café

In this unit you will learn how to

- say what you want or like
- ask others what they want or like
- ask what others want to drink
- give and ask for personal information
- say *in* and *to*
- make negative statements

Dijalog

Now that Rudolf and Jasna have met the Bryants, they invite Mark and Sandra for a drink in the hotel.

HOTEL BAR

Rudolf	Gdje živite, vi i Sandra?
Mark	Živimo u Londonu.
Rudolf	Da li volite živjeti u Londonu?
Mark	Da, volimo tamo živjeti. Volimo London.
Rudolf	Što želite popiti?
Mark	Žedan sam. Ja bih pivo, hvala.
Rudolf	Jasna, da li si žedna?
Jasna	Nisam. Što želite popiti, Sandra?
Sandra	Ja bih kavu, hvala.

Jasna   Da... kava je ovdje veoma dobra. I vino je dobro. Ja bih vino, Rudolf.

Rudolf   U redu. Ti želiš vino, Jasna, a vi želite kavu, Sandra.

Gdje živite? *Where do you live?*	**pivo** *beer*
živimo *we live*	**Da li si žedna?** *Are you thirsty?* (to
u Londonu *in London*	a female)
Da li volite... *Do you like...*	**Nisam.** *I am not.*
živjeti *to live*	**Ja bih kavu.** *I would like a coffee.*
volimo *we like* (or *love*)	**Kava je veoma dobra.** *The coffee*
tamo *there*	*is very good.*
Što želite... *What do you want...*	**ovdje** *here*
popiti *to drink*	**Vino je dobro.** *The wine is good.*
Žedan sam. *I am thirsty* (male	**u redu** *okay, all right*
speaking).	**ti želiš** *you want*
Ja bih... *I would like...*	**vi želite** *you want*

They order their drinks from the waiter and continue chatting.

Jasna   Volite li živjeti u Londonu, Sandra?
Sandra   Ne, ne volim živjeti u Londonu, ali radim tamo.
Jasna   Što radite?
Sandra   Radim u školi. Ja sam učiteljica. Radim kao učiteljica.
Jasna   Ja radim kao sekretarica u Zagrebu.
Sandra   Živite li u gradu?
Jasna   Ne, ne živim u gradu. Živim u predgrađu. Idem u grad na posao. Kamo vi idete?
Sandra   Idem u školu. Moja škola je u gradu.
Jasna   Rudolf, ideš li sutra u grad?
Rudolf   Da, idem.

ne *no*	**u predgrađu** *in a suburb*
ne volim... *I do not like...*	**idem u grad** *I go to town*
radim *I work, I do*	**na posao** *to work* (to my job)
Što radite? *What do you do?*	**Kamo vi idete?** *Where do you go?*
u školi *in school*	**u školu** *to school*
učiteljica *teacher* (female)	**moja škola je...** *my school is...*
kao *as*	**Ideš li..?** *Are you going..?*
u gradu *in town*	**sutra** *tomorrow*

Istina ili neistina?

(a)   Mark does not like living in London.
(b)   Jasna is thirsty.
(c)   Rudolf is going to town tomorrow.

———— **Objašnjenja i komentari** ————

You

In common with many other European languages, Serbo-Croat has two words for *you*. They are **ti** and **vi**. The **ti** form is used among friends, relations, to children and is generally recognised as an informal mode of address. It is only used when referring to one person. The **vi** form is always used when referring to more than one person. It is also a more formal and polite form, used to a boss at work or to a stranger.

Do not try to use **ti** to someone thinking that you are just being friendly. The conventions for choosing the correct form depend on social factors which you might not recognise. You could cause great offence. Rudolf uses **ti** when he speaks to Jasna, but **vi** when he speaks to Mark or Sandra. Always let the Croat or Serb to whom you are speaking be the first to use the **ti** form. It is, however, common for teenagers and students to use the **ti** form within their own age group.

Drinks

People might drop in at a **kavana** for a drink. The usual system is to find a table and wait for the waiter to come and take your order – which might be **kava**, **pivo**, **vino**, **sok** (*fruit juice*) or a **rakija** (*brandy*). You could try asking for **čaj** (*tea*), but you might get the herbal variety. In some of the trendy cafés in Zagreb and Belgrade, and on the coast you might find a bar with something like counter service as in a pub. These are usually small places, called a **kafić**. You can also buy snacks in some, and even proper meals. The usual place for a meal would be a **restoran** (*restaurant*), in many of which a small area is often set aside for customers who only want a drink. On a train or at a station look for the **bife** (*buffet*).

Ključne fraze

How to:

- ask what someone wants to drink. **Što želite popiti?**
- respond when offered a drink. **Ja bih kavu.**
  Ja bih pivo.
  Ja bih vino.
- ask where someone lives. **Gdje živite?**
- respond when asked where you live. **Živim/Živimo u Londonu (u Zagrebu, u gradu, u predgrađu).**
- ask if someone likes to do something. **Da li volite...** or **Volite li...**
- respond that you do like something, or **Da, volim...**
  that you do not like something. **Ne, ne volim.**
- ask what someone does for a living. **Što radite?**
- say what you do for a living. **Radim kao...**
- ask where someone is going. **Kamo ideš?**
- respond when asked where you are going. **Idem u grad (u školu, na posao)**
- say that something is here, or there. **Kava je ovdje dobra.**
  Ne volim tamo živjeti.

Jezični obrasci

1 'You' and 'we'

The two new words for referring to people in this unit are **ti** (*you*) and **mi** (*we*). They are rarely used except for emphasis. The ending of the verb changes according to the following pattern:

| ti voliš | you like/love |
| mi volimo | we like/love |

| ti ideš | you go |
| mi idemo | we go |

These endings can be added to the other verbs which you have met so far:

| ti govoriš | you speak |
| mi razumijemo | we understand |

Here is the exception:

ti si	you are
(jesi – long form)	
mi smo	we are
(jesmo – long form)	

2 I like to live in... (infinitive)

You have met verbs in one of two ways, either with a person (*I like*, *you work*, etc.) or as an infinitive (*to live*, *to drink*, etc.). The infinitive usually follows a verb with a person (I like *to live* in London). In English the infinitive is two words, but in Serbo-Croat it is one word:

| živjeti | *to live* |
| popiti | *to drink* |

Once you know both the infinitive and the **ja** parts of the verb you will be able to produce any form of a verb. You can recognise the other infinitives from the parts of the verb you already know:

govorim	govoriti	*to speak*
razumijem	razumjeti	*to understand*
učim	učiti	*to study*
radim	raditi	*to do, work*
volim	voljeti	*to like, love*
želim	željeti	*to want*

There are one or two exceptions: e.g. **ja sam** – biti (*to be*). Most infinitives end in **-ti** but some end in **-ći**: e.g. **idem** – ići (*to go*). You can find more verbs in the lists of new words following the **Dijalog** with their infinitives and **ja** forms.

3 I do not like (negation)

To say that you are not doing something (to negate a verb) simply place **ne** before the verb:

Ne volim živjeti u Londonu.	*I do not like to live in London.*
Ne želimo popiti pivo.	*We do not want a drink of beer.*

The verb **biti** as usual provides an exception. The pattern which means *I am not*, etc. is all one word:

nisam	*I am not*	nismo	*we are not*
nisi	*you are not*	niste	*you are not* (plural)

4 Thirsty/hungry (adjectives)

Adjectives change their endings like nouns: e.g. Mark says **žedan sam** (*I am thirsty*) while Sandra says **žedna sam**.

Masculine adjectives end in a consonant.
Feminine adjectives end in **-a**.
Neuter adjectives end in **-o**.

There is a rule of spelling and pronunciation that after certain consonants you write and say **e** instead of **o**. These are called soft consonants, and they are **c**, **č**, **ć**, **dž**, **đ**, **j**, **lj**, **nj**, **š** and **ž**.

If there is the letter **a** between the final two consonants it is omitted when you add the ending for feminine and neuter:

Masc.	Fem.	Neut.
dob**ar**	dob**ra**	dob**ro**
žed**an**	žed**na**	žed**no**
glad**an** (*hungry*)	glad**na**	glad**no**
mo**j**	mo**ja**	mo**je**

5 Possessive adjectives

The two possessive adjectives relevant to this unit are:

tvoj	*your* (correspond to **ti**)
naš	*our* (correspond to **mi**)

Ovo je moja kava.	*This is my coffee.*
Ovo je tvoje pivo.	*This is your beer.*
Ovo je naš grad.	*This is our town.*
Ovo je vaša žena.	*This is your wife.* (someone to whom you would normally use the **vi** form).

6 In/to

Serbo-Croat uses the same word to mean both *in* and *to*: **u**.

The difference between the two meanings is indicated at the end of the noun. Compare the following two sentences:

Idem **u** grad.	*I go to town.* (motion)
Ja sam **u** gradu.	*I am in town.* (stationary)
Idem **u** školu.	*I go to school.*
Ja sam **u** školi.	*I am in school.*

Words like **u** which relate two things together, often in a spatial way as in these examples, are called prepositions. Different prepositions require different endings. The endings indicate what are called the cases of the noun. Here there are examples of two cases: the accusative (acc.) and the dative (dat.) case. (In some grammar books this use of the dative after **u** is sometimes referred to as the locative case. However, given that the locative and dative case endings are always the same we have continued them under the dative heading in this book.) They follow the patterns below:

Masc. (e.g. **grad**)
acc.	**grad** (no change)
dat.	**gradu** (add **-u**)

Fem. (e.g. **škola**)

acc.	**školu** (change **-a** to **-u**)
dat.	**školi** (change **-a** to **-i**)

Neut. (e.g. **predgrađe**)

acc.	**predgrađe** (no change)
dat.	**predgrađu** (change **-e/-o** to **-u**)

The acc. after **u** indicates being in motion.
The dat. after **u** indicates being stationary.

Study the following examples:

Da li živiš u Londonu?	*Do you live in London?*
Idemo u London.	*We are going to London.*
Ne idem u kavanu.	*I am not going to the café.*
Mi smo u kavani.	*We are in the café.*
Idete li u predgrađe?	*Are you going to the suburb?*
Nisam u predgrađu.	*I am not in the suburb.*

Serbo-Croat has two ways of asking *where?*:

Gdje živite?	*Where do you live?*
Kamo idete?	*Where are you going?*

Gdje asks where something is (being stationary).
Kamo asks to where something goes (being in motion).
In answering a question with **gdje** you use dat.
In answering a question with **kamo** you use acc.

7 Other ways of saying 'to'

You have seen that **na** can also mean *to* in the expression:

Idem na posao.	*I am to going to work.*

The word **na** usually means *on* but is also used with certain nouns where you would not say *on* in English, such as with the word **pošta** (*post office*) and **kolodvor** (*station*) and in some idioms:

Ja sam na pošti.	*I am in the post office.*
Idem na kolodvor.	*I am going to the station.*
Idemo na kavu.	*We are going for a coffee.*
Ideš li na pivo?	*Are you going for a beer?*

The acc. after **na** indicates being in motion.
The dat. after **na** indicates being stationary.

8 Unusual noun categories

Somewhere and somehow there are always words in any language which do not behave like most of the others. For example most masculine nouns end in a consonant. **Posao** (*job*, *work*), however, is a masculine noun. Centuries ago the **-o** at the end was an **-l**, but with time its pronunciation was softened into this vowel sound. When you add case endings the old 'l' returns to replace the 'o'.

Posao also has that **-a** before the last letter which disappears as soon as you add a different ending to the word (think of **dobar dan** and the change to **dobro jutro**). The pattern of its changes looks like this:

acc.	pos**ao**
dat.	pos**lu**

Vježbe

1 Answer the following questions: positively, negatively.

   e.g. Volite li pivo?
         Volim. Ne volim.

   (a) Volite li kavu?
   (b) Govorite li engleski?
   (c) Jeste li vi Englez?
   (d) Volite li London?
   (e) Želite li živjeti u Londonu?
   (f) Želite li ići u grad?
   (g) Volite li ići na posao?
   (h) Idete li na kavu?

2 Change all the questions in Ex. 1 to the **ti** form of the verb.

3 Find the two correct forms of the verbs in the lists on the right to match the personal pronouns on the left:

   (a) **ja**   si, sam, razumijete, govorimo, učim

(b) **ti**   želiš, želite, ideš, razumijem
(c) **mi**   živim, razumijemo, učimo, volite
(d) **vi**   ste, smo, učite, učimo

4 Put the noun in brackets below into the correct case.

Kamo ideš, Rudolf?

(a) Idem u (grad).
(b) Idem u (kavana).
(c) Idem u (škola).
(d) Idem u (Zagreb).
(e) Idem na (posao).
(f) Idem na (kava).

Gdje je Jasna?

(g) Jasna je u (grad).
(h) Jasna je u (London).
(i) Jasna je u (škola).
(j) Jasna je na (posao).
(k) Jasna je u (kavana).
(l) Jasna je u (predgrađe).

5 Put the verbs and nouns in brackets into the correct forms:

e.g. (ići – ti) u (grad)
     Ideš   u grad.

(a) (željeti – mi) živjeti u (London).
(b) (željeti – ja) živjeti u (Zagreb).
(c) (ići – ti) na (kava).
(d) (živjeti – ja) u (grad).
(e) (živjeti – mi) u (predgrađe).
(f) (voljeti – vi) biti na (posao).

6 Match the following questions with the appropriate responses:

(a) Kamo idete?   (i) Ja bih kavu.
(b) Gdje želite živjeti? (ii) Idem u grad.
(c) Što želite popiti?   (iii) Radim kao učiteljica.
(d) Što radite?   (iv) Želim živjeti u Londonu.

7 Put the adjectives in brackets into the correct form:

e.g. Jasna je (gladan).
     Jasna je gladna.

(a) (dobar) večer.
(b) Sandra je (žedan).
(c) Ovo je (naš) predgrađe.
(d) Mark je (vaš) muž.
(e) Ovo je (moj) (dobar) prijateljica.
(f) Ovo je (tvoj) kavana.
(g) Rudolf je (gladan).

—————— Dopunsko štivo ——————

Two friends, Velimir and Zvonko, are chatting about Velimir's new flat.

Zvonko Gdje živiš?
Velimir Živim u gradu.
Zvonko Kako to? Imaš stan u predgrađu.
Velimir Imam nov stan u gradu.
Zvonko Voliš li živjeti u gradu?
Velimir Volim. Moj posao je u gradu.
Zvonko Ideš li sutra na posao?
Velimir Idem. Volim ići na posao.
Zvonko Gdje radiš?
Velimir Radim u školi.
Zvonko Što radiš?
Velimir Sada radim kao učitelj.

Kako to? *How come?*		**posao** *job* (work)	
imaš *you have*		**sada** *now*	
imam *I have*		**učitelj** *teacher* (masc.)	
nov stan *a new flat*			

Istina ili neistina?

(a) Velimir has a new flat.
(b) Velimir has a job in the suburbs.
(c) Velimir has a new job as a bus conductor.

3

U GRADU

In town

In this unit you will learn how to

- express basic directions
- ask where something is
- say where something is in relation to something else
- say other expressions useful in getting about a town
- express *can* and *have to*

Dijalog

Rudolf and Jasna have invited the Bryants to join them for a trip into the town. This is the first time the Bryants have had the opportunity to see something of Zagreb. Their Croatian friends call at their hotel.

Rudolf   Dobar dan, Mark. Dobar dan, Sandra. Kako ste?
Mark   Dobro smo, hvala. A, kako ste vi?
Rudolf   I ja sam dobro.
Mark   Gdje je Jasna?
Rudolf   Ona dolazi. Parkira auto ispred hotela. Evo Jasne, sada možemo ići u grad.

Ona dolazi. (dolaziti, dolazim) *She is coming.*
Parkira auto. (parkirati, parkiram) *She (or he) is parking the car.*
ispred hotela *in front of the hotel*

Evo Jasne. *Here is Jasna.*
sada *now*
možemo (moći, mogu – irregular verb) *we can, we may, we are able*

From here onwards you will find both the infinitive and **ja** forms of new verbs. (You can recognise the infinitive by the ending, and it is followed by the **ja** form.)

Sandra and Jasna walk and chat together. Rudolf and Mark walk ahead.

Sandra Gdje smo sada?
Jasna Na desno je Esplanade. To je dobar hotel. Na lijevo je Glavni kolodvor. Sada idemo ravno u centar grada. Vidite li tamo veliku zgradu? Da... Rudolf tamo radi. Njegov ured je u zgradi.
Sandra A što je tamo ispred kolodvora?
Jasna To je park. U parku je spomenik. Ovo je lijep kraj grada.
Sandra Da, lijep je. Gdje su Mark i Rudolf?
Jasna Vidim Rudolfa blizu spomenika. I Mark je tamo ispod drveta.
Sandra Što rade?
Jasna Gledaju spomenik.

na desno *on the right*
To je Hotel Esplanade. *That is the Esplanade hotel.*
na lijevo *on the left*
Glavni kolodvor *Main Station*
ići ravno *to go straight on*
centar grada *the centre of town*
vidite (vidjeti, vidim) *you see (vi form)*
veliku zgradu *large building* (acc.)
njegov ured *his office*
ispred kolodvora *in front of the station*

park *park*
spomenik *monument*
lijep kraj grada *a nice part of town*
Gdje su..? *Where are..?*
Vidim Rudolfa. *I see Rudolf.*
blizu spomenika *near the monument*
ispod drveta *under the tree*
Što rade? *What are they doing?*
Gledaju spomenik. (gledati, gledam) *They are looking at the monument.*

Mark Kamo idemo sada?
Rudolf Idemo na Jelačićev trg, a onda u Gornji grad.
Mark Gdje je pošta? Moram kupiti marke i koverte. Jesu li skupe?

Rudolf Ne, nisu skupe. Pošta nije daleko od trga. Možemo tamo otići kasnije.

Jelačićev trg *Jelačić Square*	**Jesu li skupe?** *Are they expensive?*
a onda *and then, next*	
Gornji grad *Upper Town*	**nisu** *they are not*
pošta *post office*	**Nije daleko od trga.** *It is not far from the square.*
moram... (morati) *I have to...*	
kupiti (kupim) *to buy*	**otići** *to go on to, to go away*
marke *stamps* (acc. plural)	**kasnije** *later*
koverte *envelopes* (acc. plural)	

Istina ili neistina?

(*a*) Jasna is coming to the hotel by bus.
(*b*) The Esplanade is a good hotel.
(*c*) The post office is near the main square.

——— Objašnjenja i komentari ———

Zagreb

Zagreb is the capital city of Croatia. It is the cultural, political and industrial centre of the region. Parts of **Gornji grad** (*Upper Town*) date from the medieval period. **Gornji grad** is aptly named as it sits on top of a hill overlooking the modern centre, much of which was constructed in the last century when Zagreb was a provincial capital in the Hapsburg Empire. After the Second World War the city was the capital of the Republic of Croatia within the Yugoslav Federation, and from the beginning of 1992 has been the capital of the independent state of Croatia. It has a population of about one million.

Gornji grad

The Upper Town has no bus or tram services as the streets are too narrow and such modern conveniences would spoil this old part of

Katedrala sv. Stjepana i Marijin stup, Zagreb
(Cathedral of St. Stephen and Mary's Column, Zagreb)

town. The area is well known for its small squares with their restaurants and cafés. It can be reached on foot from **Jelačićev trg** through the old streets which twist their way uphill. There is also a funicular railway which can be found not far from **Jelačićev trg** along one of the main streets called **Ilica**.

Use of capital letters

Note that in Serbo-Croat the names of places, whether names of towns or areas in a town, are spelt with a capital letter. If there is more than one word, the second word is spelt with a small letter as in the following examples:

Glavni kolodvor
Jelačićev trg
Gornji grad

 ───────── **Ključne fraze** ─────────

How to:

- say that something is on the left, or on the right.

  Ovo je na lijevo.
  Ovo je na desno.

- tell someone to go straight on.

  Idemo ravno.

- say where things are –
  in front of
  near
  under
  not far from

  ispred hotela
  blizu spomenika
  ispod drveta
  nije daleko od trga

- say *this is*,
  or *that is*.

  Ovo je lijep kraj grada.
  To je dobar hotel.

- express *can*,
  and *must*.

  sada možemo ići
  moram kupiti ...

(both verbs are followed by the infinitive of what *can* or *must be* done)

- announce that someone is here.

  Evo Jasne.

───────── **Jezični obrasci** ─────────

1 'He'/'she'/'it' and 'they'

In this unit you have learnt the final parts of the verb in the present tense. They express he/she/it does or they do. The words for the pronouns (*he*, etc.) are as follows:

	Masc.	**Fem.**	**Neut.**
singular	on	ona	ono
plural	oni	one	ona

Unlike in English, there are three forms of the plural (*they*), and the pronouns may be used to refer to both people and things depending on the gender of the noun which they are replacing as in these examples:

Spomenik (masc.) je u parku.	*The monument is in the park.*
On je u parku.	*It is in the park.*
Oni su u parku.	*They* (monuments) *are in in the park.*
Zgrada (fem.) je na trgu.	*The building is on the square.*
Ona je na trgu.	*It is on the square.*
One su na trgu.	*They* (buildings) *are on the square.*
Kazalište (neut.) je u gradu.	*The theatre is in the town.*
Ono je u gradu.	*It is in the town.*
Ona su u gradu.	*They* (theatres) *are in the town.*
Rudolf je ovdje a Jasna je tamo.	*Rudolf is here and Jasna is there.*
On je ovdje a ona je tamo.	*He is here and she is there.*
Oni su na lijevo a one su na desno	*They* (men) *are on the left and they* (women) *are on the right.*

When you are talking about two things, one masculine and one feminine, the masculine forms are used:

Spomenik i zgrada su u parku.	*The monument and the building are in the park.*
Oni su u parku.	*They are in the park.*

2 Verbal forms and categories

Now that you have all the parts of the verb you can see the complete pattern of endings in the present tense. There are just three standard types of ending depending on the vowel which occurs immediately before the **-m** of the **ja** form:

(*a*)   **i** type (dolazim)
(*b*)   **e** type (idem)
(*c*)   **a** type (gledam)

---

dolaziti   (*to come*)

ja	dolazim	mi	dolazimo
ti	dolaziš	vi	dolazite
on/a/o	dolazi	oni/e/a	dolaze

---

ići   (*to go*)

ja	idem	mi	idemo
ti	ideš	vi	idete
on/a/o	ide	oni/e/a	idu

---

gledati   (*to look at*)

ja	gledam	mi	gledamo
ti	gledaš	vi	gledate
on/a/o	gleda	oni/e/a	gledaju

These three verbs represent the three patterns of the verb in the present tense in Serbo-Croat.

There are a small number of irregular verbs which do not follow this plan. The ones which you have met so far are:

---

moći   (*may, can, able* – to do something)

ja	mogu	mi	možemo
ti	možeš	vi	možete
on/a/o	može	oni/e/a	mogu

---

biti   (*to be*)
short form   *long form*

ja	sam	mi	smo	jesam	jesmo
ti	si	vi	ste	jesi	jeste
on/a/o	je	oni/e/a	su	jest	jesu
				(**jest** also has form **jeste**)	

The negative form is spelt as one word:

nisam	nismo
nisi	niste
nije	nisu

There is one exception to the use of the short form of **biti** and that is when asking a question with **je**. In this instance the short form may come at the beginning of the question. Compare the following:

Je li Sandra u hotelu?	*Is Sandra in the hotel?*
Jesu li Sandra i Mark u hotelu?	*Are Sandra and Mark in the hotel?*

3 Where things are

New expressions are used in this unit which tell you where things are:

ispred hotela	*in front of the hotel*
Evo Jasne.	*Here is Jasna.*
blizu spomenika	*near the monument*
ispod drveta	*under the tree*
Nije daleko od trga.	*It is not far from the square.*
Daleko je od trga.	*It is far from the square.*

Each position word is followed by the genitive case (gen.). This is another of the cases in Serbo-Croat. You can see the pattern of changes from the examples below:

Masc. (e.g. **hotel**)
gen.   **hotela** (add **-a**)

Fem. (e.g. **škola**)
gen.   **škole** (change **-a** to **-e**)

Neut. (e.g. **predgrađe**)
gen.   **predgrađa** (change **-e/-o** to **-a**)

4 How to say 'of'

The genitive is not only used after certain place words. It has another important use to mean *of*.

u centru grada – *in the centre of town*
where **grada** actually means *of town*

Cases are often used when in English we would have to use one of those small words like *of*, *to*, *by*, etc. They give a greater economy to the language, although it takes a little while for the English speaker to become used to thinking about the ends of words in this way.

5 Other uses of cases

Look at these examples taken from the dialogues in this and the previous unit:

Kava je dobra.	*The coffee is good.*
Ja bih kav**u**.	*I would like a coffee.*
Vidite li tamo veliku zgrad**u**?	*Do you see the big building there?*
Vidim Rudolf**a** blizu spomenika.	*I see Rudolf near the monument.*

The words **kava**, **zgrada** and **Rudolf** all change at the end. To understand why these words change here, look at these two English sentences:

I see him.
He sees me.

When *I* comes before the verb it is called the subject because it is the one who is performing the action of the verb. When it comes after the verb it changes to *me* and is called the object because the action of the verb is carried out on it. This is the pattern of the English language and you would be unlikely to confuse *I* and *me* (or *he* and *him*). The same principle operates in Serbo-Croat with all nouns.

In Serbo-Croat, nouns which are the object of the sentence are put into the accusative case. The accusative case of masculine nouns is the same as the nominative except when masculine nouns in the singular refer to people or animals when the accusative case is the same as the genitive. Study the following examples:

Volim kavu.	*I like coffee.*
Volim pivo.	*I like beer.*
Volim London.	*I like London.*
Vidim Rudolfa.	*I see Rudolf.*
Vidim Marka.	*I see Mark.*
Vidim Jasnu.	*I see Jasna.*

The case which identifies the gender of a noun is the nominative (nom.), and is used to express the subject of a sentence. Study the following examples:

Sandra (nom.) vidi Jasnu (acc.).	*Sandra sees Jasna.*
Mark (nom.) vidi Rudolfa (acc.).	*Mark sees Rudolf.*

6 His/her/its/their (Possessive adjectives)

Jasna points out the building to Sandra where Rudolf has his office and says **Tamo je njegov ured**. The words for *his*, *her*, *its* and *their* are adjectives like **moj**, **tvoj**, **naš** and **vaš**.

njegov	*his*
njen (or njezin)	*her*
njihov	*their*

Njegov also substitutes for neut. nouns as in:

Ovo je kazalište.	*This is the theatre.*
Njegova fasada je...	*Its facade is...*

The ending of the word changes to match in gender (agreement) with the thing being owned. Examples:

Ovo je njegov ured.	*This is his office.*
Ovo je njihov hotel.	*This is their hotel.*
Ovo je njena kava.	*This is her coffee.*
Ovo je njegovo pivo.	*This is his beer.*

7 Unusual noun categories

You have seen how nouns and verbs change their form, and how all these changes fall into certain patterns, and how some words do not follow the standard patterns, like **posao** which is a masculine noun although it ends in **-o**.

Drvo (*tree*) is a neut. noun, but with a slight difference to the usual pattern. Before case endings it adds **-et-** as in **ispod drveta**. There are a small group of such nouns which follow this pattern:

nom.	**drvo**	gen.	**drveta**
acc.	**drvo**	dat.	**drvetu**

Vježbe

1 There are two correct and two incorrect verb endings given for each personal pronoun. Choose the two **correct** ones:

(a) **ja**   moram, moramo, mogu, možemo.
(b) **ti**   govoriš, razumiješ, idete, morate.
(c) **on**   idu, dolazi, radi, moraju.
(d) **mi**   vidimo, idemo, uči, radi.
(e) **vi**   ste, smo, govorite, razumiješ.
(f) **oni**   idu, rade, razumije, vidi.

2 Put the nouns in brackets below into the correct case for the preposition:

(a) Spomenik je u (park).
(b) Naš hotel nije daleko od (kavana).
(c) Pošta je na (trg).
(d) Rudolf je blizu (drvo).
(e) Mark ide u (grad).
(f) Sandra ide na (pošta).

3 Put the nouns in brackets below into the correct case for the object of the sentence:

(a) Rudolf vidi (Jasna) ispod drveta.
(b) Gledamo (spomenik) u parku.
(c) Sandra mora kupiti (kava) i (sok).
(d) Žele piti (vino).
(e) Učiteljica voli (škola) u gradu.
(f) Sekretarica vidi (gospodin) u uredu.

4 Supply the correct form of **njegov**, **njen** or **njihov** as required:

e.g. Mark je u kavani.   Ovo je _____ kava.
Ovo je njegova kava.

(a) Jasna je u kavani.   Ovo je ——— sok.
(b) Rudolf je u kavani.   Ovo je ——— vino.
(c) Sandra radi u školi.   Ovo je ——— škola.
(d) Mark i Rudolf rade u uredu. Ovo je ——— ured.
(e) Jasna i Sandra su u kavani. Ovo je ——— vino.
(f) Mark i Sandra su u Zagrebu. Ovo je ——— hotel.

5 Fill in your part of the dialogues:

Gdje je hotel?
(a) (*It is on the left in front of the station.*)
A gdje je kolodvor?
(*It is not far from the post office.*)

(b) (*Where can I buy stamps and envelopes?*)
Na pošti.
(*Where is the post office?*)
Idete ravno. Pošta je na desno.

(c) (*Where is Rudolf going?*)
Ide na posao.
(*Where does he work?*)
Radi u centru grada.

(d) Da li Mark gleda Sandru?
(*Yes, he is looking at Sandra.*)
Gdje je Sandra?
(*Sandra is near the building.*)

6 Substitute the noun or nouns in brackets for **on/ona/ono** or **oni/one/ona**:

(a) (Zgrada) je velika.
(b) (Mark) je u hotelu.
(c) (Rudolf i njegova prijateljica) su na trgu.
(d) (Pošta) je u centru grada, blizu parka.
(e) (Sandra i Jasna) su ispred kolodvora.
(f) (Drvo) nije daleko od spomenika.
(g) (Rudolf i Mark) idu u centar grada.
(h) (Spomenik) je u parku.

Dopunsko štivo 1

Marija Marinković is a tour guide in Zagreb. She is showing a group of tourists around the centre of Zagreb.

Marija   Sada smo u centru grada. Zagreb je lijep grad. To je kulturni i politički centar Hrvatske. Mi smo ispred hotela. Tamo je Glavni kolodvor. Na desno je hotel Esplanade. Idemo ravno prema trgu.
Turist   Oprostite, što je ono u parku?
Marija   To je spomenik. On se nalazi u parku.
Turist   Gdje je kazalište?

Marija Kazalište nije daleko. Idete ravno, a ono je na desno. Zgrada je velika i lijepa. Sada dolazimo na Jelačićev trg. Velika zgrada na desno je Gradska kavana. Sada idemo u Gornji grad. On je vrlo star.

Hrvatsko narodno kazalište *(Croatian National Theatre)*

kulturni i političiki centar Hrvatske *cultural and political centre of Croatia*	**ono** *that* (over there)
prema trgu *towards the square*	**On se nalazi u parku.** *It is situated* (Lit. *finds itself in the park.*)
	star *old*

Istina ili neistina?

(a) Zagreb is the cultural and political centre of Croatia.
(b) To get to the theatre you go straight on and it is on the left.
(c) The café on the square is called **Gradska kavana**.

Dopunsko štivo 2

Read the following short passage about Velimir and Zvonko and answer the questions below:

Velimir ide u grad. Na ulici vidi Zvonka. Idu zajedno kroz park i razgovaraju. Dolaze do spomenika. Onda idu na desno, prema trgu.

Zvonko   Želiš li ići na kavu, Velimire?
Velimir   Možemo ići na kavu, ali prvo moram ići na poštu. Želim kupiti marke.
Zvonko   Gradska kavana nije daleko od pošte. Idemo tamo.

Idu zajedno na poštu. Velimir ulazi u zgradu. Zgrada je velika. Velimir izlazi i idu na desno. Ulaze u kavanu.

Zvonko   Što želiš popiti?
Velimir   Ja bih kavu, hvala.
Zvonko   I ja bih kavu.

na ulici *on the street*	**do** *up to, as far as* (+ gen.)
Vidi Zvonka. *He* (i.e. Velimir) *sees Zvonko* (Zvonka is acc.).	**prvo** *first*
kroz *through* (+ acc.).	**ulaziti, ulazim** *to enter* (followed by **u zgradu**)
zajedno *together*	**izlaziti, izlazim** *to go out, come out*
razgovarati, razgovaram *to chat, have a conversation*	

Select the correct answer from (*a*), (*b*) and (*c*) for each of the questions below.

1   Kamo idu Zvonko i Velimir?
  (*a*)   Idu kroz park.
  (*b*)   Idu u kazalište.
  (*c*)   Idu na Gornji grad.

2   Što Velimir želi kupiti?
  (*a*)   Želi kupiti koverte.
  (*b*)   Želi kupiti kavu.
  (*c*)   Želi kupiti marke.

3   Što žele Zvonko i Velimir popiti?
  (*a*)   Žele popiti pivo.
  (*b*)   Žele popiti kavu.
  (*c*)   Žele popiti vino.

4
ŽELIM KUPITI...
I want to buy...

In this unit you will learn how to

- use phrases and expressions when shopping for basic items and when in the post office
- say some numbers
- use words for handling money
- use expressions relating to need or desire
  (The prices used in this unit do not reflect the real costs of such items because of recent high inflation.)

─────────────── Dijalog ───────────────

Sandra treba kupiti neke stvari.

Sandra   Želim kupiti razglednicu, Jasna. Moram pisati mami. Gdje mogu kupiti razglednicu?
Jasna   Razglednice možete kupiti u kiosku. Tamo je kiosk. Ali u svim kioscima ne prodaju razglednice.

trebati, trebam *to need, require*		**mama** *Mum*	
neke stvari *some things*		**kiosk** *kiosk*	
razglednica *postcard*		**u svim kioscima** *in all kiosks*	
pisati, pišem *to write*		**prodavati, prodajem** *to sell*	

From now onwards you will find more nouns in the nominative case, although they might appear in another case in the **Dijalog**. Adjectives are given in the masculine nominative case. The forms are as they appear in the **Dijalog** where confusion might otherwise occur.

Sandra	Molim vas, imate li razglednice?
Prodavačica	Imam i velike i male razglednice. Kakve želite?
Sandra	Trebam veliku razglednicu. Koliko košta velika razglednica?
Prodavačica	Velika razglednica košta dvanaest dinara, a mala osam dinara.
Sandra	Dajte mi, molim vas, jednu veliku razglednicu, i jednu malu.
Prodavačica	Dvadeset dinara. Još nešto?
Sandra	Ne, hvala. (**Daje novac ženi.**)
Prodavačica	Molim.
Jasna	Hoćete li još nešto, Sandra?
Sandra	Znate, trebam sapun, šampon i zubnu pastu.
Jasna	Idemo u samoposlugu.

prodavačica *saleswoman*	**dajte mi** *give to me*
imati, imam *to have*	**jednu veliku razglednicu** *one large postcard* (acc.)
molim vas *please* (Lit. *I beg you*)	**dvadeset dinara** *20 dinars*
i… i… *both… and…*	**Hoćete li još nešto?** *Do you want anything else?*
male razglednice *small postcards*	**htjeti, hoću** (irregular verb) *to want*
Kakve želite? *What kind do you want?*	**davati, dajem** *to give*
Koliko košta velika razglednica? *How much does a large postcard cost?*	**novac** *money*
velika razglednica košta *a large postcard costs*	**žena** *woman*
dvanaest dinara *12 dinars* (currency of Serbo-Croat-speaking areas – abbreviated to din., see Ex. 1)	**hvala** *thank you*
	molim *response to **hvala**, please*
	sapun *soap*
	šampon *shampoo*
osam dinara *eight dinars*	**zubna pasta** *toothpaste*
	samoposluga *self-service shop*

Mark i Rudolf ulaze u poštu.

Mark Molim vas, dajte mi tri koverte i marke za Englesku.

Čovjek Ne prodajem koverte i nemam marke. Ovo je pogrešan šalter. Trebate šalter broj sedam.

Mark Molim vas, mogu li ovdje kupiti marke i koverte?

Čovjek Kako da ne, gospodine. Ovo je pošta!

čovjek *person, man*	**pogrešan šalter** *the wrong counter*
tri koverte *three envelopes*	**šalter broj sedam** *counter number*
marke za Englesku *stamps for*	*seven*
England	**kako da ne** *of course*
nemam *I have not*	

Istina ili neistina?

(a) Small postcards cost 12 dinars at the kiosk.
(b) Mark wants to buy four envelopes.
(c) Mark goes straightaway to the correct counter.

—— Objašnjenja k komentari ——

Shops

Kiosks are dotted along the streets of towns in the whole region. They sell newspapers, cigarettes, postcards, stamps, and often other small items. When handing over change or your purchases the shop-keeper might say **izvolite** (*here you are*). When asking for something it sounds a little harsh in English to say the equivalent of *give to me* (**dajte mi**), but it is said.

Post office

In addition to selling stamps and other items obvious to a visitor from England, you can also make telephone calls from post offices. This is particularly important if making a call overseas as the rates tend to be much higher in hotels than in a post office. Simply go to the main desk in the post office, say where you want to call, you will then be told which booth (**kabina**) to use, make your call and pay on your way out.

Hvala/Molim

You have met these words before. It is polite to reply with **molim** when someone says **hvala** to you. **Molim** also has other meanings. It is the equivalent of *please* when making a polite request, or if said with a questioning intonation it means that you are asking that someone repeat what they have just said (very useful!).

 —————— **Ključne fraze** ——————

How to:

- express need or desire to different degrees.

I need	**trebam**
I may, can	**mogu**
I must	**moram**
I want	**želim**
Do you want...	**Hoćete li...**

- request something in a shop. **Molim vas, imate li..?**
  Molim vas, dajte mi...

- ask how much something costs. **Koliko košta..?**

- use some numbers. **jedna razglednica**
  osam dinara
  tri koverte

- name basic items for purchase.

postcard	**razglednica**
envelope	**koverta**
stamp	**marka**

soap	**sapun**
shampoo	**šampon**
toothpaste	**zubna pasta**
● say *thank you,*	**hvala**
and to reply politely.	**molim**

Jezični obrasci

1 Htjeti, hoću

Another common word meaning *want* is used in this unit. It follows an irregular pattern:

ja	hoću	mi	hoćemo
ti	hoćeš	vi	hoćete
on/a/o	hoće	oni/e/a	hoće

Like **biti** this verb also has a negative form which is all one word:

ja	neću	mi	nećemo
ti	nećeš	vi	nećete
on/a/o	neće	oni/e/a	neće

Hoću razglednicu.	*I want a postcard.*
Neću kupiti razglednicu.	*I do not want to buy a postcard.*
Hoćemo kavu.	*We want coffee.*
Nećete velike razglednice.	*You don't want the big postcards.*

Htjeti (**hoću**, *I want*) is an alternative to the verb **željeti** (**želim**) which was used in Unit 2. **Željeti** is a verb which follows the regular patterns which you know, but **htjeti** is also commonly used.

2 Nemam.../I have not...

The words meaning *I have not...*, etc. are also a single word:

ja	nemam	mi	nemamo
ti	nemaš	vi	nemate
on/a/o	nema	oni/e/a	nemaju

You have now met the only three verbs which form their negative as a single word (**nisam**, **neću**, **nemam**). As you know, all the others put **ne** in front of the verb:

Ne pišem.	*I'm not writing.*
Ne govore.	*They're not speaking.*

3 How to say 'to'

As seen in the previous unit, little words in English such as *of* are conveyed in Serbo-Croat by the use of cases. The dative case is used in such phrases as *to write to*, *to give to* and *to say to*, so Sandra remarks **Moram pisati mami** (*I must write to Mum*).

There is no separate word for *to* in the Serbo-Croat sentence. It is implied by the use of the dative case. Similarly, the word *for* is implied by the use of the dative case in the sentence **Moram kupiti sapun mami.** (*I must buy the soap **for** Mum*). Look at these other examples:

Jasna mora pisati Rudolfu.	*Jasna must write to Rudolf.*
Mi pišemo prijateljici.	*We are writing to our* friend* (female).
Konobar daje salatu ženi.	*The waiter gives the salad to the woman.*

*Words such as *my*, *your*, etc. are often omitted in Serbo-Croat if it is clear from the context which word is implied.

Look at the way the last example is built up of nouns with different endings (cases):

Subject nominative	Verb	Object accusative	*To...* dative
konobar	**daje**	**salatu**	**ženi**

Compare with the following sentence:

žena	**daje**	**salatu**	**konobaru**

It is important to use the correct case ending in Serbo-Croat, since to use the wrong one could make you imply that the woman did not like her salad and she was returning it!

4 Plurals

To say more than one of something in the nominative and accusative cases:

Masc. (e.g. **hotel, grad**)
nom.   **hoteli** (add **-i**)
acc.   **hotele** (add **-e**)

Masc. nouns of one syllable usually add **-ov-** before the case ending
nom.   **gradovi** (add **-ovi**)
acc.   **gradove** (add **-ove**)
                after a soft consonant (**c, č, ć, dž, đ, j, lj, nj, š, ž**) add
                -evi and **-eve** (e.g. **muž – muževi**) see spelling rule
                Unit 2, p.25.

Fem. (e.g. **škola**)
nom.   **škole** (change **-a** to **-e**)
acc.   **škole** (change **-a** to **-e**)

Neut. (e.g. **kazalište**)
nom.   **kazališta** (change **-e/-o** to **-a**)
acc.   **kazališta** (change **-e/-o** to **-a**)

Examples

Masc.
Hoteli su tamo.   *The hotels are there.*
Vidim hotele tamo.   *I see the hotels there.*

Fem.
Razglednice su na šalteru.   *The postcards are on the counter.*
Imam razglednice.   *I have the postcards.*

Neut.
Kazališta su ispred parka.   *The theatres are in front*
                                   of the park.
Vidim kazališta.   *I see the theatres.*

5 Spelling rules

There are certain rules for spelling which effect nouns. When **-i** is added after **k, g, h**, these letters change to **c, z, s**. Study the following examples:

Kios**k** je na ulici.	*The kiosk is on the street.*
Kios**ci** su na ulici.	*The kiosks are on the street.*
Idemo u samoposlu**gu**.	*We are going to the self-service shop.*
Sada smo u samoposlu**zi**.	*Now we are in the self-service shop.*

Exceptions are made for people's proper names: **Branka** (a girl's name) becomes **Branki**.

6 Unusual categories of nouns

(a) stvar

The word **stvar** (*thing*) is a feminine noun although it ends in a consonant. There is a small sub-category of these nouns with the following endings:

	singular	plural
nom.	stvar	stvari
acc.	stvar	stvari
gen.	stvari	
dat.	stvari	

(b) čovjek

The word **čovjek** refers to a person regardless of sex. It has an unusual plural in the form **ljudi** (*people, men*). Both words are masc.:

	singular	plural
nom.	čovjek	ljudi
acc.	čovjeka	ljude
gen.	čovjeka	
dat.	čovjeku	

Čovjek je na ulici.	*A person is in the street.*
Ljudi su na ulici.	*People are in the street.*

7 Numbers 1–20

jedan, jedna, jedno	1	jedanaest	11
dva/dvije	2	dvanaest	12
tri	3	trinaest	13
četiri	4	četrnaest	14
pet	5	petnaest	15
šest	6	šesnaest	16
sedam	7	sedamnaest	17
osam	8	osamnaest	18
devet	9	devetnaest	19
deset	10	dvadeset	20

The number *one* behaves like an adjective. This means that its ending changes according to the word which follows:

Masc.
jed**an** stol   *one table*

Fem.
jed**na** žena   *one woman*

Neut.
jed**no** kazalište   *one theatre*

The number *two* has different forms when it refers to masculine or neuter nouns (**dva**) and when it refers to feminine (**dvije**). Like the numbers *three* (**tri**) and *four* (**četiri**) they are followed by words in the genitive singular:

dva stola	*two tables*
dva piva	*two beers*
dvije kave	*two coffees*
tri marke	*three stamps*
četiri koverte	*four envelopes*

The numbers *five* to *20* are followed by the genitive plural. The most frequent ending for the genitive plural is **a** for all genders:

Masc.
pet dinara
šest gradova

Fem.
sedam kava
osam razglednica

Neut.
devet piva

However, when there are one or more consonants at the end, they are separated by an extra **a**:

marka   (add case ending to **mark-**)   deset maraka

Some nouns take **i** at the end
stvar   stvari
čovjek   ljudi

Vježbe

1   Write out the following prices and then add them up:

(a)

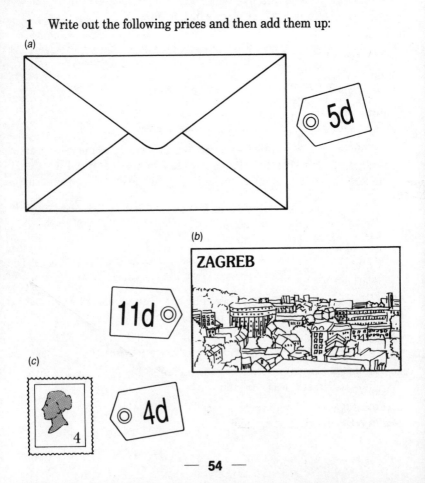

(b)

(c)

Koliko košta..?

(a) koverta
(b) razglednica
(c) marka

2   Look at this table and make up sentences similar to this:

Rudolf hoće kavu. Koliko košta kava? Kava košta devetnaest dinara.

(a) Rudolf	kava	19 din.
(b) Sandra	razglednica	8 din.
(c) Mark	pivo	20 din.
(d) Jasna	šampon	17 din.
(e) Zvonko	marka	12 din.
(f) Velimir	marka za Englesku	16 din.

3   Put the nouns in brackets into the plural and into the correct case:

(a) Moram kupiti (marka i razglednica).
(b) Vidim (park) gdje su (spomenik).
(c) (Hotel) su u centru grada.
(d) (Čovjek) vole živjeti u gradu.
(e) U centru grada su velike (zgrada).
(f) Prodajete li (koverta)?

4   Complete missing part of dialogue:

(*Hello. Do you have any postcards?*)
Dobar dan. Imamo razglednice.
(*May I see the large postcards?*)
Izvolite.
(*How much does one large postcard cost?*)
Petnaest dinara.
(*Give me three, please.*)
To je četrdeset pet dinara.
(*Thank you. Goodbye.*)
Molim. Do viđenja.

5   Make up sentences according to the following model using the information at the top of p. 56:

e.g. Sandra davati novac žena.
     Sandra daje novac ženi.

(a)	Mark	davati	kava	Rudolf
(b)	Čovjek	davati	marka	Jasna
(c)	Mi	davati	sapun	mama
(d)	Žena	davati	pivo	Velimir
(e)	Oni	davati	novac	čovjek
(f)	Konobar	davati	vino	Branka

6 Match the questions to the answers:

(a)	Trebam marke i koverte.	(i)	Gdje je Jasna?
(b)	Idem na kavu.	(ii)	Što trebate?
(c)	Evo Jasne.	(iii)	Imate li marke?
(d)	Nemamo	(iv)	Kuda ideš?

7 Complete the sentences with the most appropriate verbs chosen from the box below. If necessary the required form of the verb is indicated by **ja**, etc. in brackets, where it would not normally be included in such a sentence or question:

(a) _____ li (ja) kupiti razglednice u kiosku?

(b) _____ li vi engleski?

(c) Mark i Sandra _____ u hotelu u Zagrebu.

(d) Oprostite, _____ li vi gospođa Bryant?

(e) Kamo _____ Rudolf i Mark?

(f) Ja _____ živjeti u centru grada.

živjeti	ići	voljeti	govoriti	moći	biti

Dopunsko štivo 1

U samoposluzi Sandra traži neke stvari.

Sandra	Molim vas, gdje su sapuni i šamponi?
Prodavač	Tamo lijevo.
Sandra	Koji sapun je dobar, Jasna?
Jasna	Ja koristim ovaj sapun. Kažu da je i taj dobar. Ovdje su šamponi.
Sandra	Dobro, gdje je zubna pasta?
Jasna	Ovdje negdje. Ovo je odlična pasta.
Sandra	Hvala. Imam sve. Gdje mogu platiti?
Jasna	Na blagajni kod izlaza.

Na blagajni

Blagajnica Sapun..., šampon..., zubna pasta... Trebate još nešto, gospođo?
Sandra Ne, hvala. Do viđenja.
Blagajnica Do viđenja.

Sandra traži... *Sandra looks for...*	**negdje** *somewhere*
tražiti, tražim *to look for* (also in	**odličan** *excellent*
the sense of *to ask for*)	**sve** *everything*
prodavač *salesman*	**platiti, platim** *to pay*
koji sapun? *which soap?*	**na blagajni** *at the checkout*
koristiti, koristim *to use*	**kod izlaza** *by the exit*
ovaj sapun *this soap*	**blagajnica** *checkout operator*
kažu da... *they say that...*	(female)
taj *that, that one*	**gospođo** *madam* (from gospođa)

Istina ili neistina?

(*a*) Sandra traži sapune i šampone.
(*b*) Blagajna je kod izlaza.
(*c*) Sandra treba još nešto na blagajni.

——— Dopunsko štivo 2 ———

Read the following passage and answer the questions below.

Sandra i Mark dolaze u hotel. Idu na recepciju.

Sandra Molim vas, dajte mi ključ od sobe broj 20. To je naša soba.
Recepcija Evo ga, gospođo. Izvolite.
Sandra Hvala.
Recepcija Molim.
Sandra Oprostite, gdje se u hotelu mogu kupiti novine?
Recepcija Novine prodajemo tamo blizu lifta.

Mark i Sandra idu tamo.

Mark Molim vas, imate li engleske novine?
Prodavač Imamo *Guardian* i *The Economist*.
Mark Imate li možda *Financial Times*?

Prodavač Nemamo.
Mark Dajte mi, molim vas, *Guardian*. A prodajete li cigarete?
Prodavač Ovdje ne prodajemo cigarete. Morate ići u bar.
Mark Hvala.
Prodavač Molim.

recepcija *reception*	**broj** *number*
ključ od sobe *key to the room*	**novine** *newspaper(s)*
soba *room*	**lift** *lift*
Gdje se u hotelu mogu kupiti	**možda** *perhaps*
novine? *Where can one buy*	**cigareta** *cigarette*
newspapers in the hotel?	**bar** *bar*

Select the correct answer from (*a*), (*b*) and (*c*) for each of the questions below.

1 Što Sandra traži na recepciji?
 (*a*) Traži sapun.
 (*b*) Traži ključ od njihove sobe.
 (*c*) Želi kupiti cigarete.

2 Gdje se u hotelu mogu kupiti novine?
 (*a*) Kod izlaza.
 (*b*) Ispred bara.
 (*c*) Blizu lifta.

3 Gdje se u hotelu mogu kupiti cigarete?
 (*a*) Na recepciji.
 (*b*) U restoranu.
 (*c*) U baru.

5

U RESTORANU
In the restaurant

In this unit you will learn how to

- order a meal
- ask for and state opinions, preferences, advice
- express agreement
- attract the attention of others
- say *there is / are* and *there is / are not*

——————— Dijalog ———————

Mark i Sandra idu s Rudolfom i Jasnom u restoran. Idu na večeru. U restoranu sjede za stolom u uglu. Za drugim stolovima ima mnogo ljudi. Rudolf zove konobara.

Rudolf	Konobaru, molim vas, imate li jelovnik?
Konobar	Imamo. Izvolite, gospodine.
Rudolf	Hvala.
Konobar	Molim.
Rudolf	Konobaru, što nam preporučujete za večeru?
Konobar	Naša riba je uvijek svježa, a i meso je odlično. Preporučujem vam nacionalne specijalitete. Imamo zagrebački odrezak i lignje na ribarski način.
Rudolf	Ja znam da je sve ovdje vrlo svježe. Sandra, što ćete jesti?
Sandra	Volim meso, ali više volim ribu.
Jasna	Onda vam savjetujem lignje na ribarski način.

Mark	A što meni savjetujete, Jasna? Mislite li da je roštilj dobar?
Jasna	Pretpostavljam da jest, ali zagrebački odrezak je nacionalni specijalitet.
Mark	Dobro. Čini mi se da moram probati zagrebački odrezak. Slažete li se?
Jasna	Slažem se. I ja bih isto.
Rudolf	Možemo naručiti večeru. Hoćemo li vino?
Jasna	Naravno. Volite li više crno ili bijelo vino, Sandra?
Sandra	Više volim crno.
Jasna	Dobro, i hoćemo juhu i tri salate, Rudolf.
Sandra	Prvo, mogu li dobiti čašu vode? Žedna sam.
Jasna	I ja sam žedna. Nema vode na stolu. Konobaru, molim vas, dvije čaše vode.

jesti, jedem to eat
s (preposition with instrumental) with
večera dinner
ići na večeru to go to dinner
sjediti, sjedim to be sitting
za stolom (stol nom.) at a table
u uglu (**ugao** masc. like **posao**) in the corner
za drugim stolovima at other tables
Ima mnogo ljudi. There are many people.
zvati, zovem to call
konobar waiter
jelovnik menu
Što nam preporučujete? (preporučivati, preporučujem) What do you recommend to us?
za večeru for dinner
riba fish
svjež fresh
meso meat
odličan excellent
...vam ...to you
nacionalni specijalitet national speciality (dish)
zagrebački odrezak Zagreb schnitzel

lignje na ribarski način squid in the fisherman's way
Što ćete jesti? What will you eat?
više volim I prefer (Lit. I like more)
savjetovati, savjetujem to advise
Mislite li da..? Do you think that..?
roštilj barbecue
pretpostavljati, pretpostavljam to suppose
Čini mi se da... It seems to me that...
probati, probam to try
Slažete li se? (slagati se, slažem se) Do you agree?
I ja bih isto. I would like the same too.
naručiti to order
naravno of course
juha soup
salata salad
crno ili bijelo vino red (Lit. black) or white wine
Volite li više..? Do you prefer..?
Mogu li dobiti čašu vode? May I have a glass of water?
Nema vode. There is no water.
dvije čaše vode two glasses of water

Their conversation turns to meals and food.

Jasna	Sandra, što jedete za doručak u Londonu?
Sandra	Jedem kruh i džem, i pijem čaj s mlijekom.
Jasna	A što volite za ručak? Da li je ručak vaš glavni obrok?
Sandra	Ručak nije naš glavni obrok. Na poslu jedem sendvič.
Jasna	Što vi jedete, Mark?
Mark	Za ručak i ja jedem malo.

Što jedete?   *What do you eat?*
za doručak   *for breakfast*
Jedem kruh i džem.   *I eat bread and jam.*
Pijem čaj s mlijekom.   *I drink tea with milk.*

piti, pijem   *to drink*
za ručak   *for lunch*
vaš glavni obrok   *your main meal*
na poslu   *at work*
sendvič   *sandwich*
malo   *a little*

Istina ili neistina?

(*a*) The restaurant has fish and meat.
(*b*) Sandra prefers meat.
(*c*) Sandra drinks coffee for breakfast.

--------- **Objašnjenja i komentari** ---------

Meals

The words for meals are **doručak** (*breakfast*), **ručak** (*lunch*) and **večera** (*dinner*). Breakfast is usually eaten at about 9 am or 10 am and often eaten at work. Many people begin work earlier than in England, e.g. at 6 am, and return home from work in the middle of the afternoon. Lunch is then taken as the main meal of the day, after which follows a nap. The evening meal is usually a light supper. However, this pattern of starting the day early and having a nap in the afternoon is slowly being replaced in urban areas by a more 9.00 to 5.00 routine as found commonly elsewhere in Europe. As this new habit spreads, so the evening meal is becoming the main meal of the day.

Restaurants

There are many types of places to eat from a local **kavana** to hotels which serve international cuisine. But one of the delights of visiting a country is to try local specialities. Eating out is not expensive and each region offers different specialities. In most restaurants you will find various first courses (**predjelo**), followed by main courses (**gotova jela**, **specijaliteti**) and sweets (**slatko**) with ice-cream (**sladoled**), filled pancakes (**palačinke**) or cakes (**kolači**). You may be asked if you would like an aperitif (**aperitif**) of a local brandy such as grape brandy (**lozovača**). There are many types of wine which vary greatly in quality and price.

Ključne fraze

How to:

• ask for a recommendation.	**Što nam preporučujete?**
• suggest something.	**Preporučujem vam...**
• ask for, and give advice.	**Što mi savjetujete?** **Savjetujem vam...**
• ask for, and give agreement.	**Slažete li se?** **Slažem se.**
• ask for and give your own preference.	**Što volite više..?** **Volite li više..?** **Više volim...**
• ask for another person's opinion.	**Mislite li da..?**
• state what you think.	**Znam da...** **Čini mi se da...** **Pretpostavljam da...**
• ask for the menu.	**Imate li jelovnik?**
• request a glass of water.	**Mogu li dobiti čašu vode?**
• say *there is* or *there are*.	**Ima mnogo ljudi.**
• say *there is not* or *there are not*.	**Nema vode na stolu.**

Jezični obrasci

1 Cases

You have now met the last of the cases and the standard endings for nouns.

(a) Instrumental singular

The two prepositions **s** (*with*) and **za** (*behind*, but used in the phrase *at a table*) are followed by the instrumental case (although **za** may also be followed by the accusative when it will mean *for*). The endings are as follows:

Masc. (e.g. **grad, muž**)

ins.	**gradom** (add **-om**)
ins.	**mužem** (add **-em** before a soft consonant **c, č, ć, dž, đ, j, lj, nj, š, ž**)

Fem. (e.g. **prijateljica, stvar**)

ins.	**prijateljicom** (change **-a** to **-om**; **-om** does not change before a soft consonant for fem. nouns)
ins.	**stvari/stvarju** (add **-i** or **-ju** to fem. nouns which end in a consonant)

Neut. (e.g. **pivo, predgrađe**)

ins.	**pivom** (change **-o** to **-om**)
ins.	**predgrađem** (change **-e** to **-em**)

(b) Instrumental and dative plural

You can learn these two together as they are the same.

Masc. (e.g. **prijatelj, grad, kiosk**)

ins. + dat.	**prijateljima** (add **-ima**)
ins. + dat.	**gradovima** (add **-ov-** before the case endings for masc. nouns with one syllable)
ins. + dat.	**kioscima** (the **k** changes to **c** before **-i**)

Fem. (e.g. **žena, stvar**)

ins. + dat.	**ženama** (change **-a** to **-ama**)
ins. + dat.	**stvarima** (add **-ima** to fem. nouns which end in a consonant)

Neut. (e.g. **predgrađe**)
ins. + dat.   **predgrađima** (change **-e/-o** to **-ima**)

(c) Vocative singular and plural

This case is used when addressing people directly in speech or in a letter. It is the case used when you want to call someone (vocative). The endings in the singular are:

Masc. (e.g. **prijatelj, gospodin**)
voc.   **gospodine** (add **-e**)
voc.   **prijatelju** (add **-u** after a soft consonant and sometimes after **-r**)

Fem. (e.g. **žena, gospođica**)
voc.   **ženo** (change **-a** to **-o**)
voc.   **gospođice** (change **-a** to **-e** if ending is **-ica**)
                However, in practice, few fem. nouns change: voc. of **Jasna** is **Jasna**.

Neut. (e.g. **dijete** [*child*])
voc.   **dijete** (no change)

There are few occasions when you would use the vocative with the neuter as most words refer to inanimate objects. Theoretically, there is a vocative ending for all nouns, but there are not many occasions in life when you want to address something like a house (**kućo!**). The endings in the plural are the same as the nominative in all genders.

There is a spelling rule for masculine nouns in the vocative singular; **-g** will change to **-ž**, **-k** will change to **-č**, **-h** will change to **-š**, and you add the ending **-e**. Look at the example:

Bog (*God*)   **Bože!** (used as a mild expletive)

2 'To me'/'to you', etc (dative)

You already know the words for *I*, *you*, etc. (the personal pronouns):

ja	*I*	mi	*we*
ti	*you*	vi	*you*
on/ona	*he/she*	oni/one	*they* (masc. and fem.)
(there are also neut. forms **ono** and **ona**)			

As you also know in certain circumstances you use the dative to mean *to someone*:

Konobar daje salatu ženi. *The waiter gives the salad to the woman.*

So there are also words which mean *to me, to you*, etc.

Look at the examples given so far:

Što nam preporučujete?	*What do you recommend to us?*
Preporučujem vamș	*I recommend to youș*
Čini mi seș	*It seems to meș*

nam	*to us*	
vam	*to you*	(equivalent to **vi**)
mi	*to me*	

Here are all the forms together, both long and short forms:

	short	long		short	long
ja	mi	meni	mi	nam	nama
ti	ti	tebi	vi	vam	vama
on	mu	njemu	oni	im	njima
ona	joj	njoj	one	im	njima

(the forms for **ono** and **ona** are the same as for **on** and **oni**)

You can use these words in other phrases and expressions which you know:

Konobar joj daje salatu.	*The waiter gives the salad to her.*
Moram mu pisati.	*I must write to him.*
Pišemo joj.	*We are writing to her.*

Look at the examples above carefully and you will notice how the short forms come in second place. This is the normal word order. They behave in the same way as the short forms of **biti**.

The long forms have two basic functions.

(*a*)   They may come at the beginning to stress the person involved:

Meni se činiș	***To me*** *it seemsș*
Tebi preporučujemș	***It is to you*** *that I'm recommendingș*

(*b*)   They are used after prepositions:
u zgradi   *in the building*
u njoj   *in it*

Otherwise use the short forms.

3   Ima/Nema

Serbo-Croat has just one word to express *there is...* and *there are...*:
ima. It is the same form as the word which means *he/she has*. When
it means *there is/are* it is followed by the genitive case to mean *some*:

Ima vode.   *There is some water.*
Ima kruha.   *There is some bread.*
Ovdje **ima** Engleza.   *There are English people here.*

The negative form is **nema** (*there is not/there are not*):

Nema vode.   *There is no water.*
Nema kruha.   *There is no bread.*
Ovdje **nema** Engleza.   *There are no English people here.*

You use the genitive singular or the plural as required by the sense
of the sentence, as you use either singular or plural in English.

4   Mnogo *and words of quantity*

Mnogo (*many, much, a lot of*) is followed by the genitive case. Most
words which indicate a quantity are followed by the genitive case,
such as **čaša vode** (*a glass of water*) or **mnogo ljudi** (*many people*).

5   Unusual categories of nouns

The word **ugao** (*corner*) is masculine and it follows the same pattern
as **posao**. When adding an ending the **a** is lost and the **-o** changes
to **l**:

	singular	plural
nom.	ugao	uglovi (ugl- is one syllable)
acc.	ugao	uglove
gen.	ugla	uglova
dat.	uglu	uglovima
ins.	uglom	uglovima

Vježbe

1 Replace the pronoun in brackets with the corresponding form meaning *to me*, *to you*, etc.:

(a) Čini (on) se da Rudolf sjedi za stolom.
(b) Što (mi) preporučujete?
(c) Preporučujem (vi) crno vino.
(d) Što (ona) savjetujete?
(e) Čini (oni) se da je riba svježa.
(f) Sandra (ja) želi savjetovati.
(g) Moram (ti) pisati.
(h) Konobar (ona) daje salatu.
(i) Čovjek (ja) daje marke na pošti.
(j) Daje li (mi) bijelo vino?

2 Add the appropriate case ending to the nouns in brackets, note that some are given in the plural:

(a) (Jasna) se čini da je roštilj dobar.
(b) Što savjetuješ (konobari)?
(c) Vidim (čovjek) na ulici.
(d) Sandra vidi (zgrada) gdje radi Rudolf.
(e) Idemo li sada na (kava)?
(f) Idemo s (prijatelji) u grad.
(g) Rudolf sjedi za (stol) s (Jasna).
(h) Gledamo (konobari) u uglu restorana.
(i) Mark hoće (cigarete) i (novine).
(j) Volimo učiti (jezici).

3 Fill in the missing part of the dialogue.

(Waiter! Hello. Do you have a menu?)
Izvolite, gospodine.
(Thank you.)
Molim. Želite li naručiti?
(What do you recommend to me?)
Preporučujem naše lignje i salatu.
(I prefer meat. I would like meat and a salad, please.)
Hoćete li vino? Što više volite, crno ili bijelo?
(I prefer red, and may I have a glass of water?)

JELOVNIK

PREDJELO

GOTOVA JELA

SLATKO

4 Match the answers to the questions:

(a) Slažem se.   (i) Gdje je kruh?
(b) Na stolu je.   (ii) Mogu li dobiti čašu vode?
(c) Kako da ne.   (iii) Slažete li se sa Jasnom?
(d) Naše lignje su uvijek   (iv) Što nam preporučujete?
      dobre.

5 Imagine that you have invited some friends to a restaurant. How would you ask the waiter the following:

(a) if he has the menu.
(b) for fish and salad.
(c) for two beers.
(d) for a glass of water.

6 Look at the following advertisements:

Which one sells fish?

7 Make up questions for the following responses:

   (*a*) Da, volim pivo.
   (*b*) Ne, ne volim pivo.
   (*c*) Sutra idem u grad.
   (*d*) Želim piti crno vino.
   (*e*) Volimo ići u grad.
   (*f*) Ne, ne možeš dobiti čašu vode.

8 In the following sentences the noun in brackets is being used with either **mnogo** or **ima/nema**, put the noun into the genitive case, and either singular or plural as appropriate (all the nouns are given here in the nominative singular).

(a) Ima li (kruh) na stolu?
(b) Vidim mnogo (park) u centru grada.
(c) Konobar daje mnogo (salata) ženi.
(d) Nema (čovjek) na ulici.
(e) Mislite li da Rudolf ima mnogo (prijatelj)?
(f) Nema (vino) na stolu.
(g) Čini joj se da ima (čovjek) za stolovima.
(h) Ima li (Englez) ovdje u hotelu?
(i) Nema (kava).
(j) Tamo ima (razglednica).

Dopunsko štivo 1

Zvonko i Velimir ulaze u kavanu.

Zvonko Je li slobodno, gospodine?
Gospodin Jest, izvolite.

Sjede za stolom.

Zvonko Voliš li više pivo ili vino, Velimire?
Velimir Više volim vino. Ali znam da nije dobro piti alkohol. Dobro je piti vodu ili sok.
Zvonko Imaš pravo. Što mi preporučuješ danas? Hoćemo li piti crno ili bijelo vino?
Velimir Konobaru, što nam preporučujete danas?
Konobar Imamo dobru svježu ribu, a i meso je odlično.
Velimir Ja hoću ribu, a ti Zvonko?
Zvonko Znaš da ne volim ribu. Ja hoću meso.
Konobar Dobro. A želite li vino?
Velimir Želimo jedno bijelo, i jedno crno vino.

Je li slobodno? *Is it* (this place) *free?* (i.e. *vacant*)	**Imaš pravo.** *You are right.*
	Znaš da... *You know that...*

Istina ili neistina?

(a) Velimir prefers beer to wine.
(b) Zvonko likes fish.
(c) Velimir orders two red wines.

───────── **Dopunsko štivo 2** ─────────

Read the passage and answer the questions below.

Sandra voli doručak. Svako jutro jede kruh s džemom i pije čaj. Njen muž, Mark, ne voli čaj, više voli piti bijelu kavu ili mlijeko. Sandra ruča u školi. Ne jede mnogo za ručak. Sjedi i jede sendvič. U sendviču je salata ili meso. Mark ponekad ruča s prijateljima u gradu, ali također ne voli jesti mnogo za ručak. Navečer, kod kuće, Sandra i Mark večeraju. Spremaju ribu ili dobro meso sa salatom. Vole jesti i kolače.

svako jutro *every morning*	**navečer** *in the evening*
ili *or*	**kod kuće** *at home*
ručati, ručam *to have lunch*	**večerati, večeram** *to have dinner*
sendvič *sandwich*	**spremati, spremam** *to prepare*
također *also*	

1 Što Mark više voli piti za doručak?
(a) Više voli piti mlijeko.
(b) Više voli piti sok.
(c) Više voli piti bijelu kavu ili mlijeko.

2 Gdje Sandra ruča?
(a) Ruča u gradu s mužem.
(b) Ruča kod kuće.
(c) Ruča na poslu.

3 Što vole Mark i Sandra jesti za večeru?
(a) Vole jesti palačinke.
(b) Vole jesti kolače.
(c) Vole jesti lignje na ribarski način.

6

DOĐITE K MENI

Come to my place

In this unit you will learn how to

- give an invitation
- accept or decline an invitation
- give and ask directions
- give your address and telephone number
- express degrees of certainty and uncertainty

Dijalog

Rudolf poziva Sandra i Marka k njemu.

Rudolf   Sandra i Mark, molim vas, hoću vas pozvati k meni sutra navečer.

Mark   Žao mi je, ali ne možemo doći. Moram raditi kod nas u hotelu.

Sandra   Mark, ne možeš stalno raditi. Vrlo rado prihvaćamo poziv. Gdje stanujete?

Rudolf   Stanujem blizu centra. Moja adresa je Heinzlova ulica šezdeset šest, a moj stan je na petom katu. Od hotela idite pješice do Glavnog kolodvora. Tamo uzmite ili tramvaj dvadeset, ili autobus sedamnaest. Voze prema Autobusnom kolodvoru. Siđite na osmoj stanici. Moj blok

se nalazi odmah preko puta te stanice. To je Heinzlova
ulica. Je li jasno? Za svaki slučaj, moj telefonski broj je dva
šest sedam – sedam osam pet.

Sandra Da, u redu, imam sve podatke. Kada trebamo doći?

Rudolf Dođite sutra u sedam sati. I nemojte doći taksijem.
Morate naučiti putovati gradskim prijevozom.

Dođite k meni. *Come to my place* (house/flat).	**tramvaj** *tram*
Rudolf poziva... *Rudolf is inviting...*	**autobus** *bus*
Želim vas pozvati k meni. *I want to invite you to my place.*	**Voze prema Autobusnom kolodvoru.** *They drive towards the bus station.*
k njemu *to his place*	**siđite** (sići, siđem) *get down/get off* (bus)
Žao mi je. *I'm sorry.*	**na osmoj stanici** *at the eighth stop*
kod nas u hotelu *at our place* (room) *in the hotel*	**blok** *block* (of flats)
stalno *continuously*	**preko puta** (preposition with gen.) *opposite*
vrlo rado *very gladly*	**Je li jasno?** *Is that clear?*
Prihvaćamo poziv. *We accept the invitation.*	**za svaki slučaj** *in any event/case*
stanovati, stanujem *to live, reside*	**telefonski broj** *telephone number*
blizu (preposition with gen.) *near*	**u redu** *all right, okay*
adresa *address*	**Imam sve podatke.** *I have all the information.*
ulica *street*	**kada** *when*
šezdeset šest *sixty-six*	**u sedam sati** *at seven o'clock*
stan *flat*	**Nemojte doći taksijem.** *Don't come by taxi.*
na petom katu *on the fifth floor*	
idite pješice *go on foot*	**naučiti putovati gradskim prijevozom** *to learn to travel by city transport*
uzmite (uzeti, uzmem) *take* (a bus)	

Dijalog

Sandra i Mark idu autobusom i silaze na osmoj stanici.
(Unfortunately, they have taken the wrong bus.)

Mark Da li si sigurna da je ovdje pravo mjesto? Ne vidim blok
preko puta.

Sandra Sigurna sam. Ovo je osma stanica. Dolazi jedan
gospodin. Pitaj njega.

Mark Oprostite, gospodine, možete li mi reći gdje je Heinzlova
šezdeset šest?

Gospodin	Ovo nije Heinzlova ulica.
Mark	Možete li mi reći kako možemo tamo doći?
Gospodin	Nije teško. Idite ravno i skrenite u drugu ulicu lijevo, onda skrenite u prvu ulicu desno i opet idite ravno do glavne ceste. To je Heinzlova.
Mark	Hvala lijepo, gospodine.
Gospodin	Nema na čemu. Do viđenja i laku noć.

---

silaze (silaziti, silazim) *They get off* (the bus).	**Nije teško.** *It's not difficult.*
siguran (masc.) **sigurna** (fem.) *sure, certain*	**idite ravno** *go straight on*
da *that*	**skrenite u drugu ulicu** (skrenuti, skrenem) *turn into the second street*
pravo mjesto *the right place*	**...u prvu ulicu** *...into the first street*
pitaj njega *ask him*	**opet** *again*
pitati, pitam *to ask*	**do glavne ceste** *as far as the main road*
Možete li mi reći..? *Can you tell me..?*	**Hvala lijepo.** *Thanks very much.*
...kako možemo tamo doći? *...how we can get there?*	**Nema na čemu.** *Don't mention it.*

Istina ili neistina?

(*a*)   Mark ne prihvaća poziv.
(*b*)   Rudolf stanuje daleko od centra grada.
(*c*)   Mark i Sandra idu taksijem.

--- **Objašnjenja i komentari** ---

When writing an address you usually indicate the floor on which the addressee lives by roman numerals after the number of the house or block of flats. Such that Rudolf would write:

Heinzlova 66/v

--- **Ključne fraze** ---

How to:
● extend an invitation.   **Želim vas pozvati...**

● decline politely an invitation.   **Žao mi je...**

- accept an invitation.

Vrlo rado prihvaćamo poziv.

- give an address,
  and a telephone number.

Moja adresa je...
Moj telefonski broj je...

- ask for directions.

Možete li mi reći gdje je..?

- ask how to get somewhere.

Kako možemo tamo doći?

- give directions.

idite ravno
idite ravno do glavne ceste
skrenite u prvu ulicu desno
skrenite u drugu ulicu lijevo

- ask if someone is sure
  of something.

Da li si sigurna?
  (**ti** form asking female)
Jeste li sigurni? (**vi** form
  asking a stranger)

- reply that you are sure.

Siguran sam. (male speaking)
Sigurna sam. (female speaking)

- say *thank you very much*,
  and reply
  (alternative reply)

hvala lijepo
  nema na čemu
  molim lijepo

Jezični obrasci

1 Giving commands

There is a special form of the verb which is used when you want to tell someone what to do, or what not to do. It is called the imperative. There are a number of examples in this unit:

Dođite k meni.	*Come to my place* (home).
Siđite na osmoj stanici.	*Get off at the eighth stop.*
Nemojte doći taksijem.	*Don't come by taxi.*
Pitaj ga.	*Ask him.*

There are, as you would expect, two forms. One corresponds to the **ti** form and one to the **vi** form.

Ti form

Take the **ja** form of the verb:

(*a*) if it ends in **-am** replace the **-m** by **-j**
pitam → pitaj;

(*b*) if it ends in **-jem** remove the ending **-em**
pijem → pij;

(*c*) for all other verbs replace **-em/-im** by **-i**
idem   → idi
uzmem   uzmi
radim   radi.

Vi form

To form the more formal or polite way of giving a command simply add **-te** to the **ti** form:

pitam → pitajte
pijem   pijte
idem   idite
uzmem   uzmite
radim   radite

2   *Do not do...*

The negative imperative is a command not to do something. It is formed by putting **ne** in front of the imperative:

Ne dođite taksijem!   *Don't come by taxi!*

However, this often sounds harsh and so there is an alternative, milder way of saying the same thing formed by placing **nemoj** (for the **ti** form) and **nemojte** (for the **vi** form) in front of the infinitive. Look at these examples:

Nemojte doći taksijem.   *Don't come by taxi.*
Nemojte sići na osmoj stanici.   *Don't get off at the eighth stop.*
Nemoj pitati.   *Don't ask.*

3   *A completed and uncompleted action*

There have been a few occasions when you have been given two different verbs to mean the same thing:

dolaziti, doći	*to come*
silaziti, sići	*to get off*
piti, popiti	*to drink*
davati, dati	*to give*
uzimati, uzeti	*to take*

These pairs of verbs are important to using the system of verbs in Serbo-Croat. The differences between them can be described like this:

(*a*)   the first verb of the pair is used to express an action which is, was or will be continuous, repeated or incomplete;

(*b*)   the second verb of the pair is used to express an action which was or will be completed, which happened or will happen once only or is of a momentary nature.

Most often when you are talking in the present tense you use the first verb in the pair. If an action is still in progress then it is not yet complete. You have used the second verb of the pair in its infinitive form and in its imperative form. Look at the following examples and the differences between the pairs of verbs:

Pijem vodu kad* sam žedan.	*I drink water when I'm thirsty.* (It means that on each occasion when thirsty I drink water.)
Moram popiti čašu vode.	*I must drink a glass of water.* (It means that I must drink a glass and finish it, as in the sense of drink up.)

*Some words may be used with or without -**a** at the end depending on how easy it is to pronounce with the following word; **kada**, **kad** (*when*), **sada**, **sad** (*now*), **s**, **sa** (*with*).

Sandra daje novac ženi.	*Sandra is giving the money to the woman.* (It means that the action is still incomplete.)
Dajte mi, molim vas,...	*Give me, please,...* (It refers to a single action which you expect to be momentary.)

These pairs of verbs are called aspects. The first verb is the imperfective aspect, and the second one is the perfective aspect.

Not all verbs come in pairs like this. **Vidjeti** is both imperfective and perfective.

4 Uses of cases (instrumental)

The instrumental case is so called because it is used to name an instrument by means of which an action is carried out. So you use it in the following phrases:

Idem taksijem.	*I am going by taxi.*
Idem autobusom.	*I am going by bus.*

as the means of transport is the instrument by which the action is being carried out.

Taksi (masc.) is slightly unusual in that is adds **j** before the case ending:

	singular
nom.	taksi
acc.	taksi
gen.	taksija
dat.	taksiju
ins.	taksijem

5 I see 'him'...

The words for *me*, *him* and *us*, etc are also pronouns like the words **mi** (*to me*) or **mu** (*to him*) except that they are in the accusative case. There is an example in the first line of the **Dijalog** in this unit **Želim vas pozvati...** (*I want to invite you...*).

Consider the following sentence:

Vidim Rudolfa i Jasnu na ulici. *I see Rudolf and Jasna in the street.*

The endings of the words have changed to indicate that Rudolf and Jasna are the object of the verb. Separate forms are needed to indicate *him* and *her* too.

Here is the full list of the words for *me*, *him*, etc. These are the accusative case of the pronouns. They have both long and short forms like the dative pronouns:

	short	long			short	long
ja	me	mene	mi		nas	nas
ti	te	tebe	vi		vas	vas
on	ga	njega	oni		ih	njih
ona	ju	nju	one		ih	njih

The forms for **ono** and **ona** (neut.) are the same as for **on** and **oni**.

The same forms are used for the genitive case of the pronouns with the following exception for **ona**: **je** (short form), **nje** (long form). However, there is a preference for using **je** as the short form in the accusative.

The rules for the use of long and short forms are the same as when we looked at the dative. The long form is used for emphasis and after prepositions. The short form cannot stand at the beginning of a sentence. If you have both an accusative or genitive pronoun used with a dative pronoun, the dative always comes first. Study the following examples:

Vidim Rudolfa.	*I see Rudolf.*
Vidim ga.	*I see him.*
Gledamo Jasnu.	*We are watching Jasna.*
Gledamo je.	*We are watching her.*
Dajem novac ženi.	*I am giving the money to the woman.*
Dajem joj ga.	*I am giving it to her.*
Konobar daje salatu ljudima.	*The waiter is giving the salad to the people.*
Konobar im je daje.	*The waiter is giving it to them.*

Note that the pronouns, like the short forms of **biti**, tend to come in second place after the first word.

6 New prepositions

You have met a number of new words to indicate position or direction in this unit:

Dođite k meni.	*Come to my place.*
	(Come and see me.)

Doðite k njemu.	*Come to his place.*
	(Come and see him.)
Radim kod nas.	*I am working at our place.*

These two words distinguish between going to someone or being at someone's: **k** (followed by the dative) indicates going round to see someone; **kod** (followed by the genitive) indicates being at someone's house.

Idem k Rudolfu.	*I am going round to Rudolf's*
	(to see Rudolf).
Sad sam kod Rudolfa.	*Now I am at Rudolf's.*

The expression **kod nas** may also mean *in our country*.

Note the difference between the following two expressions (**kuća** = *house, home*):

Rudolf je kod kuće.	*Rudolf is at home.*
	(stationary)
Rudolf ide kući.	*Rudolf is going home.*
	(movement)

Other prepositons followed by the genitive are:

bez	*without*
blizu	*near*
do	*to, as far as*
iz	*out of, from*
preko puta	*opposite*

and followed by the dative:

prema	*towards.*

---

7 First, second, etc.

In addition to the numbers discussed before, there are others which are not used in counting but in ordering things (*first, second,* etc). They are called ordinal numbers. In Serbo-Croat they are all adjectives and so agree in number, case and gender with the noun which they describe:

Masc.	Fem.	Neut.	
prvi	prva	prvo	*first*
drugi	druga	drugo	*second*
treći	treća	treće	*third*
četvrti	četvrta	četvrto	*fourth*
peti	peta	peto	*fifth*
šesti	-a	-o	*sixth*
sedmi	-a	-o	*seventh*
osmi	-a	-o	*eighth*
deveti	-a	-o	*ninth*
deseti	-a	-o	*tenth*

The pattern is then repeated by simply adding an adjective ending on the following numbers (**jedanaesti**, **dvanaesti**, **trinaesti**, etc.)

✔ ──────── Vježbe ────────

1 Choose the correct command from the pair given (the first verb is always the imperfect):

(*a*) Pij/Popij mlijeko svaki dan.
(*b*) Pijte/Popijte čašu vode odmah.
(*c*) Dolazi/Dođi k meni danas.
(*d*) Uzimajte/Uzmite tramvaj dvadeset četiri.

2 Choose the correct form of the infinitive:

(*a*) Moraš silaziti/sići na trećoj stanici.
(*b*) Volim piti/popiti mlijeko.
(*c*) Želim dolaziti/doći k tebi sutra.
(*d*) Hoćete li mi davati/dati čašu vina?

3 Put the noun or nouns in the brackets in the correct case after the preposition:

(*a*) Sutra smo kod (Mark i Sandra).
(*b*) Autobus ide prema (centar) grada.
(*c*) Autobus ide u (centar) grada.
(*d*) Autobus je u (centar) grada.
(*e*) Idite ravno do (trg).
(*f*) Gradska kavana se nalazi na (trg).
(*g*) Dođite iz (hotel) do (restoran).

(*h*)   On sutra ide na (večera).
(*i*)   Njegov stan je blizu (kolodvor).
(*j*)   Rudolf stoji ispod (drvo) u (park) preko puta (stanica).

4   Put the noun or nouns in the brackets in the correct case according to the uses of cases:

(*a*)   Konobar daje (Jasna) (salata).
(*b*)   Idemo u Zagreb (autobus).
(*c*)   Trafalgar Square se nalazi u centru (London).
(*d*)   (Konobar)! Želimo naručiti večeru.
(*e*)   Sandra mora pisati (Mark).

5   Look at the diagram below. You are in the spot marked **X**.

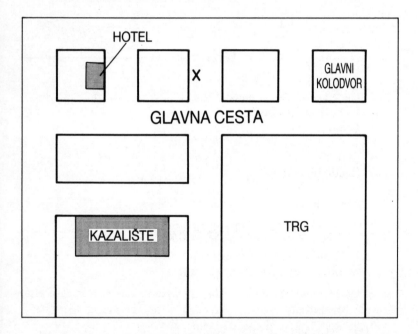

You see a man walking towards you. Stop him and ask if he knows the way to the theatre. How would he describe to you:

(*a*)   the way to the theatre?
(*b*)   the way to the Main Station?
(*c*)   the way to the hotel?
(*d*)   the way to the square?

6 Fill in the missing parts of the dialogue:

(*I want to invite you to my place today.*)
Ne mogu. Moram danas ići k mami.
(*I am sorry. Can you come tomorrow?*)
Dobro. Kada?
(*At eight o'clock.*)
Kako mogu doći k vama?
(*Take the bus number 14 or the tram number 6 opposite the park and get out at the seventh stop. My flat is in the block opposite the theatre*).
Dajte mi, molim vas, vašu adresu i telefonski broj.
(*My address is ... My telephone number is ...*)

7 Replace the nouns in brackets with the appropriate pronoun. Take care to use the long or short form as appropriate and to use the correct word order:

(*a*) Idemo k (Marku).
(*b*) Konobar daje (ribu) (Sandri).
(*c*) Gledamo (ljude) na ulici.
(*d*) Idite do (kolodvora).
(*e*) Moram kupiti (razglednice).
(*f*) (Mark i Sandra) moraju pisati (prijateljima).
(*g*) Rudolf stanuje blizu (centra grada).
(*h*) (Ljudi) piju (kavu).

—————— **Dopunsko štivo 1** ——————

Zvonko poziva Velimira na ručak.

Zvonko Velimire, dođi sutra k meni na ručak.
Velimir Na žalost, ne mogu. Moram sa ženom ići u grad. Moramo kupiti poklon za njenu mamu.
Zvonko Dovedi i ženu na ručak.
Velimir Ne znam. Ona uvijek kaže da je teško doći do tebe. Ti stanuješ daleko od glavne ceste.
Zvonko Žao mi je. Možete li doći taksijem?
Velimir Možemo. Znaš, kad idemo k tebi, moramo ići u centar tramvajem, onda uzeti autobus. Možemo doći taksijem direktno iz centra grada.

Zvonko	Dobro. Drago mi je, dođite onda u tri.
Velimir	Hvala lijepo.
Zvonko	Molim lijepo. Do viđenja.
Velimir	Do viđenja, do sutra.

na žalost	*unfortunately*	**kaže da...** (kazati, kažem)	*he/she*
poklon	*present*	*says that...*	
Dovedi i ženu.	*Bring your wife too.*	**direktno**	*directly*
uvijek	*always*	**u tri**	*at three* (o'clock)
teško	*difficult*	**do sutra**	*until tomorrow*

Istina ili neistina?

(a) Zvonko poziva Velimira na večeru.

(b) Velimir ide sutra na posao.

(c) Velimir i njegova žena mogu doći taksijem.

Dopunsko štivo 2

Read the following passage and answer the questions below.

U gradovima u Evropi čovjek danas vidi tramvaje i autobuse na ulicama. Tramvaji i autobusi voze svugdje. Tramvajem ili autobusom ljudi idu na posao i k prijateljima. Gradski transport je jedan veliki sistem. Spaja jednu stranu grada s drugom. Spaja ljude s poslom, s prijateljima, s centrom grada i s mjestima gdje se ljudi skupljaju. Naravno, nije uvijek lako putovati po gradu. Neki ljudi stanuju daleko od centra. Živjeti tamo nije lako. Teško je doći u grad. Ali neki ljudi vole stanovati daleko od grada. Život je miran kada čovjek ne gleda stalno ljude na ulicama.

Evropa	*Europe*		*people gather together*
svugdje	*everywhere*	**naravno**	*of course*
sistem	*system*	**po gradu**	*around the town*
spaja	*it links*	**život**	*life*
jednu stranu	*(acc.) one side*	**miran**	*quiet, peaceful*
gdje se ljudi skupljaju	*where*		

1 Što vidi čovjek u gradovima danas?
   (a) Vidi taksije.
   (b) Vidi tramvaje i autobuse.
   (c) Vidi samoposluge.

2 Kamo idu ljudi tramvajem ili autobusom?
   (a) U hotel.
   (b) Na posao i k prijateljima.
   (c) Na poštu.

3 Gdje je život miran?
   (a) U predgrađu.
   (b) Na Glavnom kolodvoru.
   (c) U centru grada.

7

KOLIKO IMATE GODINA?

How old are you?

In this unit you will learn how to

- give and ask for more personal information concerning age, marital status, occupation, where you are from, and about other members of your family

Dijalog

Rudolf ulazi u stan s Markom i Sandrom. Njegova majka je u sobi.

Rudolf   Da vas upoznam. Ovo je moja majka. Mama, ovo su moji prijatelji. Zovu se Sandra i Mark.

Sandra   Drago mi je. Ja sam Sandra.

Mark   Drago mi je, gospođo. Ja sam Mark Bryant.

Majka   Drago mi je, gospođo i gospodine. Sjednite, molim vas.

Mark i Rudolf izlaze iz sobe. Majka i Sandra razgovaraju.

Majka   Odakle ste vi, Sandra?

Sandra   Ja sam iz Engleske.

Majka   A gdje žive vaši roditelji?

Sandra   Žive u Londonu.

Majka   Imate li brata ili sestru?

Sandra   Imam sestru. Ona živi s roditeljima. Cijela moja obitelj živi u Londonu. Mark ima brata.

Majka	Gdje on živi?
Sandra	Njegov brat živi u Njemačkoj, u Berlinu. Radi tamo i oženjen je Njemicom.
Majka	Koliko dugo ste vi u braku?
Sandra	U braku smo već osam godina.
Majka	Moj Rudolf je još uvijek samac. Vrijeme je da se oženi, ali se Jasna neće udati... Sandra, koliko imate godina?
Sandra	Imam trideset pet godina.
Majka	A koliko ima vaš muž?
Sandra	Ima trideset sedam godina.
Majka	Moj Rudolf ima trideset devet godina. Radi već deset godina u istoj firmi. Imate li posao?
Sandra	Imam. Radim kao učiteljica u školi kod nas. Mark prodaje opremu za kompjutore i urede. On je predstavnik svoje firme u Zagrebu. Moja mama je računovođa, a tata radi u banci. Markov otac je mehaničar.

majka	*mother*	**godina**	*year*
soba	*room*	**još uvijek**	*still*
zovu se	*they are called*	**samac**	*batchelor*
sjednite (sjesti, sjednem)	*sit down*	**Vrijeme je da...**	*It is time that...*
razgovaraju (razgovarati, razgovaram)	*they talk, chat*	**oženiti se**	*to get married* (of male)
Odakle ste vi?	*Where are you from?*	**udati se**	*to get married* (of female)
roditelj	*parent*	**u istoj firmi**	*in the same firm*
brat	*brother*	**Koliko imate godina?**	*How old are you?*
sestra	*sister*	**Imam trideset pet godina.**	*I am 35.*
cio, cijela, cijelo	*whole*	**oprema za kompjutore**	*equipment for computers*
obitelj (fem.)	*family*	**predstavnik**	*a representative*
u Njemačkoj	*in Germany*	**firma**	*firm, company*
Oženjen je Njemicom.	*He is married to a German* (woman).	**računovođa**	*accountant*
koliko dugo...	(for) *how long...*	**tata**	*Dad*
u braku	*married* (Lit. *in marriage*)	**u banci** (nom. banka)	*in a bank*
već	*already*	**Markov otac**	*Mark's father*
		mehaničar	*mechanic*

Istina ili neistina?

(*a*) Sandra ima trideset jednu godinu.

(*b*) Markov brat živi u Njemačkoj.

(*c*) Markov tata je računovođa.

Objašnjenja i komentari

Gosti

To be invited as a guest (**gost**) in a family home is to be treated with all the hospitality which could be wished for. The problem is often how to refuse the excessive zeal with which food is put on plates. There are a number of phrases which can be repeated like, **Ne, hvala, ne mogu više** (*No, thank you, I can't any more*). Perhaps you could add a little later **stvarno, ne mogu više** (*really, I can't any more*). As for drink, if you don't want any more simply keep your glass full. Although the word **gost** is monosyllabic its plural form is **gosti** (without the **-ov-** typical of other such words liks **grad/gradovi**).

Obitelj

The names of the members of the family which you have met so far are:

muž (*husband*)	žena (*wife*)
otac (*father*)	majka (*mother*)
tata (*Dad*)	mama (*Mum*)
brat (*brother*)	sestra (*sister*)

You will find more in the last section of this unit. The word **obitelj** is slightly unusual in that although it ends in a consonant it is a feminine word (like **stvar**).

 ## Ključne fraze

How to:

- ask where someone is from, and say where you are from.

  Odakle ste vi?
  Ja sam iz...

- ask how long someone has been married.

  Koliko dugo ste u braku?

- say if you are married.

  Već smo osam godina u braku.

- say *to get married* (of a man), **oženiti se**
  and *he is married*. **oženjen je**

- say *to get married* (of a woman), **udati se**
  and *she is married*. **udata je**

- say that *you are married* **Oženjen sam.**
  (man speaking),
  or *not married*. **Nisam oženjen.**

- say that *you are married* **Udata sam.**
  (woman speaking),
  or *not married*. **Nisam udata.**

- ask if someone is married. **Jeste li oženjeni?**
  Jeste li udati?

There are two ways of saying you are married depending on whether you are a man or a woman. A man would use the verb **oženiti se** and a woman the verb **udati se**. They must not be mixed.

How to:

- ask about age –

  How old are you? **Koliko imate godina?**
  I am... **Imam...**
  How old is your husband? **Koliko ima godina vaš muž?**
  My husband is... **Moj muž ima...**

Jezični obrasci

1 Adjectives

You have already seen a variety of adjective endings in previous units. Your attention has not been drawn to them because we were concentrating on nouns and verbs.

There is a basic similarity in adjective and noun endings, but there are things to watch for. Look at the following patterns for the nominative singular:

Masc.
  Hotel je star. *The hotel is old.*

Fem.

Kava je vruća.   *The coffee is hot.*

Neut.

Kazalište je lijepo.   *The theatre is beautiful.*

However, notice that the masculine ending is not always a consonant, but may be **-i**:

Ovo je dobar hotel.   *This is a good hotel.*

Ovo je taj stari čovjek.   *This is the old man.*

You add **-i** to the masculine nominative case in order to add the meaning of *the*. This is the only instance in which this happens.

Several adjectives only exist in this **-i** form. For example, **prvi** and other ordinal numbers.

There are a number of adjectives to which you may *not* add **-i**. For example, **moj**, **njegov** (and the other possessive adjectives), **jedan**, etc.

The ending without **-i** is always used in the following pattern:

Hotel je star.   *The hotel is old.*
   ('something' *is* 'something')

So far you have mostly seen the nominative and accusative adjective case endings. These endings in both the singular and the plural are similar to the endings for the nouns:

Singular	Masc.	Fem.	Neut.
nom.	star(i)	stara	staro
acc.	star(i)	staru	staro
nom.	vrúć(i)	vrúća	vrúće
acc.	vrúć(i)	vrúću	vrúće

Plural	Masc.	Fem.	Neut.
nom.	stari	stare	stara
acc.	stare	stare	stara
nom.	vrúći	vrúće	vrúća
acc.	vrúće	vrúće	vrúća

2   U Njemačkoj *(dative case of adjectives)*

When Sandra says that Mark's brother lives in Germany (**u Njemačkoj**), she uses the dative case of the word for Germany. In principle it is no different from saying that he works in a school (**u**

školi). However, the word for Germany is an adjective **Njemačka**. It behaves like an adjective with feminine endings. There are a number of names for countries which behave similarly:

Engleska	*England*	u Engleskoj
Francuska	*France*	u Francuskoj
Poljska	*Poland*	u Poljskoj
Danska	*Denmark*	u Danskoj
Hrvatska	*Croatia*	u Hrvatskoj
Škotska	*Scotland*	u Škotskoj
Irska	*Ireland*	u Irskoj

Not all the names of countries behave in this way: for example

Italija	*Italy*	u Italiji
Rusija	*Russia*	u Rusiji
Amerika	*America*	u Americi
Srbija	*Serbia*	u Srbiji

The endings for dative adjectives are:

Masc. add **-om** (or **-em** to a word ending in a soft consonant)

dobar	dobrom
lijep	lijepom
vruć	vrućem

Fem. add **-oj**

dobra	dobroj
lijepa	lijepoj
vruća	vrućoj

Neut. add **-om** (or **-em** to a word ending in a soft consonant)

dobro	dobrom
lijepo	lijepom
vruće	vrućem

The plural ending is **-im** in all genders:

dobri	dobrim
lijepi	lijepim
vrući	vrućim

Look at the following examples:

Masc.

lijep grad	*a beautiful town*
u lijepom gradu	*in a beautiful town*

Fem.

vruća kava	*hot coffee*
u vrućoj kavi	*in hot coffee*

Neut.

dobro kazalište	*a good theatre*
u dobrom kazalištu	*in a good theatre*

Plural

lijepi gradovi	*beautiful towns*
u lijepim gradovima	*in beautiful towns*

3   Iz Engleske *(genitive case of adjectives)*

In answer to the question **Odakle ste vi?** you say **Ja sam iz Engleske**. You are using the preposition **iz** *(from)* followed by the genitive case of the name of the country, which is an adjective:

The endings for genitive adjectives are:

Masc.   add **-og** (or **-eg** to a word ending in a soft consonant)

dobar	dobrog
lijep	lijepog
vrúć	vrućeg

Fem.   add **-e**

dobra	dobre
lijepa	lijepe
vrúća	vrúće

Neut.   add **-og** (or **-eg** to a word ending in a soft consonant)

dobro	dobrog
lijepo	lijepog
vrúće	vrućeg

The plural ending is **-ih** in all genders:

dobri	dobrih
lijepi	lijepih
vrúći	vrućih

Study the following examples:

Ja sam iz Njemačke.	*I am from Germany.*
Rudolf izlazi iz visoke zgrade.	*Rudolf is coming out of the tall building.*

Mark izlazi iz starog kazališta.	*Mark is coming out of the old theatre.*
U Zagrebu ima lijepih parkova.	*There are some nice parks in Zagreb.*

Remember that the accusative case for masculine nouns which denote persons or animals is the same as the genitive. Adjectives which agree with these nouns also have an accusative case which is the same as the genitive. Compare the following:

Vidim lijepi park.	*I see the nice park.*
Vidim starog čovjeka.	*I see the old man.*

4 Mark's father (possession)

You can make adjectives from personal names:

for a man's name add **-ov**

Mark	Markov
Rudolf	Rudolfov
Zvonko	Zvonkov

for a woman's name replace **-a** with **-in**

Sandra	Sandrin
Jasna	Jasnin

These adjectives never take the **-i** ending in the masculine. These words are just like other adjectives:

Ovo je Markova majka.	*This is Mark's mother.*
Izlaze iz Jasnine kuće.	*They are coming out of Jasna's house.*
Ovo je Rudolfovo pivo.	*This is Rudolf's beer.*

5 Use of svoj

Look at the following sentence in English:

He is taking his money.

There is a possibility of ambiguity, because the word *his* may refer to *his own* or to *somebody else's* money. In Serbo-Croat you distinguish between these two meanings of *his*:

On uzima svoj novac. (his own)
On uzima njegov novac. (somebody else's)

When the person who possesses the object is the same as the one who also performs the action you use the possessive adjective **svoj**. Look at the following examples:

On daje jelo svojoj ženi.	*He gives the dish to his wife.*
On daje jelo njegovoj ženi.	*He gives the dish to his (i.e. not his own) wife.*
Oni gledaju svoju kuću.	*They are looking at their house.*
Oni gledaju njihovu kuću.	*They are looking at their (i.e. belonging to someone else) house.*
On uzima svoj kaput.	*He takes his coat.*
kaput	*coat*
Njegov kaput je tamo.	*His coat is there* (i.e. the coat is his own but the subject of the sentence is *his coat*).

Svoj follows the same pattern as **moj** and other adjectives which end in a soft consonant.

6 Numbers (20-99)

For numbers above 20, simply combine the numerals:

dvadeset jedan	21	pedeset	50
dvadeset dva/dvije	22	pedeset pet	55
dvadeset tri	23	šezdeset	60
dvadeset pet	25	šezdeset tri	63
dvadeset osam	28	sedamdeset	70
dvadeset devet	29	sedamdeset šest	76
trideset	30	osamdeset	80
trideset jedan	31	osamdeset jedan	81
trideset ćetiri	34	devedeset	90
trideset šest	36	devedeset devet	99
trideset sedam	37		
četrdeset	40		

The word which follows the number follows the same pattern as for the earlier numbers:

...jedan (singular)
| dvadeset jedan čovjek | *21 people* |

The word after **jedan** is always singular even when used in combination with other numbers, and **jedan** behaves like an adjective:

| dvadeset jedna kuća | *21 houses* |

...**dva/dvije, tri, četiri** (genitive singular)

trideset dva čovjeka	*32 people*
trideset dvije žene	*32 women*
osamdeset četiri godine	*84 years*

...**pet, šest, sedam**, etc. (genitive plural)

| pedeset sedam stolova | *57 tables* |
| devedeset devet ljudi | *99 people* |

The ordinal numbers (*twentieth*, etc) are adjectives:

| dvadeseti, dvadeseta, dvadeseto | *twentieth* |
| trideseti, trideseta, trideseto | *thirtieth* |

In compound numbers only the last number is treated as an adjective:

| dvadeset prvi | *twenty-first* |
| trideset deveti | *thirty-ninth* |

7 Use of već

When in English you use the past tense to ask *How long have you been married?*, in Serbo-Croat you use the present tense and include the word **već** (*already*): **Koliko dugo ste već u braku?**

| Koliko dugo ste u braku? | *How long have you been married?* |
| U braku smo već osam godina. | *We have been married for eight years.* |

8 Unusual categories of nouns

(a) Look at the pattern of case endings for **otac**:

	singular	plural
nom.	otac	očevi
voc.	oče	očevi
acc.	oca	očeve

— **95** —

gen.	oca	očeva
dat.	ocu	očevima
ins.	ocem	očevima

It is effected by the spelling rules of Serbo-Croat.

The penultimate **a** between two consonants drops out when case endings are added.

The letter **t** is the same sound as the beginning of **c** (**ts**) and this is treated as a double consonant. Double consonants are rarely tolerated and so the first **t** is also omitted.

It has a plural which is regular in its case pattern but with a stem of **očev-**.

(b) **Nijemac**: the penultimate **a**, normally lost from masculine nouns with their case endings, returns in the genitive plural form:

dva Nijemca	*two Germans* (gen. singular)
pet Nijemaca	*five Germans* (gen. plural)

The **a** returns in the genitive plural form only with all such nouns.

(c) **Tata** is unusual in that the word is feminine (like **kava** or **žena**) and it changes according to the regular pattern for such nouns. However, adjectives take the corresponding masculine endings because the word refers to a masculine person. Study the following examples:

Naš stari tata je u sobi.	*Our old Dad is in the room.*
Vidim starog tatu.	*I see the old Dad.*

9 Koliko imate godina?

The word **koliko** means *how much* or *how many*. It is followed by the genitive case like other words of quantity (such as **mnogo**). Remember the word order in the question *How old are you?*:

Koliko imate godina?

Vježbe

1 Fill in the missing adjective from the list given below (all the

adjectives are given with the correct case ending and each is therefore appropriate to just one sentence):

(a) Hotel je _____
(b) Dan je _____
(c) Riba je _____
(d) Meso je _____
(e) Jasna je _____
(f) Razglednica je _____
(g) Vino je _____
(h) Zgrada je _____

| star | velika | žedna | bijelo | svježa | vruć | odlično | skupa |

2 Add the correct case ending to the adjectives in the sentences below:

(a) Spomenik je u lijep___ parku.
(b) Čovjek izlazi iz velik___ pošte.
(c) Koverte nisu skup___.
(d) Skrenite u treć___ ulicu desno.
(e) Izlazi iz star___ hotela.
(f) Jasna hoće kupiti velik___ razglednice.
(g) Idemo na Glavn___ Kolodvor.
(h) Pijemo dobr___ kavu u Gradsk___ kavani.

3 Make up sentences from the information given below as indicated:

| | John | Englez | Engleska | banka |

John je Englez.
Živi u Engleskoj.
Radi u banci.

(a) Pierre   Francuz   Francuska   ured
(b) Vjekoslav   Hrvat   Hrvatska   restoran
(c) Branka   Srpkinja   Srbija   hotel
(d) Maša   Ruskinja   Rusija   škola

4 Change the name in brackets into an adjective and supply the correct case ending:

(a) Milivoj živi u (Branka) stanu.
(b) On izlazi iz (Mark) sobe.
(c) Gledamo (Sandra) sestru.
(d) (Mark) brat živi u Njemačkoj.

(e) (Rudolf) ured je u centru grada.

(f) Ulazimo u (Velimir) školu.

5 Complete the missing part of the dialogue:

(*Are you married, Rudolf?*)
Ne, nisam oženjen.
(*Is Jasna married?*)
Ne, nije udata.

6 Match the questions to the answers:

(a) Da li je ovo vaša kava?   (i)   Vidim ga.
(b) Da li je Jasna udata?   (ii) Ne, to je moja.
(c) Gdje je Rudolfova majka?   (iii) Sjedi u svojoj sobi.
(d) Da li vidite Marka?   (iv) Nije.

7 Supply in words the numbers given in numerals:

22, 47, 64, 29, 17, 11, 43, 38, 77, 58, 90, 61.

Dopunsko štivo 1

Sandrina sestra živi u Londonu s roditeljima. Ima dvadeset jednu godinu. Studira medicinu na sveučilištu u Londonu. Želi postati liječnica.

Markov brat živi u Berlinu. On je vojnik. Njegova žena je Njemica iz Frankfurta. Markov brat ima trideset godina, a njegova žena dvadeset devet. Imaju sina i kćerku. Sin ima pet godina, a kćerka tri.

studirati, studiram *study*	**liječnica** *doctor (woman)*
medicina *medicine*	**vojnik** *soldier*
sveučilište *university*	**sin** *son*
postati *become*	**kćerka** *daughter*

Istina ili neistina?

(a) Sandrina sestra ima dvadeset dvije godine.
(b) Žena Markovog brata je Njemica.
(c) Njihov sin ima pet godina.

—————— **Dopunsko štivo 2** ——————

Read the following passage and answer the questions below:

Rudolf govori Marku o svojoj obitelji. Brat njegove majke je njegov ujak. Njegova žena je Rudolfova ujna. Brat njegovog tate je njegov stric. Njegova žena je Rudolfova strina. Rudolfovi roditelji imaju i sestre. Sestre majke i oca su Rudolfove tetke. Njihovi muževi su Rudolfovi teci – to znači da ako je tetka udata, njen muž je Rudolfov tetak. Dijete jednog ujaka, strica ili tetke je Rudolfov brat ili sestra. Kaže se da je brat od strica, ili sestra od tetke. Koliko Mark razumije obiteljske odnose?

ujak	*uncle*	**tetak**	*uncle* (her husband)
ujna	*aunt* (his wife)	**to znači**	*that means*
stric	*uncle*	**ako**	*if*
strina	*aunt* (his wife)	**kaže se**	*it is said, one says*
tetka	*aunt*	**obiteljski odnosi**	*family relations*

1 Brat Rudolfovog oca je...
   (a) Rudolfov stric.
   (b) Rudolfov ujak.
   (c) Rudolfov brat od tetke.

2 Sestra Rudolfove majke je...
   (a) Rudolfova tetka.
   (b) Rudolfova strina.
   (c) Rudolfova ujna.

3 Žena Rudolfovog strica je...
   (a) Rudolfova strina.
   (b) Rudolfova sestra.
   (c) sestra Rudolfove majke.

8

KAKAV STAN IMATE?

What kind of flat do you have?

In this unit you will learn how to

- describe a room, your house or flat
- describe your day's routine
- use more question words
- tell the time
- use expressions for the divisions of the day

Dijalog

Sandra i Mark su na večeri kod Rudolfa. Rudolf pokazuje Marku stan. U dnevnoj sobi su dva naslonjača, veliki kauč i dva stolića za kavu. Namještaj je udoban. U uglu je televizor. Oni izlaze iz dnevne sobe, dok Sandra razgovara s Rudolfovom majkom.

Mark   Kakav stan imate? Koliko imate u stanu soba?

Rudolf Imamo četiri sobe, kupaonicu i kuhinju. Ovo je blagovaonica. Vidite da u sredini stoji veliki stol. Oko njega su stolice. Kroz vrata vidite kuhinju gdje su frižider, zamrzivač i ormari. U ormarima su tanjuri, šalice, vilice, noževi, žlice i tave.

Mark Koliko spavaćih soba imate?
Rudolf Imamo dvije. Ovo je mamina soba, a to je moja. Moja soba je velika. To je i moja radna soba. Tamo imam kompjutor, radni stol i police s knjigama.

pokazuje Marku (pokazivati, pokazuje) *he shows to Mark*	**oko njega** *around it*
dnevna soba *living room*	**stolica** *chair*
naslonjač *armchair*	**kroz vrata** *through the door*
kauč *couch*	**frižider** *fridge*
stolić *little table*	**zamrzivač** *freezer*
namještaj *furniture*	**ormar** *cupboard*
udoban *comfortable*	**tanjur** *plate*
dok *while*	**šalica** *cup*
Kakav imate stan? *What kind of flat do you have?*	**vilica** *fork*
	nož *knife*
Koliko imate soba? *How many rooms do you have?*	**žlica** *spoon*
	tava *saucepan*
kupaonica *bathroom*	**spavaća soba** *bedroom*
kuhinja *kitchen*	**radna soba** *study* (work room)
blagovaonica *dining room*	**radni stol** *desk*
u sredini *in the middle*	**polica s knjigama** *bookshelf*
stoji (stojati, stojim) *he/she/it is standing*	**knjiga** *book*

Dijalog

Sandra i Rudolfova majka razgovaraju. Majka je pita o njenom životu u Londonu.

Majka U koliko sati počinje vaš radni dan?
Sandra Počinje u sedam sati kad obično ustajem. Stižem u školu oko osam i pol i radim od deset do devet do podne.
Majka Imate li pauzu?
Sandra Imamo pauzu prije podne. Ta pauza traje dvadeset minuta. Imamo i pauzu za ručak. Poslije ručka škola počinje u jedan i petnaest. Kao i prije podne, učenici imaju četiri sata sa pauzom poslije drugog sata.
Majka To znači da se škola završava oko četiri sata.
Sandra Da, onda idem kući. Kod kuće obično večeram s Markom oko pola osam.

o *about* (preposition followed by dat.)	**trajati, traje** *to last*
u koliko sati *at what time*	**prije podne** *in the morning* (before noon)
počinjati, počinjem *to begin*	**poslije ručka** *after lunch*
obično *usually*	**poslije** (preposition followed by gen.) *after*
ustajati, ustajem *to get up*	
stizati, stižem *to arrive*	**jedan i petnaest** *quarter past one*
oko osam i pol *about half past eight*	**učenik** *pupil*
	sat *hour, o'clock, class, lesson*
deset do devet *ten to nine*	**završavati se** *to finish*
podne *midday*	**oko četiri sata** *about four o'clock*
pauza *pause, break*	**oko pola osam** *about half past seven*

Istina ili neistina?

(*a*)   Rudolf i njegova majka imaju dvije spavaće sobe.
(*b*)   Veliki stol je u kuhinji.
(*c*)   Poslije ručka Sandrina škola počinje u jedan i pet.

—— Objašnjenja i komentari ——

Housing

Most people in big cities live in flats. Huge building programmes began after the Second World War which have resulted in the creation of new districts (**naselja**). Both Zagreb and Belgrade (**Beograd** in Serbo-Croat) have areas built since the war which have extended the city boundaries far beyond their original limits. These areas are, in fact, called Novi Zagreb and Novi Beograd. In villages it is more common to find the road lined with family houses rather than the typically urban blocks (**blokovi**).

—— Ključne fraze ——

How to:

● describe rooms in your house/flat.   **kupaonica**
                                        kuhinja

	dnevna soba **blagovaonica** **spavaća soba** **radna soba**
● show someone round your house/flat.	**pokazivati stan Marku** (dat.).
● name some divisions of the day.	**prije podne** **podne**
● ask/say at what time something happens.	**U koliko sati?/U sedam** **sati.**
● give an approximate time.	**Oko pola osam.**

Jezični obrasci

1 Adjectives (instrumental case)

Look at this example of an adjective used in the instrumental case after the preposition **s**:

Sandra govori sa njegovom majkom.   *Sandra speaks with his mother.*

The endings for adjectives in the instrumental are:

Masc. add **-im**

dobar	dobrim
lijep	lijepim
moj	mojim

Fem. add **-om**

dobra	dobrom
lijepa	lijepom
moja	mojom

Neut. add **-im**

dobro	dobrim
lijepo	lijepim
moje	mojim

The plural ending is **-im** in all genders:

dobri	dobrim
lijepi	lijepim
moji	mojim

2 Telling the time

In official contexts, such as railway timetables, the 24-hour clock is used. Thus,

dva sata i pet minuta

pet sati i petnaest minuta

deset sati i dvadeset minuta

četrnaest sati i četrdeset minuta

dvadeset sati i pedeset pet minuta

In most everyday circumstances a different system is used.

Minutes past the hour:
Here the pattern resembles the 24-hour clock:

jedan (sat) i pet (minuta)
dva (sata) i deset (minuta)
tri (sata) i petnaest (minuta)
pet (sati) i dvadeset pet (minuta)
šest (sati) i trideset (minuta)

The words for hours and minutes are usually omitted. Here, they have been put in brackets. After **jedan** the word for hour is in the nominative (**sat**), after **dva**, **tri** and **četiri** in the genitive singular (**sata**) and after the other numbers in the genitive plural (**sati**). The word for *minute* is **minuta**.

Alternative ways of expressing *half past the hour*:

(a)   4.30   četiri i pol
       9.30   devet i pol
(b)   5.30   pola šest
      11.30   pola dvanaest

(In this way you are saying: *It is now half of the sixth hour*)

Minutes to the hour:

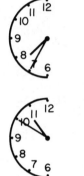

dvadeset pet do osam
dvadeset do devet
petnaest do deset
deset do jedanaest
pet do dvanaest

3   What time is it?

Koliko je sada sati?   *What time is it now?*

To state the time simply put **Sada je...** in front of the time:

Sada je jedan sat.   *It is now one o'clock.*
Sada je tri i petnaest.   *It is now quarter past three.*
Sada je šest i pol.   *It is now half past six.*
Sada je pola sedam.   *It is now half past six.*
Sada je deset do dvanaest.   *It is now ten to twelve.*

To give an approximate time add **oko**:

Sada je oko šest.   *It's about six. (It's sixish.)*
Sada je oko pola jedanaest.   *It's about half ten.*

4 At what time?

U koliko sati...   *At what time...*

To say *at what time...* put **u** before the time:

u pet sati	*at 5 o'clock*
u šest i pol	*at six thirty*
u deset do dvanaest	*at ten to twelve*
u dvanaest	*at twelve o'clock*
u podne	*at noon*

To give an approximate time, again use **oko**, but without **u**:

oko osam sati	*at about eight o'clock*
oko tri i dvadeset	*at about twenty past three*
oko petnaest do pet	*at about quarter to five*

To say *from... to...* use **od... do...**:

od pet do šest	*from five to six o'clock*
od petnaest do sedam	*from quarter to seven*
do osam sati	*to eight o'clock*

5 Divisions of the day

jutro	*morning*	**večer**	*evening*
jutros	*this morning*	**večeras**	*this evening*
ujutro	*in the morning*	**uvečer** (or **navečer**)	*in the evening*
prije podne	*morning*	**poslije podne**	*afternoon*
dan	*day*	**noć**	*night*
danas	*today*	**noćas**	*tonight*
danju	*during the day*	**noću**	*at night*
podne (u podne)	*noon*	**ponoć** (u ponoć)	*midnight*

po podne is often used instead of **poslije podne**

The following are approximate times:

jutro	*6am to 10am*
dan	*10am to 6pm*
večer	*6pm to 12pm*
noć	*12pm to 6am*

Take care not to invite someone to meet you **noćas**, when you really mean **večeras**!

The divisions of the day are used to clarify time by the clock:

osam sati ujutro	*eight o'clock in the morning*
deset sati prije podne	*nine o'clock in the morning*
u četiri poslije podne	*at four in the afternoon*
u šest i pol večeras	*at half past six this evening*

You can add to these divisions of the day with the following:

prekjučer	*day before yesterday*	**sutra**	*tomorrow*
jučer	*yesterday*	**prekosutra**	*day after tomorrow*
sinoć	*last night*		

u šest sati sutra ujutro	*at six o'clock tomorrow morning*
u sedam i petnaest sinoć	*at quarter past seven last night*
oko tri poslije podne	*at about three in the afternoon*
prekjučer	*the day before yesterday*

6 More prepositions

There are four more prepositions in this unit.

(*a*) followed by the accusative:
kroz (*through*)

Idem kroz kuću	*I'm going through the house.*

(*b*) followed by the genitive:
oko (*around, about*)

Gosti sjede oko stola.	*The guests are sitting around the table.*

poslije (*after*)

Škola počinje poslije ručka.	*School begins after lunch.*

(*c*) followed by the dative:
o (*about*)

Govore o školi.	*They are speaking about school.*

7 Kakav

Kakav is an adjective, so, it changes its ending according to the noun. It has two meanings:

(a) What kind of...?

Kakav naslonjač stoji u dnevnoj
  sobi?
Kakvu juhu više volite?
Kakve knjige su na stolu?

What kind of an armchair?
  stands in the living room?
What kind of soup do you prefer?
What kind of books are on
  the table?

(b) What a...!

Kakav čovjek!
Kakva kuća!

What a person!
What a house!

8 This/that

Sandra says:

Ta pauza traje dvadeset minuta.   *That break lasts for 20 minutes.*

The adjectives meaning *this* and *that* are **ovaj**, **taj** and **onaj**. They do
not have the masculine nominative ending with **-i**. Add endings for
other genders and cases on to **ov-**, **t-** and **on-**:

Ulaze u **ovu** zgradu.
Vidite li **tog** čovjeka?
Novine se mogu kupiti u **onoj**
  prodavaonici na uglu.

They are entering this building.
Do you see that man?
One can buy newspapers in
  that shop on the corner.

Both **taj** and **onaj** mean *that*, with the difference than **onaj** refers to
an object which is further away.

9 Unusual noun categories: Vrata (door)

Vrata is one of the words in Serbo-Croat which only exists in a plural
form. It ends in **-a**, and it is neuter plural.

All adjectives and verbs agree with the neuter plural form of the
word.

Vrata su lijepa.
Ideš kroz crna **vrata** u hodnik.

The door is beautiful.
You go through the black door
  into the corridor.

Novine also exists only in this feminine plural form, although it may refer to one, or more than one, newspaper:

To su dobre **novine**.   *That is a good newspaper.*

Vježbe

1   Choose the most appropriate adjective to fit the gaps in the following sentences. The adjectives are in the masculine nominative form, you will have to put them in the correct gender, case and number (i.e. singular or plural). You may use each adjective only once:

(*a*)   Nije daleko od _____ ceste do našeg bloka.
(*b*)   Ona govori sa _____ majkom u kuhinji.
(*c*)   Više volim _____ vino, ali mogu piti i bijelo.
(*d*)   Možemo ići pješice od hotela do _____ zgrada u centra grada.
(*e*)   Danas idemo u _____ školu, a ne u moju školu.
(*f*)   Gosti sjede na _____ stolicama u blagovaonici.

udoban	tvoj	glavan	velik	crn	njegov

2   Choose the most appropriate preposition to fit the gaps in the following sentences. Make sure that you consider the case endings of the nouns and adjectives:

(*a*)   Idem kući _____ škole.
(*b*)   Radim od šest sati ujutro _____ tri poslije podne.
(*c*)   Pošta se nalazi _____ trgu.
(*d*)   Ideš _____ velika vrata tamo u njihov stan.
(*e*)   Jasna govori sa Rudolfovom majkom _____ kuće.
(*f*)   Oni izlazi _____ kavane u šest sati uvečer.

do	iz	na	kroz	kod	poslije

3   Answer the questions below by referring to the drawings:

(*a*) Kakav namještaj imate u dnevnoj sobi?

(I have three armchairs, one small table and a television set in the corner.)

(*b*) Što imate u kuhinji?

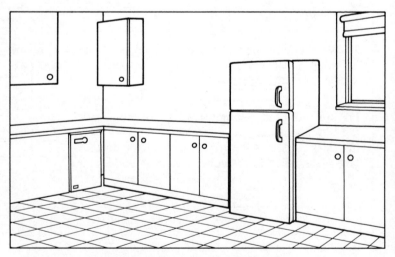

(In the kitchen I have a fridge, a freezer and cupboards.)

(c) Radite li u spavaćoj sobi?
Da, moram raditi u spavoćoj sobi. Imam tamo...

(a desk and two shelves for books.)

(d) Kakav namještaj imate u blagovaonici?

(I have a large table and six chairs for guests.)

4 Match the questions to the answers:

(a) Kakvu dnevnu sobu imate? (i) Počinje u sedam.
(b) U koliko sati počinje film? (ii) Idem k tetki.
(c) Što radite sutra? (iii) Jasna ne može doći.
(d) Tko ne dolazi na ručak danas? (iv) Velika je sa stolom.

5 Write out the times given below on the clock faces:

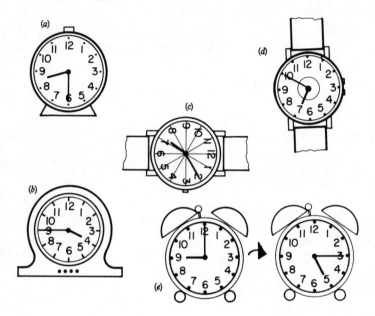

6 Fill in the gaps with the most appropriate divisions of the day from the box below.

(a) Učenici počinju raditi u školi _____.
(b) Idemo _____ u kazalište.
(c) Autobusi ne idu kroz grad _____.
(d) Danas i _____ idem k bratu.

sutra	večeras	prije podne	noću

——————— Dopunsko štivo 1 ———————

Jasna Kušan je sekretarica u velikoj zagrebačkoj firmi. Ovdje govori o svom tipičnom radnom danu.

Ustajem u pola sedam. Znam da je rano, ali moram se istuširati i popiti kavu prije posla. Na posao idem autobusom. Put traje oko dvadeset minuta. U uredu odmah počinjem raditi, uvijek me nešto čeka na radnom stolu. U devet i petnaest idem na doručak. Kupujem sendviče i pijem kavu. Radim do tri. Ponekad idem u grad kupiti nešto ili možda rezervirati karte za kazalište ili kino. Ručam kod kuće ili s prijateljicama u restoranu.

zagrebački *of Zagreb*	**nešto** *something*
tipičan *typical*	**čekati, čekam** *wait*
radni dan *working day*	**kupovati, kupujem** *to buy*
rano *early*	(imperfective; **kupiti** perfective)
istuširati se, istuširam se *shower*	**možda** *perhaps*
prije *before*	**rezervirati, rezerviram** *reserve*
put *road, journey*	**karta** *ticket*

Istina ili neistina?

(*a*) Jasnina firma je u Zagrebu.
(*b*) Put na posao traje oko dvadeset minuta.
(*c*) Jasna radi do tri po podne.

——————— Dopunsko štivo 2 ———————

Read the passage below and answer the following questions:

Poslije lijepe večere kod Rudolfa i njegove majke, Sandra razmišlja o svom i Markovom životu u Zagrebu. Sjeća se njihovog stana u Londonu. U tom stanu imaju dnevnu sobu sa zelenim tepihom i zavjesama iste boje. Stan nije velik, ali ima kuhinju i spavaću sobu za goste. Koliko dugo su već u Zagrebu? Hotel nije loš, ali je teško stanovati u jednoj sobi. Kaže mužu, "Moram priznati, sviđa mi se Rudolfov stan. Možemo li mi tražiti stan u Zagrebu? Ne volim živjeti stalno u hotelu." Mark sluša ženu i kaže, "Moramo čekati. Ne znam koliko dugo ostajemo u Zagrebu."

razmišljati, razmišljam *to consider, think about*	**loš** *bad*
sjećati se, sjećam se (followed by gen.) *remember*	**teško je** *it is difficult*
zelen *green*	**kazati, kažem** *to say, tell*
tepih *carpet*	**priznati** *to confess, admit*
zavjesa *curtain*	**Sviđa mi se Rudolfov stan.** *I like Rudolf's flat.*
iste boje *of the same colour*	**slušati, slušam** *to listen to*
Koliko dugo su već u Zagrebu? *How long have they been in Zagreb?*	**Koliko dugo ostajemo u Zagrebu?** *For how long are we staying in Zagreb?*

1 Kakve su zavjese u Rudolfovoj dnevnoj sobi?
- (*a*) Lijepe su.
- (*b*) Zelene su.
- (*c*) Loše su.

2 Gdje Sandra ne može stanovati?
- (*a*) Ne može stanovati u Zagrebu.
- (*b*) Ne može stanovati u Londonu.
- (c) Ne može stanovati u jednoj sobi.

3 Što misli Mark?
- (*a*) Misli da je to dobra ideja.
- (*b*) Ne zna koliko dugo ostaju u Zagrebu.
- (*c*) Misli da hotel nije udoban.

9

SVIĐA MI
SE PLIVANJE

I like swimming

In this unit you will learn how to

- describe hobbies, sports and free time
- use other expressions of time, days of the week and months of the year

Dijalog

Mark govori sa Rudolfom o sportovima i o slobodnom vremenu.

Mark   Rudolf, bavite li se sportom?

Rudolf   Da, bavim se sportom. Volim igrati tenis i nogomet. Sviđa mi se plivanje. Idem na bazen svakog ponedjeljka.

Mark   I meni se sviđa plivanje. U Londonu idem dva-tri puta tjedno. Gdje je vaš bazen?

Rudolf   Idem u Sportsko-rekreacijski centar. Zatvoren bazen radi svaki dan i zimi i ljeti. Imaju i otvoren bazen, radi od početka lipnja do kraja rujna.

Mark   Što još ima tamo?

Rudolf   Ima terena za sve sportove. Imaju stadion za hokej na travi i stadion za hokej na ledu. Ljudi igraju košarku. Imaju rukometno igralište, i terene za tenis i za nogomet.

ŠPORTSKI
TERENI

ZAGREB

Stadioni za hokej rade svaki
dan, rukometno igralište
radi subotom i nedjeljom.

Mark   Volim igrati badminton.

Rudolf   Imaju teren za igranje badmintona. Radi srijedom od devet
sati do podne, i subotom po podne.

Mark   Da li se Jasna bavi sportom?

Rudolf   Igra badminton. A bavi li se Sandra sportom?

Mark   Sandri se sviđa plivanje.

Rudolf   Morate doći u Centar.

Mark   Kada idete?

Rudolf   Da vidim… Danas je četvrtak. Idem prekosutra.

Mark   Dobro. Ja sam u subotu slobodan.

sport *sport*	**do kraja rujna** *to the end of September*
slobodno vrijeme (o slobodnom vremenu… without '..ij..') *free time* (*leisure*)	**teren** *pitch, court* (for sports)
	za sve sportove *for all sports*
baviti se, bavim se (followed by instrumental case) *to be occupied with, take part in*	**stadion za hokej na travi** *stadium for grass hockey*
	hokej na ledu *ice hockey*

igrati, igram *to play*	**rukometno igralište** *handball pitch*
tenis *tennis*	**rukomet** *handball*
nogomet *football*	***teren za tenis*** *tennis court*
bazen *swimming-pool*	**svaki dan** *every day*
svakog ponedjeljka *every Monday*	**subotom** *on Saturdays*
dva-tri puta *two or three times*	**nedjeljom** *on Sundays*
tjedno *weekly*	**igranje** *playing*
Sportsko-rekreacijski centar	**srijedom** *on Wednesdays*
Sports Centre	**Sandri se sviđa plivanje.** *Sandra*
zatvoren bazen *covered pool*	*likes swimming.*
zimi *in winter*	**Da vidim...** *Let me see...*
ljeti *in summer*	**četvrtak** *Thursday*
otvoren bazen *open-air pool*	**Ja sam slobodan.** *I am free*
od početka lipnja *from the*	*(available).*
beginning of June	**u subotu** *on Saturday*
košarka *basketball*	

Mark čita informacije o Sportsko-rekreacijskom centru:

ZATVORENI BAZENI (olimpijski i mali)
Radno vrijeme: radnim danom od **12.00** do **19.00** sati, subotom od **10.00** do **20.00** sati. Nedjeljom ne radi.

RUKOMETNO IGRALIŠTE
Radno vrijeme: svake subote i nedelje od travnja do listopada.

ATLETSKI STADION
Tečaj atletike traje 15 sati (3 tjedna x 5 dana) od **15.30** do **16.30** sati

čitati, čitam *to read*	**svake subote** *every Saturday*
informacija (usually used in plural	**od travnja do listopada** *from April*
informacije) *information*	*to October*
radnim danom *on working days*	**atletski stadion** *athletics stadium,*
Nedjeljom ne radi. *It does not work*	*track*
on Sundays (i.e. it is not open).	**tečaj** *course*

Istina ili neistina?

(*a*) Rudolf se bavi tenisom, nogometom i plivanjem.
(*b*) Mark voli igrati košarku.
(*c*) Zatvoreni bazeni rade svaki dan.

Objašnjenja i komentari

Sportsko-poslovni kompleks »Cibona«
(Cibona Sports and Offices Complex)

Sport and recreation

Zagreb, as the main city of Croatia, has many sporting facilities. Many of them are modern, having been built to accommodate the World Student Games which were held there in 1987. There are opportunities for winter sports too such as skating (**klizanje**), and just outside the city there is a popular spot for skiing (**skijanje**).

Ključne fraze

How to:

● use more expressions of time –

every day	**svaki dan**
every Monday	**svakog ponedjeljka**
every Saturday	**svake subote**
on Saturdays	**subotom**
on Sundays	**nedjeljom**
on Wednesdays	**srijedom**
weekly	**tjedno**
today is...	**danas je...**
on Saturday	**u subotu**
in winter	**zimi**
in summer	**ljeti**
from the beginning of June	**od početka lipnja**
to the end of September	**do kraja rujna**
from April to October	**od travnja do listopada**

● express involvement with sport.　**bavim se sportom**
● say that you play a sport.　**igram tenis**
● say that you like a sport.　**volim tenis**
　or　**sviđa mi se plivanje**

⊡ ———— Jezični obrasci ————

1 Sviđa mi se plivanje

You have already met the phrase **volim...** to express that you like something. There is another common expression used: **sviđa mi se...** This expression literally means *It is pleasing to me* and is formed by using the dative case of the relevant person (i.e. *me*).

Sviđa mi se plivanje.	*I like swimming.*
Sviđa joj se Zagreb.	*She likes Zagreb.*
Marku se sviđa plivanje.	*Mark likes swimming.*
Sandri se sviđa Zagreb.	*Sandra likes Zagreb.*

The verbal part **sviđa** is an **-a** verb like **gledati**. Look what happens when more than one thing is liked, **sviđa** is transormed into a plural form **sviđaju**:

Sviđaju mi se te knjige.	*I like those books.*

2 Reflexive verbs

In this unit you have met more verbs which are called reflexive verbs. These verbs include **se** when used: (**baviti se**, **sjećati se**, etc.). The short word **se** never changes.

Se is roughly equivalent to the English *oneself*, although it is not always immediately apparent in English that this word has to be used with the verb.

These verbs are never followed by the accusative case:

Bavim se sportom.	*I am engaged in sport.*
(instrumental – **sportom**)	(I involve *myself* in sport.)
Sjećam se stana u Londonu.	*I remember the flat in London.*
(genitive – **stana**)	
Ženi se Njemicom.	*He is getting married*
(**ženiti se** – *to be getting married*)	*to a German.*
(followed by the instrumental – **Njemicom**)	

The word **se** is like the short forms of **biti** or of **ja**, **ti**, etc. It never comes as first word, but as second word in the sentence:

Kako se zovete?	*What is your name?*
	(Lit. *How do you call yourself?*)
Zovem se Mark.	*My name is Mark.*
	(*I call myself Mark.*)

3 Word order

The words like **se** which never come at the beginning of the sentence are called enclitics. There is a strict order for the enclitics when more than one occurs together. The order is **li**, dative enclitic, genitive enclitic, accusative enclitic, **se**. Study the examples below.

Sjećam ga se.	*I remember him.*
Dajem joj ga.	*I give it to her.*
Sviđa mi se plivanje.	*I like swimming.*
Da li vam se sviđa plivanje?	*Do you like swimming?*
Sviđaju li vam se nogomet i košarka?	*Do you like football and basketball?*

In other instances word order is fairly flexible in Serbo-Croat. The case endings mean that you cannot get the meaning wrong, whatever the order of words. Look at these examples which mean the same because Sandra is nominative case each time:

Sandra daje ženi novac.	*Sandra gives the money*
Sandra daje novac ženi.	*to the woman.*
Novac Sandra daje ženi.	

4 Days of the week

The days of the week are:

ponedjeljak	*Monday*	**petak**	*Friday*
utorak	*Tuesday*	**subota**	*Saturday*
srijeda	*Wednesday*	**nedjelja**	*Sunday*
četvrtak	*Thursday*		

Days are always spelt with a small letter in Serbo-Croat.

To say *every...* use the genitive case with the adjective **svaki** (*every*):

| svakog ponedjeljka | *every Monday* |
| svake subote | *every Saturday* |

(Sometimes the accusative case is used with **dan: svaki dan**.)

To say *on Tuesdays*, etc. simply use the word in the instrumental case (singular):

| utorkom | *on Tuesdays* |
| četvrtkom | *on Thursdays* |

To say *on a day* use the preposition **u** followed by the name of the day in the accusative case

| u utorak | *on Tuesday* |
| u subotu | *on Saturday* |

The word for *week* is **tjedan** and for *weekly* is **tjedno**.

5 Months of the year

There are two sets of names for months of the year.

western	eastern	
siječanj	januar	*January*
veljača	februar	*February*
ožujak	mart	*March*
travanj	april	*April*
svibanj	maj	*May*
lipanj	jun	*June*
srpanj	jul	*July*
kolovoz	avgust	*August*
rujan	septembar	*September*
listopad	oktobar	*October*
studeni	novembar	*November*
prosinac	decembar	*December*

The first set are more common in the western variant of the language, and the second set (similar to the English names) are more commonly used in the eastern variant.

The names of the month are always spelt with a small letter in Serbo-Croat. To say in a month use **u** followed by the name of the month in the locative case:

u siječnju	*in January*
u veljači	*in February*
u ožujku	*in March*

The word **studeni** is an adjective in form:

u studenom	*in November*

The word for *month* is **mjesec** and for *monthly* is **mjesečno**.

6 Seasons of the year

The seasons of the year are:

proljeće spring	**jesen** autumn
ljeto summer	**zima** winter
u proljeće in spring	**u jesen** in autumn
ljeti in summer	**zimi** in winter

7 Dva-tri puta

To say *two or three* in Serbo-Croat you join the two numbers together with a hyphen. Look at the following examples:

pet-šest ljudi	*five or six people*
sedam-osam terena za tenis	*seven or eight tennis courts*

--- Vježbe ---

1 Replace the verb **voljeti** with the corresponding phrase taken from **sviđati se** as in the example:

Examples: Mark voli nogomet.   Marku se sviđa nogomet.

Take care to choose the correct person in the dative case and to choose the correct endings for both the verb (**sviđa** or **sviđaju**) and the thing which is liked.

(*a*) Vole ove knjige.

(b) Volim nogomet.
(c) Da li volite plivanje?
(d) Rudolf voli košarku.
(e) Sandra i Jasna vole badminton.

2 Replace the noun or nouns in bold in the following sentences with the appropriate pronouns.

Example: Konobar daje **nož ženi**. Konobar joj ga daje.

Take care with choosing the correct case for each person and take care to position each short enclitic form correctly.

(a) Čovjek daje **marke Marku**.
(b) Da li žena daje **Sandri** novac?
(c) Vidim **Rudolfa** blizu spomenika.
(d) Ljudi piju **kavu** u kavani.
(e) Mark gleda **ženu**.
(f) Pišemo **mami**.
(g) Dajem **knjige ljudima**.
(h) Sjeća se **stana** u Londonu.

3 Fill in the missing parts of the dialogue:

(*Do you like swimming?*)
Ne, ne sviđa mi se.
(*Do you involve yourself in a sport?*)
Da, bavim se rukometom.
(*I like to play handball too. Where is the handball court?*)
Ima rukometno igralište u sportsko-rekreacijskom centru.
(*Do they have a covered swimming-pool there?*)
Ima. Zatvoren bazen radi svaki dan.
(*At what time is it working?*)
Radi od devet sati prije podne do dva sata po podne.
(*When are you going to the sports centre?*)
Idem u srijedu. Dođite u Centar u srijedu!

4 Supply the expression of time as indicated in English in brackets to complete the sentences below:

Example: Igram tenis. (*on Thursdays*) Četvrtkom.

(a) Pijem kavu. (*every day*)
(b) Volim igrati badminton. (*every Saturday*)
(c) Idem u Zagreb. (*on Wednesday*)
(d) Ljudi idu na skijanje. (*in winter*)

(e) Otvoren bazen radi. (*from May to September*)
(f) Jedemo ribu. (*on Fridays*)
(g) Više vole igrati tenis. (*in spring*)
(h) Mark i Sandra idu u grad. (*on Sunday*)
(i) Jasna ide u London. (*in March*)
(j) Zvonko se ženi Marijom. (*on Saturday*)

───────── **Dopunsko štivo 1** ─────────

Dva dana kasnije Sandra i Jasna idu na kavu.

Sandra Jasna, što radite kada niste na poslu?
Jasna Kod kuće gledam televiziju ili čitam.
Sandra Bavite li se sportom?
Jasna Bavim se sportom.
Sandra Kakav sport volite?
Jasna Volim igrati badminton i tenis.
Sandra Kada ih igrate?
Jasna Ovaj tjedan idem u sportski centar u subotu. Igram tenis subotom.
Sandra Kada igrate badminton?
Jasna Teren za badminton radi utorkom i nedjeljom po podne. Tamo idem nedjeljom.
Sandra A, imaju li tamo otvoren bazen?
Jasna Ima. Otvoren bazen radi ljeti, od početka srpnja do kraja kolovoza.
Sandra Što radite zimi?
Jasna Zimi idem na skijanje.
Sandra Kamo idete na skijanje?
Jasna Idem na Sljeme. To nije daleko od Zagreba. Možete ići tamo autobusom iz centra grada.

ići na skijanje	*to go skiing*

Istina ili neistina?

(a) Jasna igra košarku.
(b) Ovaj tjedan Jasna ide u sportski centar u subotu.
(c) Zimi Jasna ide na skijanje.

Dopunsko štivo 2

Read the following passage and answer the questions below.

Velimir i njegova žena su na odmoru. Oni su u hotelu na moru.
Na recepciji su informacije o sadržajima hotela. Velimir ih čita.

VAŠ HOTEL

PRIZEMLJE
Zatvoren bazen radi svaki dan od 8.00 do 21.30 sati.
Uz bazen gosti imaju trim kabinet, salon za masažu i saunu.
Radno vrijeme: Trim kabinet od 10.00 do 20.00 sati
Salon za masažu od 11.00 do 18.00 sati
Sauna od 10.00 do 20.30 sati.
(salon za masažu **ne radi** subotom i nedjeljom)
(sauna **ne radi** nedjeljom)

PRVI KAT
Četvorostazna automatska kuglana radi svaki dan od 10.00 do
21.00 sati. Pored kuglane je Noćni klub **'Vašeg hotela'**. Radno
vrijeme: od 21.00

ČETVRTI KAT
Stolni tenis radi od 12.00 do 23.00 sati svaki dan osim poned-
jeljka.
Ljeti gosti imaju i druge mogućnosti za sport u okolini hotela.
Mini-golf.
Badminton i tenis igrališta.
Sportovi na vodi.

na odmoru *on holiday*	**noćni klub** *night club*
na moru *by the sea*	**stolni tenis** *table-tennis*
sadržaj *facility, content*	**osim ponedeljka (osim** preposition
prizemlje *ground floor*	with gen.) *except Monday*
uz bazen *along with the pool*	**druge mogućnosti** *other possibilities*
trim kabinet *exercise room*	**u okolini hotela** *in the vicinity of*
salon za masažu *massage salon*	the hotel
četvorostazna automatska kuglana	**sportovi na vodi** *water sports*
four-lane automatic bowling alley	
pored *next to* (preposition followed	
by gen.)	

1 Kada radi trim kabinet?
   (*a*) Od deset sati ujutro do šest sati navečer.
   (*b*) Od deset sati ujutro do osam sati navečer.
   (*c*) Od jedanaest sati ujutro do pola devet navečer.

2 Kada radi Noćni klub?
   (*a*) Od sedam sati navečer.
   (*b*) Od devet sati navečer.
   (*c*) Od jedanaest sati navečer.

3 Kada ne radi stolni tenis?
   (*a*) Ponedjeljkom.
   (*b*) Subotom.
   (*c*) Nedjeljom.

10

NA IZLETU
On an excursion

In this unit you will learn how to

● use more phrases to express agreement and disagreement
● express further degrees of certainty
● express satisfaction
● talk about travelling, the weather and the countryside

━━━━━━━━ Dijalog ━━━━━━━━

Danas Sandra i Mark idu s prijateljima u planine. Putuju kolima.
Jasna vozi kola.

Mark   Kako je dobro biti izvan grada u prirodi! Kako su lijepe ove
planine!

Rudolf   U pravu ste. Planine su lijepe kad sunce sija.

Sandra   Da, slažem se. Vidimo planine, šumu, rijeku i polja.

Rudolf   Međutim, kad je loše vrijeme, kad pada kiša ili snijeg, nije
lijepo biti na planinama.

Mark   Ali, danas je dobro vrijeme. Ja sam zadovoljan ovim pogle-
dom na planine.

Jasna   Slažem se s vama. Pogled je zaista divan. Sada dolazimo u
selo. Tko ima kartu?

Sandra   Ja je imam. Ne mogu naći selo.

Rudolf   Dajte mi kartu, mislim da znam gdje smo. Idemo prema
Varaždinu.

Mark   Gdje je Varaždin?

Rudolf Varaždin je grad u sjeverozapadnoj Hrvatskoj.
Mark Znači, mi smo na sjeveru Hrvatske.
Rudolf Idemo u tom pravcu, prema sjeveru. Ali, mislim da je već vrijeme da skrenemo na lijevo. Kako se zove ovo selo? Nije mi jasno gdje smo. Po mom mišljenju, autoput je na lijevo. Mi smo na krivom putu.
Jasna Nemaš pravo, Rudolf. Ovo je pravi put.
Rudolf Nisam baš siguran.
Jasna Ja jesam sigurna.
Rudolf U pravu si. Slažem se s tobom. Nije daleko do autoputa. Je li to kavana pored ceste?
Jasna Da. Ja sam žedna.
Rudolf I ja sam žedan. Putujemo već dva sata. Možemo ovdje napraviti kratku pauzu.

planina *mountain*	**s vama** *with you*
putovati, putujem *to travel*	**zaista** *really*
kola (neut. pl.) *car*	**divan** *wonderful*
kolima *by car*	**selo** *village*
voziti, vozim *to drive*	**karta** *map*
Kako su lijepe ove planine! *How*	**naći, nađem** *to find*
beautiful these mountains are!	**u sjeverozapadnoj Hrvatskoj**
izvan (preposition with gen.)	*in north-west Croatia*
outside	**na sjeveru** *in the north*
priroda *nature, countryside*	**u tom pravcu** *in that direction*
U pravu ste. *You are right.*	**prema sjeveru** *toward the north*
sunce *sun*	**Nije mi jasno.** *It is not clear to me.*
sijati, sija *to shine*	**po mom mišljenju** *in my opinion*
šuma *forest*	**autoput** *motorway, trunk road*
rijeka *river*	**na krivom putu** *on the wrong road*
polje *field*	**Nemaš pravo.** *You are not right.*
međutim *however*	**pravi put** *right road*
loše vrijeme *bad weather*	**Nisam baš siguran.** *I am not*
pada kiša *it rains, it is raining*	*quite sure.*
pada snijeg *it snows, it is snowing*	**U pravu si.** *You are right.*
dobro vrijeme *good weather*	**s tobom** *with you*
zadovoljan (with ins.) *pleased with,*	**napraviti kratku pauzu** *to make a*
satisfied with	*short break*
pogled na (with acc.) *view of*	

Istina ili neistina?

(a) Lijepo je biti na planinama kada pada snijeg.
(b) Sandra daje kartu Rudolfu.
(c) Jasna je u pravu kada kaže da su na pravom putu.

——— **Objašnjenja i komentari** ———

Excursions around Zagreb

There are many places to visit in and around Zagreb. To the north-west is the old town of Varaždin, once the capital of Croatia. It is fast becoming an industrial town but the centre still retains its old world charm. The castle and the town hall both date from the sixteenth century.

Gradska Vijećnica, Varaždin *(Town Hall, Varaždin)*

To the south is the Plitvice National Park. This is one of the most beautiful spots in inland Croatia with numerous lakes connected by waterfalls surrounded by dense forests. Both places are within a couple of hours' drive from Zagreb. The coast is not really accessible on a one-day trip.

Motoring

Large numbers of tourists visit Croatia by car. It is easy, if somewhat expensive, to hire a car from any one of a number of international hire companies which operate there. If you are driving and you need petrol (**benzin**) stop at a **benzinska pumpa**. The road network is good on the whole and connects all major places of interest. Tourists that go straight to the coast are missing out on the historic towns, relaxing spa sites and countryside of inland Croatia. Visitors to such places can usually find accommodation in hotels, motels and private rooms at moderate rates.

Ključne fraze

How to:

- say that you agree with someone.

  Slažem se s vama.
  (to someone with whom you use **vi**)
  Slažem se s tobom.
  (to someone with whom you use **ti**)

- say that someone is *right*, or that someone is *wrong*.

  U pravu si (ti).
  Nemate pravo. (vi).

- say that you are sure of something.

  Ja jesam siguran.
  (male speaking, using the long form of **biti** for added emphasis)
  Ja jesam sigurna.
  (female speaking)

- say that you are not quite sure of something.

  Nisam baš siguran.
  (male speaking)
  Nisam baš sigurna.
  (female speaking)

- say that it is not clear to you.

  Nije mi jasno.

- say that *in your opinion...*

  po mom mišljenju

- express satisfaction.

Zadovljan sam.
(male speaking)
Zadovoljna sam.
(female speaking)

- use expressions relating to
  the weather.

loše vrijeme
dobro vrijeme
sunce sija
pada kiša
pada snijeg

- use expressions relating to
  direction and position.

u sjeverozapadnoj Hrvatskoj
na sjeveru
prema sjeveru
u tom pravcu
na krivom putu
na pravom putu

Jezični obrasci

1 S vama/with you (Personal pronouns in the instrumental case)

You already know that after **s** (*with*) you use the instrumental case.
So in the sentence **Slažem se s vama** you are using the instrumental case of **vi**. The pattern of cases for all the personal pronouns is as
follows with some revision notes below:

nom.	acc.	gen.	dat.	ins.
ja	me, mene	me, mene	mi, meni	mnom(e)
ti	te, tebe	te, tebe	ti, tebi	tobom
on	ga, njega	ga, njega	mu, njemu	njim(e)
ona	je, ju nju	je, nje	joj, njoj	njom(e)
mi	nas, nas	nas, nas	nam, nama	nama
vi	vas, vas	vas, vas	vam, vama	vama
oni	ih, njih	ih, njih	im, njima	njima

(*a*) The short form of the pronoun comes first.
(*b*) The forms for **ono** are the same as for **on**.

(c)   The preferred short form of **ona** in the accusative is **je**.
(d)   Sometimes an **e** is added to the end of the pronoun in the instrumental case.
(e)   The extra letter is added when the pronoun is used without a preposition (e.g. **Idem s njim. Zadovoljan sam njome**).
(f)   The short forms are unstressed.
(g)   The forms which are spelt the same (e.g. **nas, nas**) are stressed when used as long forms.
(h)   The cases for **one** and **ona** are the same as for **oni**.

2   Nije mi jasno *and word order*

This kind of expression is called an impersonal expression. The phrase **nije jasno** (*it is not clear*) is formed by taking the neuter nominative form of the adjective **jasan** and using the **je** form from the verb **biti**. You have already come across some examples:

Lako je.	*It is easy.*
Teško je.	*It is difficult.*
Jasno je.	*It is clear.*

The **je** comes in second place because it is a short form and so cannot come at the beginning. The negative **nije** is not a short form.

Nije lako.	*It is not easy.*
Nije teško.	*It is not difficult.*
Nije jasno.	*It is not clear.*

You can add to these expressions the dative case of the personal pronouns to mean *to me* or *for me*, etc. Take care with the order of the short forms as **je** must come after the dative:

Lako mi je.	*It is easy for me. (I find it easy.)*
Teško mu je.	*It is difficult for him. (He finds it difficult).*
Jasno im je.	*It is clear to them.*
Nije joj lako.	*It is not easy for her.*
Nije nam teško.	*It is not difficult for us.*

Study the word order in the following questions:

Je li ti jasno?	*Is it clear to you?*
Da li vam je jasno?	*Is it clear to you?*

Remember that **je** is an exception as far as short forms are concerned as it may occur at the beginning when introducing a question with the form **Je li..?**

3 Points of the compass

The basic points of the compass are:

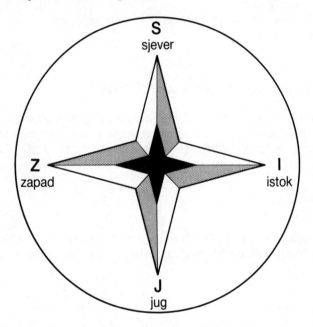

To say *in the north,* etc. you use the preposition **na** (and dat.):

na sjeveru	*in the north*
na istoku	*in the east*

To say *towards the south,* etc. you use the preposition **prema** (and dat.):

prema jugu	*towards the south*
prema zapadu	*towards the west*

The adjectives *northern,* etc. are:

sjeverni	*northern*
istočni	*eastern*

južni	*southern*
zapadni	*western*

They only have the definite forms which end in **-i**. And you can make compounds like *northwestern*:

sjeverozapadni	*northwestern*
jugoistočni	*southeastern*

4 Idioms

(*a*) There are a number of ways of saying *you are right/wrong* (**U pravu** followed by short from of **biti**):

U pravu ste.	*You are right.*
U pravu je.	*S/He is right.*
U pravu su.	*They are right.*

(negative of **biti** followed by **u pravu**):

Niste u pravu.	*You are wrong.*
Nismo u pravu.	*We are wrong.*

(**Imat**i followed by **pravo**):

Imaš pravo.	*You are right.*

(negative of **imati** followed by **pravo**):

Nemaju pravo.	*They are wrong.*

There are also adjectives:

kriv *wrong*	**prav** *right*	

Mi smo na pravom putu.	*We are on the right road.*
Ovo je krivi telefonski broj.	*This is the wrong telephone number.*

(*b*) The intensifying **baš** which may be added after many words to mean *quite* or *really*:

Nisam baš siguran.	*I am not quite sure.*
Baš sam zadovoljan.	*I am quite satisfied.*
Baš smo žedni.	*We are really thirsty.*

(*c*) To form the expression *in my opinion*, etc.:

The expression **po mom mišljenju** is formed from the preposition **po** followed by the dative case of **moj** and of the word **mišljenje** (opinion).

The words **moj** and **tvoj** are often shortened:

moj + em = mom	tvoj + em = tvom

Study the following examples:

po njegovom mišljenju	*in his opinion*
po našem mišljenju	*in our opinion*

This expression is similar in meaning to

čini mi se	*it seems to me*
mislim da...	*I think that...*

☑ ——————— Vježbe ———————

1 Supply the correct cases of the personal pronoun indicated in the brackets:

   (*a*) Zadovoljni smo (oni).
   (*b*) Konobar (ona) daje jelovnik.
   (*c*) Idu s (mi) u kino.
   (*d*) Zadovoljna je (ja).
   (*e*) Da li (oni) gledate?
   (*f*) Nisu zadovoljni (on).
   (*g*) Gledaš li (ja).
   (*h*) Idem u kazalište s (vi).
   (*i*) Ne gledaju (ja).
   (*j*) Je li zadovoljan (ti)?

2 Form a question for the following answers?

   (*a*) Teško mi je.
   (*b*) Nije joj lako.
   (*c*) Nije im jasno.
   (*d*) Jasno mi je.

3 Answer the following questions affirmatively and then negatively:

(*a*) Da li vam je teško?
(*b*) Je li im jasno?
(*c*) Je li mu jasno?
(*d*) Je li ti lako?

4 Fit the correct question words taken from the box below to the following questions (you must use all the question words only once):

(*a*) _____ se zovete?
(*b*) _____ soba imaju u stanu?
(*c*) _____ kompjuter imate?
(*d*) _____ ide Rudolf sutra?
(*e*) _____ ideš u grad?
(*f*) _____ govori hrvatski?
(*g*) _____ je Varaždin?
(*h*) _____ Sandra želi kupiti?

Koliko	Tko	Što	Kamo	Kakav	Kako	Gdje	Kada

5 Match the answers to the questions:

(*a*) Je li Jasna u pravu?   (i) Ne, nismo.
(*b*) Da li ste u pravu?   (ii) Ne, nisam u pravu.
(*c*) Tko ima pravo?   (iii) Da, u pravu je.
(*d*) Jesmo li na pravom putu?   (iv) Rudolf ima.

6 Change the following sentences to include the phrase **po**̧ **mišljenju**. Look at the examples and take care to use the adjective of the name of the person, or the correct form of **moj**, etc.:

Examples: Jasni se čini da pada kiša.
Po Jasninom mišljenju, pada kiša.

Mislimo da idemo prema Zagrebu.
Po našem mišljenju, idemo prema Zagrebu.

(*a*) Rudolf misli da su Sandra i Mark u hotelu.
(*b*) Čini joj se da je Rudolf na poslu.
(*c*) Sutra idem, čini mi se, u kazalište.
(*d*) Sandra i Mark misle da otvoren bazen radi svaki dan.

7 The map on p. 138 shows Bosnia, Croatia, Montenegro and Serbia where Serbo-Croat is spoken. Say where the four towns are according to the points of the compass:

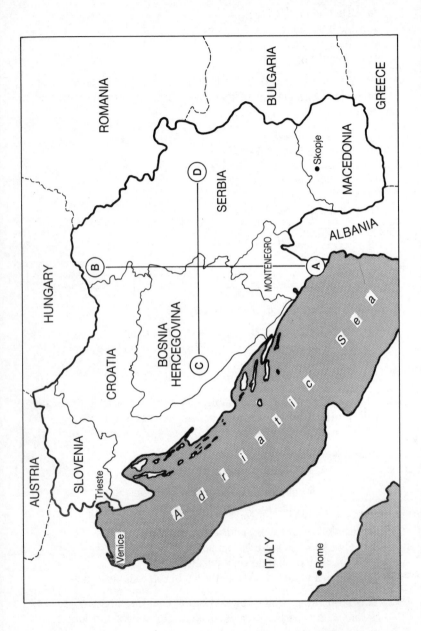

———— Dopunsko štivo 1 ————

Zagreb je glavni grad Hrvatske. Privredni je i kulturni centar s oko milijun stanovnika. U Zagrebu je park Maksimir sa zoološkim vrtom. Zoološki vrt otvoren je od devet sati do sumraka. U blizini parka Maksimir i Zooloošćkog vrta nalaze se sportski tereni: Stadion i kompleks "Dinamo" i Sportsko-rekreacijski centar.

Ako putujete prema sjeveru od Zagreba stižete do Slovenije. Ako putujete prema istoku stižete do Srbije. Ako putujete prema zapadu i prema jugozapadu stižete do Jadranskog mora. Ljeti tamo ima mnogo turista. Glavni gradovi na obali su Dubrovnik, Split, Zadar i Rijeka. Blizu obale su otci – Hvar, Brač, Mljet Korčula... Obala je divna, otoci su lijepi i more je plavo.

privredni *economic*	**u blizini** *in the vicinity*
kulturni *cultural*	**stizati, stižem** *to arrive*
milijun *million*	**Jadransko more** *Adriatic Sea*
stanovnik *inhabitant*	**obala** *coast*
zoološki vrt *zoo*	**blizu** (preposition with gen.) *near*
otvoren *open*	**otok** *island*
sumrak *dusk*	**plav** *blue*

Istina ili neistina?

(*a*) U Zagrebu živi oko milijun stanovnika.
(*b*) Dubrovnik je jedan od glavnih gradova na obali.
(*c*) Mnogo turista dolazi na more.

———— Dopunsko štivo 2 ————

Read the passage and answer the questions below.

When they stop during their excursion at the café, Mark asks Jasna about the weather on the coast. Sandra joins in their conversation.

Mark	Jasna, kakvo je vrijeme na moru?
Jasna	Toplo. Ljeti sunce sija skoro svaki dan. Volite li more?
Mark	Da. Volim ga, i volim plivati u moru.
Jasna	Sandra, slažete li se s Markom?

Sandra Da, slažem se s njim. Baš mi se sviđa ovdje u Zagrebu i u blizini Zagreba. Ali želimo također vidjeti obalu i Jadransko more.

Jasna Jadransko more je jako lijepo. Rudolf i ja idemo na odmor u kolovozu. Idemo na more. Hoćete li poći s nama?

Sandra Hvala na pozivu. To je dobra ideja. Idemo s vama.

Jasna Sandra, da prijeđemo na ti. Idemo zajedno na more, sad smo prijatelji.

Sandra U pravu si, Jasna.

toplo *warm*	**Hvala na pozivu.** *Thanks for the invitation.*
skoro *almost*	
plivati *to swim*	**dobra ideja** *a good idea*
jako *very*	**Da prijeđemo na ti.** *Let's start to use **ti** to one another.*
ići na odmor *to go on holiday*	
poći *to go, set off*	

1 Kakvo je vrijeme na obali?
   (*a*) Loše.
   (*b*) Pada kiša.
   (*c*) Toplo je.

2 Što Sandra i Mark žele vidjeti?
   (*a*) More.
   (*b*) Planine.
   (*c*) Zagreb.

3 Kada idu Jasna i Rudolf na odmor?
   (*a*) Idu na more.
   (*b*) Idu u kolovozu.
   (*c*) Idu svaki mjesec.

11

POVRATNE KARTE
Return tickets

In this unit you will learn how to

- express that things happened in the past (using the past tense form of the verb)
- talk more about travelling
- ask what happened
- ask how long ago something happened

─────────────── **Dijalog** ───────────────

Prijatelji su govorili o odmoru. Htjeli su ići na otok Hvar. Jasna je išla u putničku agenciju s Markom i Sandrom. Htjeli su kupiti avionske karte za Split. U Splitu će kupiti karte za brod.

Jasna   Dobar dan. Molim vas, koliko koštaju avionske karte za Split?

Agent   Da li hoćete povratne karte ili u jednom smjeru?

Jasna   Povratne. Idemo slijedeći tjedan u petak, a vraćamo se dva tjedna kasnije.

Agent   Jedna povratna karta košta tri tisuće dinara. Petkom ima dva aviona. Prvi ide prije podne u deset i petnaest sa zagrebačkog aerodroma. Drugi ide poslije podne u petnaest i trideset.

Jasna	Koliko dugo traje put avionom od Zagreba do Splita?
Agent	Četrdeset minuta.
Jasna	Mislim da moramo rezervirati karte za prvi avion.
Sandra	Imaš pravo, jer poslije dolaska u Split moramo stići na brod za otok. Molim vas, gospodine, želimo četiri povratne karte za prvi avion u petak idućeg tjedna. Vraćamo se natrag dva tjedna kasnije, u petak.
Agent	Dobro...

The vocabulary layout changes here: we shall give imperfective and perfective forms of the infinitives of new verbs where appropriate (not every verb has two forms). We shall also give the **ja** forms when the present tense is not formed directly from the infinitive. Don't forget that in any pair of verbs the imperfective always comes first.

putnička agencija *travel agency*
avionska karta *air ticket*
U Splitu će kupiti... *In Split they will buy...*
za (preposition with acc.) *for*
brod *boat*
povratna karta *return ticket*
karta u jednom smjeru *one-way ticket*
slijedeći tjedan *next week*
vraćati se, vratiti se *to return*
kasnije *later*

avion (avionom) *aeroplane* (by air – instrumental)
aerodrom *airport*
Koliko dugo traje put...? *How long does the journey last...?*
od... do... (followed by gen.) *from... to...*
jer *since, for*
stizati, stići, (stižem, stignem: stizao, stigao/stigli) *to arrive*
natrag *back*

Čovjek je gledao u kompjutorski ekran i rezervirao njihove karte. Jasna je platila i izašli su iz agencije. Te večeri, išla je k Rudolfu.

Rudolf	Što se desilo danas u agenciji? Je li sve bilo u redu?
Jasna	Sve je bilo u redu. Nisam imala problema. Kupili smo karte.
Rudolf	Onda, idemo u petak. Sjajno. Bili smo na Hvaru prije tri godine. Sjećaš li se?
Jasna	Da, sjećam se. Ali smo tada išli u hotel. Možemo li iznajmiti privatne sobe u Hvaru?
Rudolf	Možemo. Moramo odlučiti s Markom i Sandrom gdje želimo boraviti. Jedan kolega na poslu rekao mi je da je iznajmio privatnu sobu u Hvaru kod ljubazne gazdarice. Moram ga sutra pitati za njenu adresu.

kompjutorski ekran *computer screen*	**boraviti** *to stay*
plaćati, platiti *to pay*	**kolega** *colleague, person at work*
te večeri *that evening*	(like **tata** this is a masculine word
dešavati se, desiti se *to happen*	which has feminine endings,
Sve je bilo u redu. *Everything was OK.*	see Unit 7)
problem *problem*	**reći** (past tense rekao, rekli) *to tell*
onda *then*	**ljubazan** *kind*
sjajno *wonderful, smashing*	**gazdarica** *landlady*
prije tri godine *three years ago*	**adresa** *address*
privatna soba *private room*	(Verbs which end in **-ovati** and **-ivati**
iznajmljivati, iznajmiti (iznajmljujem, iznajmim) *to rent*	regularly form the present tense by changing to **-ujem, uješ**, etc:
odlučivati, odlučiti (odlučujem, odlučim) *decide*	**putovati-putujem; iznajmljivati-iznajmljujem.**)

Istina ili neistina?

(a) Jasna je kupila avionske karte u putničkoj agenciji.
(b) Put avionom od Zagreba do Splita traje trideset minuta.
(c) Rudolf i Jasna su bili na Hvaru prije tri godine.

—————— **Objašnjenja i komentari** ——————

Travel

Many people find it more convenient to travel by air within the country. Rail or road transport can be slow because of the mountains. The flight from Zagreb to, say, Split or Dubrovnik on the coast does not take long. Once there you can take the airport bus into town and quickly get tickets for the boats which sail regularly to the islands.

Hvar

The town of Hvar is on the island of Hvar: when talking about the island you say **Idem na Hvar** or **Ja sam na Hvaru** using the preposition **na**. The preposition **na** is the one normally used when talking about islands in general. However, when talking about the town of Hvar you say **Idem u Hvar** or **Ja sam u Hvaru** using the preposition **u**. Generally speaking, the preposition **u** is used when talking about towns with one or two exceptions such as the town of **Rijeka** (**Idem na Rijeku**).

Privatna soba

There are basically two types of accommodation (**smještaj**) available to tourists on the coast. There are hotels used by all the large tour companies, and private rooms. Many people who live on the coast or on one of the Adriatic islands have converted their houses to take in paying guests during the summer. This is a relatively inexpensive form of accommodation. You can book such rooms at a travel agency on arrival at your destination. They are regularly checked to ensure that standards are maintained and you can book either a room (**soba**) or a small holiday flat (**apartman**).

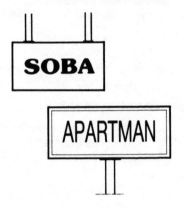

Ključne fraze

How to:

● use words for travelling on holiday.
odmor
avion
brod
aerodrom

● use words for tickets and reservations.
avionska karta za Split
povratna karta
karta u jednom smjeru
kupiti karte za brod
rezervirati kartu

- use words for the journey.

Koliko dugo traje put?
Idemo u Split.
Vraćamo se iz Splita.

- use words for staying.

boraviti
hotel
privatna soba
gazdarica

- ask what happened and
  how long ago?

Što se desilo?
Je li sve bilo u redu?

Jezični obrasci

1 Past tense

Prijatelji su govorili o...	*The friends spoke about...*
Htjeli su ići...	*They wanted to go...*
Jasna je išla...	*Jasna went...*
Čovjek je gledao...	*The man looked at...*
Sve je bilo u redu.	*Everything was OK.*
Nisam imala problema.	*I did not have any problems.*
Kupili smo karte.	*We bought the tickets.*

The past tense is formed using two parts: one taken from the infinitive of the verb indicating something in the past and the other from **biti** (*to be*).

(a) One part is formed using a part of the infinitive. There are three types of infinitive:

- Infinitives which end in a vowel before **-ti**, remove the **-ti** at the end:

govori**ti**	**govori-**
gleda**ti**	**gleda-**

Treat this part like an adjective which agrees with the subject of the verb:

masc. singular add **-o**	masc. plural add **-li**
gledao, govorio	**gledali, govorili**
fem. singular add **-la**	fem. plural add **-le**
gledala, govorila	**gledale, govorile**
neut. singular add **-lo**	neut. plural add **-la**
gledalo, govorilo	**gledala, govorila**

There is a small sub-group of verbs which end in **-jeti** in the infinitive which have an exception in the masculine singular (**vidjeti, željeti, živjeti, htjeti**):

masc. singular	masc. plural
vidio	**vidjeli**
želio	**željeli**
živio	**živjeli**
htio	**htjeli**

● Infinitives which end in **-sti**, remove the **-sti** then follow the same pattern as above:

    je**sti**-   **je-**

masc. singular	masc. plural
jeo	**jeli**
fem. singular	fem. plural
jela	**jele**
neut. singular	neut. plural
jelo	**jela**

● Infinitives which end in **-ći**, learn the past tense forms separately:

moći	**moga-**
ići	**iša-**
reći	**reka-**

masc. singular	masc. plural
mogao, išao, rekao	**mogli, išli, rekli**
fem. singular	fem. plural
mogla, išla, rekla	**mogle, išle, rekle**
neut. singular	neut. plural
moglo, išlo, reklo	**mogla, išla, rekla**

The **-a-** which appears just before the adjective ending in the masculine singular disappears in the other forms in this category.

(b) Along with this part of the past tense taken from the infinitive use the relevant form of **biti**:

Morali su kupiti avionske karte.	*They had to buy air tickets.*
Čovjek je gledao u kompjutorski ekran.	*The man looked at the computer screen.*
Sve je bilo u redu.	*Everything was OK.*
Kupili smo karte.	*We bought the tickets.*

The part of **biti** you use depends on the subject of the verb. So, if the subject is **ja** you use **sam**, if it is **ti** you use **si**, etc. If Jasna wanted to say *I spoke...* she would use the form **ja sam govorila** (or **govorila sam** without **ja**), whereas Rudolf would say **ja sam govorio**.

2 Word order with the past tense

The rules for the order of enclitics (short forms) apply when forming the past tense in Serbo-Croat and care has to be taken. The short forms of **biti** cannot occur as the first word of the sentence or phrase. So you say:

On je gledao u komjutorski ekran.	*or* Gledao je u kompjutorski ekran.
Ja sam govorila o odmoru. (fem.)	*or* Govorila sam o odmoru.
Mi smo bili na Hvaru.	*or* Bili smo na Hvaru.

The word order, when using the short forms of the personal pronouns, follows a set pattern which you first met in Unit 9, e.g. **Rekao mi je** (*he told me*, using **mi** the dat. case of **ja**). The pattern is:

(i) short form of **biti** (except **je**)
(ii) dat. case
(iii) gen. case
(iv) acc. case
(v) **se** (reflexive verbs only)
(vi) **je** (short form from **biti**)

Look at the following examples:

Dala sam joj knjigu.	*I gave a book to her.*
Dala sam joj je.	*I gave it to her.*
Dali smo mu sok.	*We gave a fruit juice to him.*
Dali smo mu ga.	*We gave it to him.*

Dao mi je knjigu.   *He gave a book to me.*
Dao mi ju je.   *He gave it to me.*

(**ju** is used as the accusative case when the **je** form from **biti** is present)

Rekli su nam.   *They told us.*
Vratili smo se.   *We returned.*
Vratio se.   *He returned.*

(reflexive verbs usually omit **je** in the **on/ona/ono** forms of the past tense)

3 Negative past tense

To form the negative of the past tense in Serbo-Croat replace the short forms of **biti** with their negative equivalents. Note the effect this has on word order as the negative forms are not enclitics (short forms):

Rekao mi je.   *He told me.*
Nije mi rekao.   *He did not tell me.*

Dali smo mu ga.   *We gave it to him.*
Nismo mu ga dali.   *We did not give it to him.*

Vratio se.   *He returned.*
Nije se vratio.   *He did not return.*

Rekli su nam.   *They told us.*
Nisu nam rekli.   *They did not tell us.*

Dala sam joj je.   *I gave it to her.*
Nisam joj je dala.   *I did not give it to her.*

4 Asking a question in the past tense

You make questions in the past tense by following the patterns for asking questions with **biti**. There are two ways of forming a question.

(*a*) Using the short form:

Da li ste bili na Hvaru?   *Have you been on Hvar?*
Da li smo rekli Rudolfu?   *Did we tell Rudolf?*

(*b*) Using the long form:

Jeste li bili na Hvaru?	*Have you been on Hvar?*
Jesmo li rekli Rudolfu?	*Did we tell Rudolf?* (or *Have we told Rudolf?*)

The normal rules for the order of short forms still apply:

Da li ste mu dali knjigu?	*Did you give a book to him?*
Jesu li vam rekli?	*Did they tell you?*

With **je** as an exception:

Je li vam dao kavu.	*Did he give you a coffee?*

5 Aspect with the past tense

The English language has a variety of forms in the past tense:

I did return.
I have returned.
I was returning.
I had returned.
etc.

Serbo-Croat only has the one form, based on the infinitive and **biti**. However, it can express all the varieties of English because of aspects. As you have already seen Serbo-Croat has two aspects, an imperfective and a perfective. You have seen the differences between them in the infinitive and the imperative (command forms). They have similar differences in the past tense: the imperfective describes an incomplete or continuous action and the perfective describes a completed or momentary action. The first verb in the list below is the imperfective of the pair:

davati, dati	*to give*
vraćati se, vratiti se	*to return*
pisati, napisati	*to write*
piti, popiti	*to drink*
čitati, pročitati	*to read*
uzimati, uzeti	*to take*

Jučer je čitao knjigu, a njegov brat je gledao televiziju.	*Yesterday he was reading, and* *his brother watched television.*

(i.e. both actions occur at the same time and without indicating when they were concluded)

Pila je mlijeko svaki dan, ali je danas popila sok.	*She drank (used to drink) milk every day, but today she drank fruit juice.*

(i.e. drinking milk was a daily occurrence, not limited to one completed occasion, but today she drank (up) a juice)

Jučer je pročitao knjigu.	*He read the book yesterday.*

(i.e. the action was completed)

Kad se vratio kući, napisao je bratu pismo.	*When he returned home he wrote a letter to his brother.*

(i.e. both actions were completed one after the other)

Some verbs only have one form which is both imperfective and perfective. These are verbs taken from foreign languages (e.g. rezervirati, telefonirati) and a small group of others (e.g. ručati, vidjeti).

6 Using vi *in the past tense*

Vi can be used to refer either to one person or to many people. When it is used to refer to one person you must always use the masculine plural form:

Jasna, da li ste bili na Hvaru?	*Jasna, have you been on Hvar?*
Rudolf, jeste li rekli Jasni?	*Rudolf, have you told Jasna?*

The same rule applies to using adjectives with **vi**:

Jasna, jeste li sigurni?	*Jasna, are you sure?*

7 Nisam imala problema

The **-a** ending on **problem** tells you that this word is being used in the genitive case meaning *I didn't have **any** problems*. The genitive case in Serbo-Croat can be used to indicate what in English would be expressed by *some* or *any*, as opposed to a single object. Compare the following sentences:

To nije moj problem.	*That is not my problem.*
Nisam imala problema.	*I didn't have any problems.*

Gdje je kruh?	*Where is the bread?*
Imate li kruha?	*Have you got any bread?*

8 Unusual noun categories

The word **večer** is unusual in that it is a masculine noun in the nominative (**dobar večer** – *good evening*) but becomes a feminine noun ending in a consonant in all other cases, and thus ends like **stvar**:

te večeri   *on that evening* (gen. singular)

◢———— Vježbe ————

1 Answer the following questions based on the **Dijalog** on pages 141-142:

  (*a*) Kamo je Jasna išla s Markom i Sandrom?
  (*b*) Što su tamo htjeli kupiti?
  (*c*) Da li su kupili povratne karte ili u jednom smjeru?
  (*d*) U koliko sati ide prvi avion iz Zagreba?
  (*e*) Koliko košta karta?
  (*f*) Što moraju kupiti u Splitu?
  (*g*) Kada se vraćaju?
  (*h*) Kada je Jasna išla k Rudolfu?
  (*i*) Kada su Jasna i Rudolf bili na Hvaru?
  (*j*) Tko je uzeo privatnu sobu u Hvaru?

2 Formulate questions for the following answers:

  (*a*) Pio sam mlijeko svaki dan.
  (*b*) Napisao sam pismo.
  (*c*) Rudolf mi je dao knjigu.
  (*d*) Da, bio sam na Hvaru.
  (*e*) Ne, nisam bila u Dubrovniku.
  (*f*) Rezervirali su karte u putničkoj agenciji.
  (*g*) Otišli su na odmor u subotu.
  (*h*) Bili smo u Dubrovniku prije pet godina.
  (*i*) Povratna karta za Split košta tri tisuće dinara.
  (*j*) Ne, Rudolf nije radio u toj zgradi.

3 Choose the correct emboldened aspect in the sentence below:

(a) **Pisao/Napisao** sam mami svaki dan.
(b) Da li vam je konobar **davao/dao** kavu?
(c) Kad smo se vratili u Zagreb **uzimali/uzeli** smo taksi.
(d) Pijem mlijeko svaki dan, ali sam danas **pio/popio** čašu vode.

4 Make the following sentences negative (take care with the word order):

(a) Išli smo na Hvar prije tri godine.
(b) Konobar mi je dao salatu.
(c) Konobar mi ju je dao.
(d) Kupili su avionske karte u putničkoj agenciji.
(e) Kupili su ih u putničkoj agenciji.
(f) Vratila sam se jučer iz Dubrovnika.
(g) Čitao je novine.
(h) Čitao ih je.

5 Complete the missing parts of the dialogue:

Dobar dan.
(*Hello. I want to buy a plane ticket to Dubrovnik.*)
Da li hoćete povratnu kartu ili u jednom smjeru?
(*A one-way ticket, please. How much does it cost?*)
Karta u jednom smjeru za Dubrovnik košta dvije tisuće dinara.
(*At what time is there a plane on Mondays from Zagreb?*)
Ima tri aviona. Prvi ide prije podne u deset sati. Drugi ide poslije podne u petnaest sati i petnaest minuta. Treći ide navečer u dvadeset sati.
(*I want a ticket for Monday in the evening.*)
Mogu vam, ako želite, rezervirati hotel.
(*I have a private room in Dubrovnik.*)
Dobro. Izvolite kartu.
(*Thank you. Goodbye.*)
Molim. Do viđenja.

Izvolite kartu.	*Here is your ticket.*

6 Make up sentences, based on the picture on p. 153, as in the example:

(a) Koliko dugo traje put avionom od Zagreba do Splita?
Četrdeset minuta.

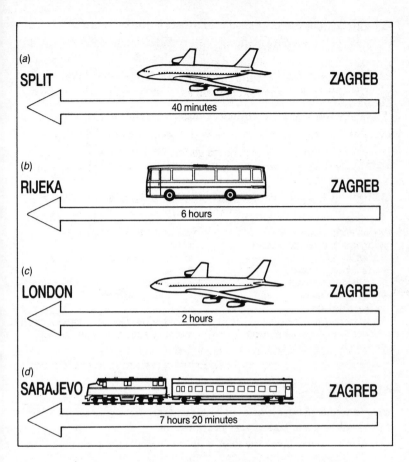

(a) SPLIT — ZAGREB — 40 minutes

(b) RIJEKA — ZAGREB — 6 hours

(c) LONDON — ZAGREB — 2 hours

(d) SARAJEVO — ZAGREB — 7 hours 20 minutes

———— Dopunsko štivo 1 ————

Zvonko je jučer išao na Glavni kolodvor. Tamo je htio kupiti voznu kartu.

Zvonko Molim vas, želim rezervirati kartu za Sarajevo.
Čovjek Da li hoćete kartu prvog ili drugog razreda?
Zvonko Prvog. Idem prekosutra.
Čovjek Prekosutra je nedjelja. Prvi vlak ide u osam i trideset ujutro.

Zvonko	Kada ide drugi?
Čovjek	Drugi ide u jedanaest sati. A onda vlakovi idu skoro svaki sat.
Zvonko	Dajte mi, molim vas, jednu kartu za vlak u jedanaest sati.
Čovjek	Da li hoćete povratnu kartu ili u jednom smjeru?
Zvonko	Ne znam kada se vraćam.
Čovjek	Nije važno, gospodine. Karta vam važi mjesec dana.
Zvonko	Moram se vratiti do srijede. Mogu li rezervirati mjesto u Sarajevu kad saznam točan datum povratka?
Čovjek	Možete, gospodine. Idite na kolodvor u Sarajevu dan prije povratka.
Zvonko	Dajte mi, molim vas, jednu povratnu kartu za Sarajevo.

---

vozna karta   *train ticket*
karta prvog razreda   *first-class ticket*
karta drugog razreda   *second-class ticket*
vlak   *train* (**vlakovi** – plural)
skoro   *almost*
Karta vam važi mjesec dana.   *Your ticket is valid for a month.*
do srijede   *by Wednesday*

rezervirati mjesto   *to reserve a seat*
saznati, saznam   *to get to know, find out*
kad saznam   *when I know* (find out)
točan datum povratka   *the exact date of return*
dan prije povratka   *the day before you come back* (Lit. *the day before return*)

Istina ili neistina?

(a) Prvi vlak za Sarajevo ide u 10.00 ujutro.
(b) Zvonko ne zna kad se vraća iz Sarajeva.
(c) Zvonko mora ići na kolodvor u Sarajevu dva dana prije povratka.

———— **Dopunsko štivo 2** ————

Read the following passage and answer the questions below:

Rudolf je otišao na posao. Razgovarao je sa svojim kolegom o sobama u Hvaru. Rudolf je htio saznati sve o tim sobama. Pitao ga je koliko koštaju privatne sobe i kakve su. Njegov kolega mu je rekao da sobe nisu skupe. Dao mu je adresu jedne žene koja izdaje apartman. Apartman je na prvom katu s velikom kuhinjom, kupaonicom i dvije spavaće sobe. Ima pogled na more i na jednu staru crkvu. U blizini kuće nalazi se dobar riblji restoran.

Blizu Hvara se nalaze mali otoci. Iz Hvara na te otoke svaki dan voze čamci. Tamo se možete sunčati i kupati. U Hvaru je sve lijepo.

koja izdaje *who lets out, rents*	**čamac** *boat*
izdavati, izdajem *to let, rent out*	**sunčati se** *to sunbathe*
crkva *church*	**kupati se** *to bathe*

1 Što gazdarica izdaje?
  (*a*) Privatnu sobu.
  (*b*) Hotel.
  (*c*) Apartman.

2 Kakav restoran je blizu njene kuće?
  (*a*) Ribliji restoran.
  (*b*) Kavana.
  (*c*) Restoran s roštiljem.

3 Što možete raditi na malim otocima?
  (*a*) Igrati nogomet.
  (*b*) Sjediti na obali.
  (*c*) Sunčati se.

12
IMAM TELEFONSKI BROJ

I have the telephone number

In this unit you will learn how to

- talk about future events
- ask questions about the future
- talk on the telephone
- report on events
- make indirect questions
- express *my/your* in other ways

Dijalog

Prijatelji su rezervirali apartman kod gospođe Bilčić. Stigli su u Split avionom. Otišli su direktno u luku, gdje su kupili karte za brod. Sada stoje na pristaništu u Hvaru sa prtljagom.

Sandra   Što ćemo raditi večeras? Nadam se da nećemo biti suviše umorni.

Jasna   Tko će biti umoran? Ići ćemo u grad i naručit ćemo lijepu večeru u nekom restoranu. Rudolf, znaš li put do gospođe Bilčić?

Rudolf   Ne mogu naći njenu adresu. Mislio sam da mi je tu negdje u džepu. Bio sam siguran da ništa nisam zaboravio. Imam njen telefonski broj. Javit ću joj se. Idem na poštu. Čekajte me ovdje.

luka *harbour*	**...da mi je tu negdje u džepu**
stajati, stojim *to be standing*	*...that it's here somewhere in*
pristanište *quay*	*my pocket*
prtljaga *luggage*	**ništa** *nothing*
nadati se, nadam se *to hope*	**zaboravljati, zaboraviti** *to forget*
suviše *too much*	**Javit ću joj se.** *I'll call her.*
umoran *tired*	**javljati se, javiti se** *to contact,*
neki *some, a certain*	*be in touch*
misliti, mislim *to think*	**čekati, čekam** *to wait*

Na pošti Rudolf razgovara s gospođom Bilčić preko telefona.

Bilčić Halo.

Rudolf Halo. Molim vas, možete li mi reći da li je gospođa Bilčić kod kuće?

Bilčić Na telefonu je. Tko govori?

Rudolf Ovdje Rudolf Šimunić, iz Zagreba. Rezervirao sam apartman kod vas. Rekao sam da ćemo stići danas.

Bilčić Oprostite, gospodine. Ne sjećam se. Jeste li mi pisali?

Rudolf Nisam. Telefonirao sam.

Bilčić Da, sada se sjećam. Ja sam vas pitala da li možete stići prekosutra.

Rudolf Da, a nismo mogli...

Bilčić Sve je u redu. Apartman je spreman. Gdje ste?

Rudolf Stigli smo u Hvar. Međutim, izgubio sam vašu adresu.

Bilčić Nema problema. Adresa mi je Dalmatinska ulica broj 5. Da li ste je zapisali?

Rudolf Jesam. Hvala vam lijepo. Doći ćemo odmah.

Bilčić Molim lijepo. Do viđenja.

Rudolf Do viđenja.

halo (on the telephone) *hello*	**međutim** *however*
na telefonu je *speaking* (Lit. *she's*	**gubiti, izgubiti** *to lose*
on the telephone)	**nema problema** *no problem*
telefonirati *to telephone*	**Adresa mi je...** *My address is...*
Pitala sam da li možete... *I asked*	**zapisivati, zapisati** (zapisujem,
if you could...	zapišem) *to note down*
spreman *ready, prepared*	**odmah** *immediately*

Istina ili neistina?

(a) Rudolf traži adresu gospođe Bilčić.
(b) Rudolf je rezervirao apartman preko telefona.
(c) Gospođa Bilčić je rekla da apartman nije spreman.

——— **Objašnjenja i komentari** ———

Preko telefona *(over the telephone)*

When making a telephone call, whoever picks up the phone at the other end may just say **halo** (*hello*), a greeting largely reserved for use on the phone. Otherwise, the first word might be simply **Molim?** An alternative way for Rudolf to begin would have been **Ovdje Rudolf Šimunić. Molim vas, dajte mi gospođu Bilčić**. When you have asked for the person you wish to speak to, the response may be **Tko ga/je traži?** (*Who wants him/her?*), or **na telefonu je** (*he/she is on the telephone*).

When calling another town or country you'll need the **pozivni broj** (*code number*), and when calling an office or a firm you may need to ask **Molim vas, dajte mi lokal ...** (*Please give me extension number ...*).

The verbs to telephone are **telefonirati** (**telefoniram joj**: with dat.), **zvati** (**zovem je**: with acc.) and **javljati se, javiti se** (**javljam joj se**: with dat.). Don't forget that when making a call you may find that the line is engaged (**linija je zauzeta**) or that you have dialled the wrong number (**krivi broj**).

——— **Ključne fraze** ———

How to:

• make telephone calls and
  to respond on the phone.

  halo
  Molim vas, dajte mi...
  Tko ga/je traži?
  Na telefonu je.
  preko telefona

- use ways of expressing *my*, etc.   **adresa mi je**

- say *somewhere, nothing*.   **negdje mi je u džepu**
                                         ništa nisam zaboravio

- report events and questions.   **Rekao sam da ćemo stići...**
                                         Pitala sam da li možete stići...
      or   **Pitala sam možete li stići...**

Jezični obrasci

1 Future tense

When expressing the future you use the short form of **htjeti** (the same as the long form without the initial **ho-**). You have already met some of these forms in the **Dialogue**s of Units 4 and 11:

ja	ću	mi	ćemo
ti	ćeš	vi	ćete
on/a/o	će	oni/e/a	će

This is used together with the infinitive of another verb:

    Ja ću ići.   *I shall go.*
    Rudolf će telefonirati.   *Rudolf will telephone.*

As this is a short form it may not come at the beginning of a sentence. If you omit the personal pronoun, the short form comes after the infinitive. If the infinitive ends in **-ti**, omit the **-i** at the end and pronounce it as one word with a silent **-t**:

    naručit ćemo   *we shall order*

Infinitives which end in **-ći** are not shortened:

    ići ćemo   *we shall go*

The short form of **htjeti**, like the short form of **biti**, takes second place and goes in front of other short forms:

    Javit ću joj se.   *I shall contact (telephone) her.*
    Odmah ću joj se javiti.   *I shall contact her immediately.*

When asking a question use either the long form or the short form following the patterns which you already know with **Da li...** or **... li ...**, unless there is a question word when you use the short form:

Hoćemo li ići?	*Shall we go?*
Da li ćemo ići?	*Shall we go?*
Što ćemo raditi večeras?	*What shall we do this evening?*
Tko će biti umoran?	*Who will be tired?*

The negative is simply formed by using the negative of **htjeti** in front of the infinitive of the other verb:

Nećemo biti kod kuće.	*We shall not be at home.*
Nećemo ići na izlet.	*We shall not go on the excursion.*

As with the past tense, aspects are important in the future tense to distinguish between actions intended to be either continuous or incomplete (imperfective) and completed or momentary (perfective):

Pit ću mlijeko.	*I'll drink milk.* (not just once)
Pisat ćemo ti.	*We'll write to you.*
Naručit ćemo večeru.	*We'll order dinner.* (completed)
Odmah ćemo doći.	*We'll come immediately.*

2 Indirect speech

The following is an example of indirect (or reported) speech, compare it with the same in direct speech:

Indirect

Rekao sam da ćemo stići danas.	*I said that we would arrive today.*

Direct

'Stići ćemo danas,' rekao sam.	*'We shall arrive today,' I said.*

In English, when you say *I said that...* or *I am telling you that...* we have a set of rules which determines the tense which follows. In Serbo-Croat the situation is simpler. You use the tense of the verb which was used or would have been used in the original statement. So:

Indirect

Rekao je da će doći.	*He said that he would come.*

Direct
'Doći ću,' rekao je.   *'I'll come,' he said.*

The same pattern is followed in all similar sentences in Serbo-Croat, for example:

Mislim da...	*I think that...*
Siguran sam da...	*I am sure that...*
Nadam se da...	*I hope that...*

Recreate what was originally said or thought and use the tense from that recreated sentence.

3   Indirect questions

Here is an example of an indirect question, compare it with the direct question:

Indirect
Možete li mi reći da li je   *Can you tell me if Mrs Bilčić*
gđa Bilčić kod kuće?   *is at home?*

Direct
Da li je (Je li) gđa Bilčić   *Is Mrs Bilčić at home?*
kod kuće?

In English, you use the word *if* in indirect questions. In Serbo-Croat, you begin the second part of the sentence with the question form **da li** (or **li** on its own after the verb as in an ordinary question) and use the tense of the verb from the original question:

Indirect
Pitala sam možete li stići   *I asked if you could arrive*
prekosutra.   *the day after tomorrow.*

Direct
Možete li stići prekosutra?   *Could you arrive the day*
                                after tomorrow?

4   Negdje, ništa

Look at the box (p. 162) to see how these words are formed in Serbo-Croat:

gdje	*where*	**tko**	*who*
negdje	*somewhere*	**netko**	*someone*
nigdje	*nowhere*	**nitko**	*nobody*
igdje	*anywhere*	**itko**	*anyone*
što	*what*	**kada**	*when*
nešto	*something*	**nekad**	*once, formerly*
ništa	*nothing*	**nikad**	*never*
išta	*anything*	**ikad**	*anytime*

There are other forms for *anywhere*, etc. formed with either **bilo** or **god** in this pattern: bilo gdje (*anywhere*), gdje god (*anywhere*), što god (*anything*), bilo tko (*anyone*), etc.

Uzeo je nešto.	*He took something.*
Netko je došao.	*Someone came.*

If the verb or any other part of the sentence is negative you must use the negative word from the above list. This is sometimes heard in colloquial speech in English (e.g. *He didn't tell me nothing* rather than *He did not tell me anything* or *He told me nothing*):

Ništa nisam zaboravio.	*I have forgotten nothing.*
Nije bio nigdje.	*He has not been anywhere.*
Nikad nije uzeo ništa.	*He has not taken anything ever.*

5   Use of personal names and cases

People's names follow the normal rules for case endings where possible. Men's names follow the masculine and women's names the feminine pattern of endings. Foreign names also change if they fit the usual pattern, i.e. men's names ending in a consonant and women's names in **-a**. Surnames also change according to the normal patterns, but surnames which end in a consonant do not change when they are used for a woman. Study the following examples:

Ići ću s Rudolfom.	*I shall go with Rudolf.*
Dala je novac Marku.	*She gave the money to Mark.*
Gledaju Zvonka.	*They are looking at Zvonko.*
Vidio sam Sandru.	*I saw Sandra.*
Gledaju Rudolfa Šimunića.	*They are looking at Rudolf Šimunović.*
Gledaju Jasnu Kušan.	*They are looking at Jasna Kušan.*
Javio se gospođi Bilčić.	*He called Mrs Bilčić.*

6 Tko će biti umoran?

After the word **tko** verbs and adjectives are always singular and take masculine endings:

Tko će biti umoran?	*Who will be tired?*
Tko je došao?	*Who has come?*

The same rule applies to **netko**:

Netko je došao.	*Someone has come.*

7 *More about possession*

The dative case of **ja**, etc. may be used in order to show possession:

Adresa mi je...	*My address is...*
	(Lit. *the address to me is...*)

This is normally to express something close such as personal possessions or members of the family:

Sestra joj je u Londonu.	*Her sister is in London.*
Roditelji su mi u Zagrebu.	*My parents are in Zagreb.*

8 Moj, *etc. and cases*

The possessive adjectives **moj**, **tvoj**, **svoj** are unusual as they generally omit the **-je-** which you would expect in the middle of the word. Here is the full pattern of endings, along with the optional vowels which are sometimes added to all adjectives:

Singular	Masc.	Fem.	Neut	Masc. plural	Fem. plural	Neut. plural
nom.	moj	moja	moje	moji	moje	moja
acc.	nom/gen	moju	moje	moje	moje	moja
gen.	mog(a) mojeg (a)	moje	mog(a) mojeg(a)	mojih	mojih	mojih
dat.	mom(e) mojem(u)	mojoj	mom(e) mojem(u)	mojim(a)	mojim(a)	mojim(a)
ins.	mojim	mojom	mojim	mojim(a)	mojim(a)	mojim(a)

The accusative of masculine adjectives is either the same as the nominative (for inanimate objects) or the same as the genitive (for people and animals).

All adjectives have the optional extra letters at the end, e.g. **dobrog(a)**, **starom(e)** and **starom(u)**. They are added when the adjective is used without a noun:

Jeste li vidjeli mladog čovjeka?	*Did you see the young person?*
Ne, vidio sam staroga.	*No, I saw the old one.*

Vježbe

1 Put the following into the future tense:

(a) Išli smo u dobar restoran.

(b) Javio joj se.

(c) Našli smo stolicu u blagovaonici.

(d) Tko je stigao?

(e) Što ste radili na odmoru?

(f) Da li si mu dao ključ?

(g) Nisu došli k nama.

(h) Nisam bio na Hvaru.

2 Put the following into indirect speech, beginning with **Rekao/Rekla je da...** as in the example. Imagine that you have asked the receptionist in your hotel for information. You have to report the answer to your friend who is waiting by the door. Remember to take care with the order of short forms which have to come immediately after **da...**:

Example: Sigurno će vaše pismo stići sutra.
         Rekao/Rekla je da će naše pismo sigurno stići sutra.

(a) Možete kupiti novine tamo kod lifta.

(b) Zaboravio sam vaše avionske karte.

(c) Dobit ćete ih sutra.

(d) Dat ću vam vaš novac sutra.

(e) Prodajemo razglednice, koverte i marke u hotelu.

(f) Ovo nije vaše pismo.

(g) Danas će biti lijepo vrijeme.

(h) Nismo izgubili ključ od vaše sobe.

(i) Netko vas je tražio u hotelu.

(j) Ne znam odakle je bio.

3 Make the following into an indirect question, beginning with **Pitao/Pitala sam da li...** You have asked the question as below, and now you have to tell someone what you asked, as in the example (**vi** is here used to refer to one person politely):

Example: Hoćete li doći sutra na večeru?
Pitao/Pitala sam da li će doći sutra na večeru.

(*a*) Da li ste zaboravili gdje stanujemo?
(*b*) Da li će danas biti lijepo vrijeme?
(*c*) Je li gospođa Bilčić kod kuće?
(*d*) Znaš li gdje mi je ključ?
(*e*) Da li će Rudolf doći u London?
(*f*) Da li ste bili u Engleskoj?
(*g*) Da li si bila u Engleskoj?
(*h*) Mogu li dobiti čašu vode?
(*i*) Možete li doći sutra?
(*j*) Idemo li k tvom bratu sutra?

4 Pick the most appropriate form of **negdje**, **ništa**, etc. out of the box to fit these sentences. Only use each word once:

(*a*) ———— je došao.
(*b*) Mislio sam da ———— nisam zaboravio.
(*c*) Naša prtljaga mora biti ———— u našoj sobi.
(*d*) ———— nisam uzeo tvoju knjigu.
(*e*) Našao je ———— u svom džepu.
(*f*) Nije bio ———— u Engleskoj.

negdje	netko	nigdje	ništa	nikad	nešto

5 Match the questions to the answers below:

(*a*) Gdje je bio vaš novac?   (i) Nikad nisam bila.
(*b*) Jesi li bila u Engleskoj?   (ii) Vaš telefonski broj.
(*c*) Tko je došao?   (iii) Jasna.
(*d*) Što ste našli u džepu?   (iv) U mom džepu.

6 Fill in the missing part of the telephone conversation:

Molim?
(*Good day. Is Mr Šimunić at work?*)
Da, na poslu je. On je u svom uredu.
(*Put me through to his extension, please.*)

Halo. Rudolf Šimunić ovdje.
(*Hello. 'Your name' here.*)
Da, sjećam vas se.
(*I have forgotten your address. Could you tell me where you work?*)
Moja zgrada je u Ilici, broj dvanaest.
(*May I come to you today?*)
Naravno. Dođite u dva sata. Čekat ću vas.
(*Thank you. Goodbye.*)
Molim. Do viđenja.

Ilica is one of Zagreb's main streets

Dopunsko štivo 1

Barry Smith je Englez. On je na odmoru u Hvaru. Ušao je u poštu i prišao šalteru.

Barry   Dobar dan. Želim nazvati Englesku.
Službenik Kabina tri je slobodna. Uđite i okrenite broj.
Barry   Molim vas, recite mi koji je pozivni broj za Englesku. Zaboravio sam ga.
Službenik Pozivni broj je devet devet četiri četiri.
Barry   Hvala.
Službenik Molim.

Barry se javio mami da joj kaže da je stigao na otok i da je sve u redu. Izašao je iz kabine. Opet je prišao šalteru i platio račun.

ušao je (ući) *he went in*	**slobodan** *free*
prišao je *he went up to*	**okrenuti broj** (okrenem) *to dial the*
(prići – the verb is used without **je** as	*number*
it is contained in the first part of the	**koji je pozivni broj...** *which is the*
sentence **ušao je**)	*code number*
šalter *counter*	**izašao je** (izaći) *he went out*
nazvati *to call*	**platiti** *to pay*
službenik *clerk*	**račun** *bill*

Istina ili neistina?

(*a*) Barry Smith je ušao u poštu.
(*b*) Htio je nazvati sestru.
(*c*) Platio je račun.

—————— **Dopunsko štivo 2** ——————

Read the following passage and answer the questions below:

Barry Smith je učio srpskohrvatski u Engleskoj. Kad je bio u Hvaru, našao je vrlo dobar riblji restoran. Nije znao sve riječi iz jelovnika. Konobarica je bila djevojka iz Zagreba, i govorila je engleski.

Barry	Molim vas, što znači ova riječ 'dagnje' na engleskom?
Konobarica	Na engleskom to znači 'mussels', gospodine.
Barry	A kako se kaže 'zubatac' na engleskom?
Konobarica	Ne znam. 'Zubatac' je jedna vrsta morske ribe. Da li znate, gospodine, kako se kaže na hrvatskom 'squid'?
Barry	Naravno. To su 'lignje'.

---

vrlo *very*
konobarica *waitress*
djevojka *girl, young lady*
  (unmarried woman)
Što znači ova riječ? *What does this word mean?*

na engleskom *in English*
Kako se kaže..? *How is ... said?/How do you say ..?*
vrsta *kind, sort*
morska riba *salt water* (Lit. *sea*) *fish*
na hrvatskom *in Croatian*

---

1 Što Barry uči u Engleskoj?
   (*a*) Francuski.
   (*b*) Srpskohrvatski.
   (*c*) Engleski.

2 Kako se kaže 'dagnje' na engleskom?
   (*a*) Squid.
   (*b*) Mussels.
   (*c*) Sea fish.

3 Što je 'zubatac'?
   (*a*) To je vrsta ribe.
   (*b*) To su lignje.
   (*c*) To je salata.

13

NA PLAŽI

On the beach

In this unit you will learn how to

- express dates, numbers above 100 and further expressions of time
- express feelings, intentions and moods
- say *oneself*

Dijalog

Svi ljudi na odmoru u Hvaru vole *Paklene otoke*. Danas se Sandra i Jasna sunčaju na plaži jednog od tih otoka. Provode dan u razgovoru.

Sandra Jasna, koji je danas datum?
Jasna Danas je dvadeset prvi kolovoz.
Sandra Kad smo stigli u Hvar?
Jasna Stigli smo desetog kolovoza.
Sandra Ne ostaje nam mnogo vremena. Ponekad sanjam da ćemo ostati mjesecima na otoku.
Jasna Znam što hoćeš reći. Zaista je ovdje divno. Kad sam bila dijete, imala sam namjeru živjeti na nekom otoku, negdje daleko od mojih roditelja.

Sandra A što sad misliš?
Jasna Više nemam tu namjeru. Sad sam pesimist.
Sandra Kad si rođena?
Jasna Rođena sam tisuću devetsto pedeset devete godine.
Sandra Ne smiješ biti pesimist. Još si mlada. Što ti je! Jutros si
bila dobro raspoložena. Lijepo si pjevala u apartmanu.
Mislila sam da ćeš mi biti veselo društvo cijeli dan.

---

svi ljudi *all people*
Pakleni otoci *Hell's Islands*
plaža *beach*
jedan od tih otoka *one of those islands*
provoditi, provesti (provodim, provedem: provodio, proveo) *to spend* (of time)
Koji je danas datum? *What is the date today?*
Danas je dvadeset prvi kolovoz. *Today is the 21st August.*
desetog kolovoza *on the 10th August*
Ne ostaje nam... *There does not remain for us...*
ostajati, ostati (ostajem, ostanem) *to remain, stay*
mnogo vremena *much time*
ponekad *sometimes*
sanjati *to dream*
mjesecima *for months*

htjeti reći *to want to say, to mean*
namjera *intention*
sam (adj. sama, samo) *alone*
(note this word is pronounced with a long falling tone and sounds completely different from the short form of **biti, ja sam**)
Nemam više tu namjeru. *I no longer have that intention.*
rođen sam *I was born*
tisuću devetsto pedeset devete godine *in 1959*
pesimist *pessimist*
Ne smiješ biti... *You mustn't be...*
mlad *young*
Što ti je! *What's with you!, What's up!*
dobro raspoložen *in a good mood*
pjevati *to sing*
biti veselo društvo *to be jolly company*
cijeli dan *for the whole day*

Jasna Nemoj misliti da sam tužna. Sretna sam. Međutim, ne
radujem se povratku u Zagreb.
Sandra Zašto?
Jasna Zato što ne znam koliko još dugo mogu podnositi
Rudolfovo ponašanje. Ljutim se na njega. Njegova majka
misli da sam ja kriva zato što nismo u braku. Ali, on se
nije htio vjenčati. Pričali smo o toj mogućnosti u prošlosti.
Ali kasnije više nije htio razgovarati o tome. Ovih dana me
je pitao da li ja želim da se mi vjenčamo. Po mom mišljen-
ju, još jednom moramo iskreno razgovarati o budućnosti.
Bit će sve u redu čim počnemo govoriti o našim osjećajima.
Sandra Slažem se. Moraš misliti na sebe, a ne na njega.

Jasna   Dobro mi je sada. Htjela sam ti ispričati što se dešava. Što
ćemo raditi sad? Hoćeš li da se idemo kupati?

Sandra   Da, kupa mi se.

tužan *sad*	**ovih dana** *these days, recently*
sretan *happy*	**još jednom** *once more*
radovati se, radujem se (with dat.)	**iskreno** *sincerely*
to look forward to	**budućnost** (fem. noun) *the future*
Zašto? *Why?*	**čim** *as soon as*
zato što *because*	**počinjati, početi** (počinjem, počnem)
Koliko još dugo..? *For how much*	*to begin*
longer..?	**osjećaj** *feeling, emotion*
podnositi *to tolerate*	**misliti na sebe** *to think of/about*
ponašanje *behaviour*	*oneself*
ljutiti se na (with acc.) *to be angry*	**Dobro mi je.** *I'm OK, I feel fine.*
with	**dešavati se, desiti se** *to happen*
kriv *wrong, guilty, at fault*	**kupati se** *to bathe*
vjenčati se *to get married*	**Kupa mi se.** *I feel like going for a*
pričati *to tell, talk*	*swim.*
prošlost (fem. noun) *the past*	
Više nije htio da... *He no longer*	
wanted to...	

Istina ili neistina?

(*a*)   Jasna je imala namjeru živjeti daleko od kuće.

(*b*)   Jasna nije lijepo pjevala.

(*c*)   Rudolfova majka misli da je njen sin kriv zato što nije oženjen.

Objašnjenja i komentari

Hvar

The island of Hvar is one of a group of larger islands including Brač
and Korčula off the Adriatic coast between Split and Dubrovnik. Hvar
is the furthest to reach from a port on the mainland, but the journey
still takes only a couple of hours by ferry. The larger islands are
surrounded by smaller ones, and the so-called **Pakleni otoci** (*Hell's*

Islands) are only a few hundred yards from the entrance to Hvar's small fishing port. They have the best beaches on Hvar and there are always boats waiting to take you over.

Ključne fraze

How to:

- ask the date today, and reply.

  Koji je danas datum?
  Danas je dvadeset prvi kolovoz.

- ask when something happened, and reply.

  Kad...
  Desetog kolovoza...

- state the year when someone was born.

  Rođena (fem.) **Rođen** (masc.)
  sam tisuću devetsto...

- use further expressions of time.

  mjesecima
  mnogo vremena
  cijeli dan
  čim
  u prošlosti
  u budućnosti
  ovih dana

- use expressions which show intentions.

  Znam što hoćeš reći.
  Imam namjeru...
  Ne smiješ...
  Kupa mi se.

- use expressions related to mood.

  Što ti je!
  tužna sam/tužan sam
  sretna sam/sretan sam
  ljutim se na njega/nju
  radujem se povratku
  dobro sam raspoložen/
  raspoložena
  biti veselo društvo
  on je kriv/ona je kriva
  osjećaj

- say *oneself*.

  moraš misliti na sebe

Jezični obrasci

1 Numbers – above 100

sto	100	sto devedeset jedan	191
dvjesta	200	dvjesta tri	203
trista	300	trista sedamdeset	370
četiristo	400	četiristo osamnaest	418
petsto	500	petsto šezdeset devet	569
šeststo	600	šeststo trideset dva	632
sedamsto	700	sedamsto dvadeset četiri	724
osamsto	800	osamsto osamdeset osam	888
devetsto	900	devetsto četrdeset pet	945
tisuća	1 000	tisuća sto jedan	1 101
milijun	1 000 000		
tri milijuna petsto pet tisuća šeststo pedeset tri			3 505 653

The word for *thousand* is often used in its accusative form **tisuću**.

2 Dates

To express dates you use ordinal numbers (see Unit 6), remembering that only the last part of such a number becomes an adjective. To say *today is...* use the nominative case, and to say *on a date* use the genitive case:

Koji je datum danas?	*What is the date today?*
Danas je treći siječanj.	*Today is the 3rd January.*
Danas je osamnaesti travanj.	*Today is the 18th April.*
Danas je dvadeset osmi prosinac.	*Today is the 28th December.*

Kad smo stigli?	*When did we arrive?*
Stigli smo...	*We arrived...*
trinaestog veljače.	*on the 13th February.*
dvadadeset prvog srpnja.	*on the 21st July.*
tridesetog travnja.	*on the 30th October.*

To express a year use the formula *one thousand nine hundred..*, and to say *in a year* use the ordinal numeral and the word for year **godina**, in the genitive case:

Kada ste rođeni?	*When were you born?*
Tisuću devetsto sedamdeset druge godine.	*In 1972.*
Tisuću devetsto pedeset sedme godine.	*In 1957.*
Tisuću devetsto dvadeset prve godine.	*In 1921.*

3 Expressions of time

Mjesecima (*for months*) is expressed by using the instrumental plural case of the word **mjesec**. Similar expressions can be formed for other periods of time:

Čekali smo te satima.	*We waited for you for hours.*
Tražili su ga danima.	*They searched for him for days.*
tjednima	*for weeks*
godinama	*for years*

Other expressions of time can be formed by using *still, yet, more*:

Nemam više tu namjeru.	*I no longer intend to* (Lit. *have the intention*).
Više nije htio da...	*He no longer wanted to...*
Dok sam još bio dijete...	*While I was still a child...*
Još nije došao.	*He has not come yet.*
Još jednom.	*Once more.*
više with negative	*no longer*
još (uvijek)	*still*
još with negative	*yet*

4 Adverbs

Adverbs are words which often end in *-ly* in English: sincerely, beautifully, etc. They are formed in one of two ways in Serbo-Croat:

(*a*) use the nominative neuter form of the adjective:

Masc.	**Fem.**	**Neut.**
lijep	lijepa	lijepo
iskren	iskrena	iskreno
tužan	tužna	tužno
sretan	sretna	sretno

(b) use the nominative masculine form of adjectives which end in **-ski**:

Masc.	Fem.	Neut.
engleski	engleska	englesko
prijateljski	prijateljska	prijateljsko

They are frequently used to add meanings to verbs (whereas adjectives add meanings to nouns).

Lijepo si pjevala.	*You sang beautifully.*
Razgovarali smo iskreno.	*We talked sincerely.*
Tužno su me gledali.	*They looked at me sadly.*
Govorim engleski.	*I speak English.*
Govorila je sa mnom prijateljski.	*She spoke with me in a friendly fashion.*

5 Hoćeš li da se idemo kupati?

You know that the verbs **željeti** and **htjeti** are used in a similar way to the English *I want to...* A difference occurs when talking about what we want others to do. Compare the following:

Hoćeš li da se idemo kupati?	*Do you want us to go for a swim?*
Ovih dana me je pitao želim li ja da se mi vjenčamo.	*Recently he's been asking if I want **us** to get married.*

(emphasis added by use of pronouns **ja** and **mi** in Serbo-Croat)

In English we still use a construction with the infinitive, but in Serbo-Croat we say the equivalent of *I want that you do something.*

6 Kupa mi se

You don't have to say that *you want* all the time, you can add more of an inner feeling by saying *you feel like*. The equivalent expression in Serbo-Croat is formed by making the verb reflexive and using the dative case for the person concerned:

Kupa mi se.	*I feel like bathing.*

(**kupa** – **on** form of verb: **mi** – dat. of **ja**: **se** – reflexive enclitic)

Jede mi se.	*I feel like eating.*
Ide mi se u kino.	*I feel like going to the cinema.*
Pije mi se čaj.	*I feel like (a drink of) tea.*

7 To say 'oneself'

In English there are a number of words like *myself, yourself* and *one-self*, etc. In Serbo-Croat there is just one word which has all these meanings. It changes according to case in the following pattern:

nom. acc. gen.	sebe
dat.	sebi
ins.	sobom

The meaning of the word depends on the context of the sentence:

Misli na sebe.	*Think about yourself.*
Pogledaj sebe.	*Look at yourself.*
Zadovoljan je sobom.	*He is pleased with himself.*
Kupio je sebi novine.	*He bought a newspaper for himself.*

8 Aspects with početi

After the verb **počinjati, početi** (and others which mean *to begin* or ones which mean *to finish*) you must use an imperfective infinitive:

On počinje čitati.	*He is beginning to read.*
Počeo sam piti mlijeko.	*I began to drink my milk.*

9 Jedan od tih otoka

The phrase *one of...* is made up of **jedan** followed by **od** and the genitive case. Remember that **jedan** is an adjective and its ending will depend on what is being discussed:

jedan od tih otoka	*one of those islands*
otok (masc.), jedan (masc.)	
jedna od tih kavana	*one of those cafés*
kavana (fem.), jedna (fem.)	
u jednoj od tih kavana	*in one of those cafés*
(use the feminine dative as you are saying *the equivalent of*)	
u jednoj kavani od tih	*in one café out of those*

10   Unusual categories of nouns (vrijeme)

Vrijeme is unusual in that it adds **-en-** before its neuter case endings:

	Singular	Plural
nom.	vrijeme	vremena
acc.	vrijeme	vremena
gen.	vremena	vremena
dat.	vremenu	vremenima
ins.	vremenom	vremenima

It also loses **-ij-** when it adds case endings.

There are a small group of nouns which follow the same pattern as **vrijeme** and add **-en-** before the case endings: e.g. **ime** (*name*), **breme** (*burden*). They are all neuter nouns which end in **-me**.

11   Unusual categories of adjectives

In this unit some adjectives do not strictly follow the patterns which you have learnt so far:

Svi	Singular			Plural		
	Masc.	Fem.	Neut.	Masc.	Fem.	Neut.
nom.	sav	sva	sve	svi	sve	sva
acc.	nom/gen	svu	sve	sve	sve	sva
gen.	sveg(a)	sve	sveg(a)		svih	
dat.	svem(u)	svoj	svem(u)		svim(a)	
ins.	svim	svom	svim		svim(a)	

The adjective is treated as if it has a soft ending, and **e** is used in place of **o** in masculine and neuter singular endings.

Remember that   **svi** (masc. plural) also means *everyone* and
               sve (neut. singular) also means *everything*.

Svi su došli.	*Everyone came.*
Sve je bilo na stolu.	*Everything was on the table.*

Veselo			
Singular	Masc.	Fem.	Neut.
nom.	veseo	vesela	veselo

The masculine nominative ends in **-o**, while all other endings are added to **vesel-**.

A similar adjective to **veseo** is **topao** (*warm*)

Topao Singular	Masc.	Fem.	Neut.
nom.	topao	topla	toplo

Vježbe

1   Write out the following numbers in words: 567, 239, 807, 301, 1 500, 3 790.

2   Write out the dates below. Take care with getting the right case to match the meaning of the sentence:

(a) Danas je   (14th March).
(b) Danas je   (1st June).
(c) U četvrtak bit će   (8th August).
(d) Vratit ćemo se   (on 3rd September).
(e) Englezi su stigli u Dubrovnik   (on 25th June).
(f) Idemo u Zagreb   (on 27th December).
(g) Rođen sam   (in 1950).
(h) Rođena je   (in 1962).
(i) Rođen sam   (on 25th May) (in 1971).
(j) Rođena je   (on 11th January) (in 1935).

3   Fill in the most appropriate words from the list below to complete the time expressions in the following sentences. Use each word only once:

(a) Radujem se povratku na Hvar u _____.
(b) Živjeli su na Braču _____.
(c) _____ nisu došli.
(d) Ne ostaje nam mnogo _____.
(e) To se dešavalo u _____.
(f) Sunčaju se na plaži po _____ dan.
(g) _____ dođe Rudolf, recite mu da sam se javio.

budućnosti	čim	prošlosti	još	vremena	godinama	cijeli

4 Complete the sentences with the correct form of **htjeti**:

(a) _____ li vi da idemo u Varaždin vlakom?

(b) Pitao me je, _____ li ja da dođe na večeru!

(c) Rudolf mi je rekao da Mark _____ ostati cijeli dan na plaži.

(d) Sandra je _____ da joj Jasna priča o svemu.

5 In the sentences below make an adverb from the adjective given in brackets. All the adjectives are given in the nominative masculine form:

(a) (Tužan) je išao prema trgu.

(b) Bilo smo u kavani i (veseo) smo pjevali.

(c) Mogu ti (iskren) reći da nikad nisam bio tamo.

(d) Mi smo razgovarali vrlo (prijateljski) cijeli dan.

6 Match the questions to the answers:

(a) Mogu li ti reći nešto?   (i) Htio sam te vidjeti.

(b) Ideš li na odmor?   (ii) Dobro sam raspoložena, hvala.

(c) Zašto si došao?   (iii) Ne moraš, ako ne želiš.

(d) Kako si danas?   (iv) Imala sam namjeru, a sada nisam sigurna.

7 Replace the verbs **htjeti** and **željeti** with a phrase meaning *I feel like* in the following sentences:

(a) Hoću piti čaj.

(b) Hoćemo ići u grad danas.

(c) Ona se želi kupati.

(d) Hoću ići na plažu danas.

8 Complete the missing parts of the dialogue below:

Što vam je?

(*I am sad.*)

Zašto?

(*Because I do not feel like going home.*)

Možete se vratiti iduće godine.

(*I intend to return.*)

Onda, nemojte se ljutiti na mene.

(*I am not angry with you. I am looking forward to my return.*)

Vidim da ste sada sretni.

9 Provide the correct form of **sebe** in the sentences below:

(a) Jasna je pogledala _____.

(b) Jesu li zadovoljni _____?

(c) On misli samo na _____.

(d) Kupili smo _____ avionske karte za Dubrovnik.

───────── **Dopunsko štivo 1** ─────────

Sandra i Mark nisu imali mnogo vremena dan prije polaska na Hvar. Sandra je spakovala majice, šorceve, kupaće kostime, čarape, donje rublje, sandale i cipele za njih. Mark je uzeo ljetne hlače, laganu crvenu jaknu i košulje. Ima jednu zelenu košulju s kratkim rukavama. Nije uzeo svoje sivo odijelo. Sandra je uzela svoju žutu jaknu, suknju i crnu haljinu. Bili su sigurni da nisu ništa zaboravili. Ali nisu znali de će biti tako toplo. Morali su kupiti šešire i mlijeko za sunčanje u prodavaonici u Hvaru.

dan prije polaska *the day before departure*	**crven** *red*
pakovati, spakovati (pakujem, spakujem) *to pack*	**jakna** *jacket*
	košulja *shirt*
majica *T-shirt*	**zelen** *green*
šorc *shorts*	**s kratkim rukavama** *with short sleeves*
kupaći kostim *swimming costume*	
čarapa *sock*	**sivo odijelo** *grey suit*
donje rublje *underwear*	**žut** *yellow*
sandale (fem. plural noun) *sandals*	**suknja** *skirt*
cipele (fem. plural noun) *shoes*	**haljina** *dress*
ljetne hlače (fem. plural noun) *summer trousers*	**tako** *so*
	šešir *hat*
lagan *light*	**mlijeko za sunčanje** (or **ulje za sunčanje**) *sun-tan lotion*

Istina ili neistina?

(a) Sandra je spakovala cipele za njih.

(b) Mark ima jednu crvenu košulju s kratkim rukavama.

(c) Kupili su mlijeko za sunčanje u Zagrebu.

Dopunsko štivo 2

Here are some descriptions of resorts and hotels. Given high levels of inflation and currency reforms the prices are not realistic. Read the descriptions and then answer the questions below:

Pag je turistički grad. Smješten je u tihom zaljevu, u blagoj mediteranskoj klimi s mnogo sunčanih dana, kristalnim morem s malim i velikim plažama.

Hotel Bellevue (B kategorija) kapacitet: 320 kreveta. Svaka soba ima tuš, WC. Svaki balkon ima pogled na more. Hotel ima vlastitu plažu, rekreacioni centar i frizerski salon.

Turističko naselje Medena smješteno je u Segetu, malom ribarskom mjestu (4km od Trogira, 30km od Splita i 7km od aerodroma). Naselje ima restoran, grill-bar s terasom, terasu za ples, salu za konferenciju, frizerske salone, supermarket, bazen s toplom morskom vodom, terene za sport i dječje igralište.

Hotel Kompas: Cjenovnik po osobi/danu

	noćenje/doručak	polupansion	puni pansion
jednokrevetna soba	din 421,00	din 512,00	din 602,00
dokrevetna soba	din 295,00	din 358,00	din 421,00
trokrevetna soba	din 240,00	din 300,00	din 341,00

turistički *tourist* (adj.)	**sala za konferenciju** *conference hall*
Smješten je... *It is situated...*	**morska voda** *salt water*
u tihom zaljevu *in a quiet bay*	**dječje igralište** *children's*
u blagoj mediteranskoj klimi *in a*	*playground*
gentle Mediterranean climate	**cjenovnik po osobi/danu** *price list*
sunčan dan *sunny day*	*per person/day*
krevet *bed*	**noćenje/doručak** *overnight/*
svaki *each, every*	*breakfast*
tuš *shower*	**polupansion** *half board*
WC *toilet* (pron. ve-tse)	**puni pansion** *full board*
balkon *balcony*	**jednokrevetna soba** *one-bedded*
vlastit *own*	*room*
frizerski salon *hairdressing salon*	**dvokrevetna soba** *two-bedded*
ribarski *fishing* (adj.)	*room*
terasa *terrace*	**trokrevetna soba** *three-bedded*
ples *dance, dancing*	*room*

1   Kakav grad je Pag?
    (a) Ribarski.
    (b) Industrijski.
    (c) Turistički.

2   Gdje je smješteno turističko naselje 'Medena'?
    (a) U malom mjestu.
    (b) U gradu.
    (c) Na plaži.

3   Koliko košta po osobi/danu dvokrevetna soba, polupansion, u
    Hotelu 'Kompas'?
    (a) din 512,00.
    (b) din 358,00.
    (c) din 295,00.

14

AKO PADA KIŠA

If it rains...

In this unit you will learn how to

- say *if* using different levels of possibility and the conditional
- further understand aspects
- use expressions for the weather and verbs of movement
- say that you can *see / hear* somebody doing something

───── Dijalog ─────

Jasna je ustala rano. Odlučila je da ide u grad. Ostavila je poruku za Rudolfa.

Rudolf
Izašla sam po kruh za doručak. Kad ustaneš, stavi ručnike na balkon da se osuše. Da smo ih sinoć stavili na balkon, bili bi već suhi. Ako vidiš Sandru ili Marka, reci im da sam otišla u grad po kruh. Imam prijedlog za danas. Ako bude toplo, možemo ići na plažu. Ako bi padala kiša, mogli bismo ići u samostan.

Tvoja Jasna

IF IT RAINS ...

ustajati, ustati (ustajem, ustanem) *to get up*	**Da smo...** *If we had...*
rano *early*	**bili bi** *they would be*
odlučiti *to decide*	**suh** *dry*
ostavljati, ostaviti *to leave*	**reci im** tell them (imperative of **reći**)
poruka *message*	**odlaziti, otići** (odlazim, odem: odlazio, otišao) *to go away*
izlaziti izaći (izlazim, izađem: izlazio, izašao) *to go out*	**prijedlog** *suggestion*
po kruh *for bread*	**Ako bude toplo...** *If it is warm...*
stavi (stavljati, staviti) *put* (command form)	**Ako bi padala kiša...** *If it were to rain...*
ručnik *towel*	**mogli bismo ići** *we could go*
sušiti se, osušiti se *to dry*	**samostan** *monastery*

Kad je Rudolf pročitao poruku, čuo je kako Jasna ulazi u apartman. Ušla je u njihovu sobu.

Jasna   Zdravo, Rudolfe. Gdje su Sandra i Mark? Nema ih u sobi.
Rudolf Ne znam. Ja sam se upravo probudio.
Jasna   Previše spavaš.
(Gleda kroz prozor.)
Evo ih. Vidim kako dolaze s obale. Možda su išli rivom u grad.
Rudolf Misliš li da će danas padati kiša? Vjetar ne puše, nebo je vedro i nema oblaka.
Jasna   Sve je moguće. Vjerojatno neće padati. Ako bude toplo, nema problema. Kada bi bilo hladno, ne bismo išli na plažu. Moramo imati i drugi plan.
Rudolf U pravu si. Jesi li jutros vidjela gospođu Bilčić?
Jasna   Koga?
Rudolf Našu gazdaricu. Hoću platiti račun.
Jasna   Zašto?
Rudolf Zato što se vraćamo prekosutra. Da postoji mogućnost, ostali bismo još. Ali ne postoji, jer imam sastanak početkom idućeg tjedna u Zagrebu.

Čuo je kako Jasna ulazi. *He heard Jasna coming in.*	**Nema ih u sobi.** *They're not in their room.*
ulaziti, ući (ulazim, uđem: ulazio, ušao) *to enter, come in*	**upravo** *just now*
	buditi se, probuditi se *to wake up*

previše *too much* (also *too...*)	**oblak** *cloud*
spavati *to sleep*	**mogući** *possible*
pogledati kroz prozor (gledati, pogledati) *to glance through the window*	**vjerojatno** *probably, likely*
	Kada bi bilo hladno... *If it were cold...*
s obale *from the coast*	**drugi plan** *another plan*
možda *perhaps*	**koga** *whom*
riva (rivom) *promenade, esplanade* (along the promenade – instrumental)	**račun** *bill, account*
	postojati, postojim *to exist*
Vjetar ne puše. *The wind is not blowing.*	**mogućnost** (fem. noun) *possibility*
	ostali bismo *we would stay*
Nebo je vedro. *The sky is clear.*	**sastanak** *meeting*
	početak *beginning*

Istina ili neistina?

(a) Jasna je ustala kasno.
(b) Sinoć nisu stavili ručnike na balkon.
(c) Moraju se vratiti u Zagreb jer Rudolf ima sastanak.

———— Objašnjenja i komentari ————

Jasna need not worry about the weather on Hvar. All the islands of the Adriatic have excellent weather, but Hvar is particularly known for having no rain all summer. It is said that hotels are even prepared to refund money for each day of rain. So, it is unlikely that she would need her **kišobran** (*umbrella*) or her **kaput**.

———— Ključne fraze ————

How to:

● describe levels of possibility.
možda
vjerojatno
moguće

- use types of sentences using *if*.

Ako vidiš Sandru...
Ako bude toplo...
Ako bi padala kiša...
Kada bi bilo hladno...
Da smo ih stavili...

- use expressions about the weather.

toplo je
hladno je
vjetar puše
nebo je vedro
nema oblaka

- say you can *see/hear* someone doing something.

Čuo je kako Jasna ulazi u sobu.
Vidim kako dolaze s obale.

- use verbs of motion.

Izašla je iz sobe.
Otišla je u grad.
Ušla je u sobu.

Jezični obrasci

1   To say 'if'

You need to know what is called the conditional part of the verb. This is formed by taking the past tense from the infinitive (**čitao**, **išli**, etc.) and combining it with the following short forms:

ja	bih	mi	bismo
ti	bi	vi	biste
on/a/o	bi	oni/e/a	bi

The conditional means *would* in English. It is often found in more formal and polite language, as a waiter might ask you in a restaurant **Što biste željeli, gospodine/gospođo?** (*What would you like, sir/madam?*) or as you first saw in Unit 2 in the phrase **ja bih kavu** (*I would like coffee*).

These short forms, like others, tend not to come in first place in a sentence.

Like other short forms which are verbs they come before short forms from personal pronouns.

In conversation all forms of the verb are sometimes reduced to **bi**: **ja bi**, **vi bi**, etc.

The negative is formed by adding **ne** before the short form, which then allows it to come in first place:

Volio bih.	*I would like.*
Ne bih volio.	*I would not like.*

Questions are formed in one of two ways:
(*a*) Da li biste htjeli...   *Would you like...*
(using the **da li** formula)
(*b*) Biste li htjeli...   *Would you like...*
(using the **li** formula, but this time the short form comes first).

There are three levels of possibility expressed in Serbo-Croat *if* sentences:

● Ako je toplo, idemo na plažu.   *If it is warm, we go to the beach.*
i.e. if A (it is warm) occurs, B (we go to the beach) occurs. Tenses are the same as in English. Note that when talking about one specific occasion in the future say **Ako bude toplo...** This is further explained below.

● Ako bi padala kiša, mogli bismo   *If it were to rain, we could go*
   ići u samostan.   *to the monastery.*
i.e. I don't believe A will occur, but it might. Conditional in both parts of the sentence. In such sentences **kada** may also be used to mean *if*.

● Da postoji mogućnost,   *If the possibility existed,*
   ostali bismo.   *we would stay.*
   Da smo ih sinoć stavili na   *If we had put them on the*
   balkon, bili bi suhi.   *balcony last night, they*
                                 would be dry.
i.e. A is not possible or was not done, so the condition is not met for B which will not or did not occur. The verb with **da** is in the appropriate tense, and the second verb is in the conditional.

2   Other tenses in Serbo-Croat

You have learnt all the most-used parts of the verb in Serbo-Croat. There are four other tenses: pluperfect, aorist, imperfect, future exact. The first three are used rarely.

The pluperfect is formed by adding the past tense of **biti** to another verb in the past tense (e.g. **Bio sam napisao pismo bratu.** *I had written a letter to my brother*).

The aorist and imperfect are also past tenses (e.g. **rekoh** *I said* – aorist; **Kako to bješe?** *How was that?* – imperfect).

The future exact is sometimes used with *if* clauses. It is formed in two parts by joining another part of the verb **biti** (given in the following pattern) –

ja	budem	mi	budemo
ti	budeš	vi	budete
on/a/o	bude	oni/e/a	budu

– with the past tense from the infinitive in the following way:

Ako bude padala kiša,	*If it rains we shall go to*
ići ćemo u kino.	*the cinema.*

It is used to indicate a precise point in the future, hence the formula **Ako bude toplo...**

i.e. if A will occur then B will happen. Both parts of the sentence are in future tenses, but it is not possible to use the future formed from the short form of **htjeti** with **ako**.)

3 Verbal aspect

You have now met a number of aspectual pairs. If we take the imperfective (the first in any pair) as the basic verb, then we can see three main trends in forming the perfective:

(*a*) The perfective verb is a shortened version of the imperfective:

ustajati	ustati	*to get up*
počinjati	početi	*to begin*
ostavlajati	ostaviti	*to leave*

(*b*) The perfective verb is formed by adding a prefix to the imperfective:

piti	popiti	*to drink*
čitati	pročitati	*to read*
pisati	napisati	*to write*

(c)   The perfective verb belongs to a different type, often being an **i** verb:

sjećati se	sjetiti se	*to remember*
vraćati se	vratiti se	*to return*

4   Verbs of movement

The verb *to go* is **ići**. From this verb you can form a number of other verbs by adding prefixes which specify the direction of the movement. From **ići** you form the perfective form of the compound verb, and an imperfective is formed by adding the same prefix to **-laziti**:

izlaziti	izaći	(followed by preposition **iz** + gen.)
(to go out)		
ulaziti	ući	(followed by preposition **u** + acc.)
(to go in, enter)		
odlaziti	otići	(prepositions vary)
(to go away, leave)		

Also:

dolaziti	doći	*to come, arrive*
izlaziti	izići	(same as **izaći**)
polaziti	poći	*to set off*
prijelaziti	prijeći	*to cross*
prolaziti	proći	*to pass by*
silaziti	sići	*to go down, get off*
zalaziti	zaći	*to go behind*

They all follow the same verbal patterns. The **-laziti** forms are regular. The other forms end in **-đem**, etc. (except **otići**):

izaći	izađem
ući	uđem
otići	odem

In the past tense they all follow the same pattern: on je izašao, ona je ušla, oni su otišli (like **išao**).

Examples:

Izašao je iz sobe.	*He came out of the room.*
Dolaze kući.	*They are coming home.*

Prešli su most.   *They crossed the bridge.*
Sunce je zašlo.   *The sun set.*

5 *It is warm*

When specifying that *I am warm* you add the relevant person in the dative case to the expression **toplo je** (which is the adverb form – Unit 13). This is the same principle as we had with the phrases **lako mi je** and **Je li vam jasno?**

Toplo mi je.   *I am warm.*
Je li vam hladno?   *Are you cold?*
Vruće im je.   *They are hot.*

6 Tko/koga

The words **tko** and **što** have case endings which resemble adjective endings:

nom.	tko	što
acc.	kog(a)	što
gen.	kog(a)	čeg(a)
dat.	kom(u/e)	čem(u)
ins.	kim(e)	čim(e)

The required case and ending are determined by the same rules as for all nouns and adjectives:

Koga si vidjela?   *Whom did you see?*
Kome je dao novac?   *To whom did he give the money?*
S kim su došli u grad?   *Who did they come to town with?* (or *With whom..?*)

Iz čega izlazimo?   *What are we getting out of?*
Čime ste zadovoljni?   *What are you satisfied with?*

Netko/nešto and **nitko/ništa** change according to these patterns too. **Netko** and **nitko** lose the **t** in other cases, e.g. **nekog(a)/nikog(a)**.

When you use a preposition with **nitko** and **ništa** the word is split. Look at the following examples:

Jasna je sama.   *Jasna is alone.*
Nije došla ni s kim.   *She came with nobody.*
Nisam dobio pismo ni od koga.   *I received a letter from nobody.*

7   Idiomatic phrases

● *to fetch*

Idem po kruh   *I am going for the bread. (or*
    I am going to fetch the bread.)

The normal way of saying *to fetch* is to say **ići po** followed by the accusative case.

● *To go along...*

Idu rivom u grad.   *They are going along the*
    promenade to town.

The place along which one moves is put into the instrumental case: **Išli su ulicom...** *They went down the street...*

● *They are not in*

Nema ih u sobi.   *They are not in their room.*

You know **nema** followed by the genitive case to mean *there is not* or *there are not*. It is also commonly used to mean *they are out* (i.e. not at home).

Nema ga.   *He is not in / not at home / not here.*

● *At the beginning of...*

This is often expressed by the word **početkom** (instrumental case of **početak** *beginning*) followed by the genitive case:

Početkom mjeseca.   *At the beginning of the month.*

The phrase **na početku** is also used.

The expression **krajem** and **na kraju** is used to mean *at the end*:

Krajem idućeg tjedna.   *At the end of next month.*

● *To see / hear someone doing something*

Čuo je kako Jasna ulazi u   *He heard Jasna coming into*
    apartman.   *the apartment.*

Vidim kako dolaze s obale.   *I can see them coming from*
    the beach.

In Serbo-Croat you express this by literally saying *he heard how Jasna comes into the apartment, I can see how they come*. The verb of perception is followed by **kako** and the other verb is in the present tense.

Gledali su kako ti ljudi   *They watched those people*
    razgovaraju ispred hotela.   *talking in front of the hotel.*

🐾 ——————— **Vježbe** ———————

1 Supply the word for *if* (**ako**, **ako/kad**, **da**) in each of the following sentences:

(a) _____ smo bili u Hvaru, bilo bi nam previše vruće.
(b) _____ dođeš k meni, vidjet ćeš ga.
(c) _____ si došao k meni, vidio bi ga.
(d) _____ pada kiša, išli bismo u kino.
(e) _____ bi padala kiša, išli bismo u kino.
(f) _____ imate moj novac, ostavite ga na stolu za mene.
(g) _____ je vidiš, reci joj da ću sutra biti kod kuće.
(h) _____ je znao kamo je otišla, rekao bi mi.
(i) _____ je vrijeme lijepo, išli bismo rivom.
(j) _____ biste htjeli ići u kazalište, dao bih vam moju kartu.

2 You are on holiday with a friend. Leave him/her a note and say the following:

I woke up early this morning.
I decided to go to the beach before breakfast.
If I return at 9 o'clock we can go to breakfast together.
If I do not return at 9, do not wait for me.
Go to breakfast. I shall buy something at the beach.
I shall see you at 10 o'clock in our room.

3 Complete the sentences below with the most appropriate verb of motion from the box. Each verb is given in its correct form.

(a) Autobusi su _____ most.
(b) Kamo _____?
(c) Jasna je _____ iz sobe.
(d) Ja ću _____, čim budem mogla.
(e) Sunce _____ na Zapadu.
(f) Mi _____ kuću gdje sam rođen.

zalazi	izašla	prolazimo	idete	doći	prešli

4 Complete the sentences below with the most appropriate prepositions. Pay attention not only to the sense of the sentence but also to the case ending of the noun which comes after the preposition:

(a) Neki ljudi vole gledati _____ prozor.

  (b) Satima smo stajali _____ trgu.
  (c) Rudolf, idite _____ kruh.
  (d) Ja sam _____ Engleske.
  (e) Sutra idemo _____ Korčulu.
  (f) Gosti su sjedjeli _____ stolom.
  (g) Dolazimo _____ obale.
  (h) Rudolf je _____ kuće.

5 Replace the words in brackets with their correct case forms:

  (a) (tko) pišete pismo?
  (b) (što) je Rudolf zadovoljan?
  (c) (nitko) nisam vidio.
  (d) (što) se sjećaš?
  (e) Nisam se sjećao (ništa).
  (f) Na (tko) se ljutiš?
  (g) (tko) je hladno?
  (h) Jesi li dao moj novac (netko)?

6 Match the questions to the answers:

  (a) Da li vam je hladno?   (i)   Ne znam, nema je od kuće.
  (b) Hoće li padati kiša danas? (ii) Početkom rujna.
  (c) Gdje je Jasna?   (iii) Nije, hvala.
  (d) Kad idete kući?   (iv) Možda.

Dopunsko štivo 1

These are weather forecasts covering different regions of Croatia:

VRIJEME
Danas: toplo
Središnja Hrvatska
Ujutro slab mraz i kratkotrajna magla. Danju sunčano sa slabim vjetrom. Jutarnja temperatura od –3 do 2, a dnevna od 11 do 15C.

Slavonija i Baranja
Ujutro mraz i magla. Danju sunčano i toplo. Jutarnja temperatura od –2 do 5, a dnevna od 12 do 16C.

Gorski kotar i Lika
Ujutro magla, a danju sunčano. Vjetar slab. Jutarnja temperatura od –3 do 2, a dnevna od 10 do 15C.

Istra i Hrvatsko primorje
Ujutro u obalnom području sumaglica, a danju vedro ili malo oblačno. Vjetar slab. Jutarnja temperatura od 3 do 7, a dnevna od 11 do 16C.

Dalmacija
Sunčano. Vjetar slab. Jutarnja temperatura od 3 do 10, a dnevna od 12 to 16C.

slab *weak, light*	**obalan** *coastal*
mraz *frost*	**područje** *region*
kratkotrajan *short-lived*	**sumaglica** *mist*
magla *fog*	**oblačno** *cloudy*
jutarnji *morning* (adj.)	

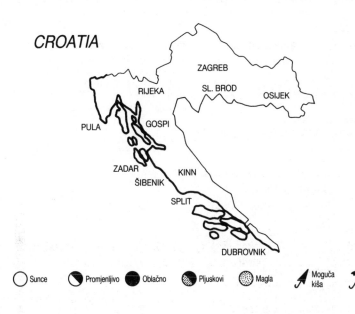

Istina ili neistina?

(*a*) U Središnjoj Hrvatskoj vrijeme je danju sunčano.
(*b*) Nema sumaglice u Istri.
(*c*) Slab vjetar puše u Dalmaciji.

Dopunsko štivo 2

Read the following passage and answer the questions below:

Margaret Turner je turistkinja iz Engleske. One je na odmoru u hotelu na Korčuli. Jednog dana, poslije doručka, nije mogla naći svoju tašku. Pitala je konobara da li je vidio njenu tašku. Rekao je da nije. Izašla je iz restorana i prišla recepciji.

Margaret	Molim vas, gdje je policijska stanica?
Recepcija	Zašto, gospođo? Što vam se desilo?
Margaret	Netko mi je ukrao tašku.
Recepcija	Što ste imali u taški?
Margaret	Imala sam novčanik, pasoš i putničke čekove.
Recepcija	A koje je boje vaša taška?
Margaret	Crvena.
Recepcija	Netko ju je predao recepciji. Evo je. Ne trebate policajca. Mislim da ćete naći sve svoje stvari u njoj.

---

turist (masc.) **turistkinja** (fem.)
  tourist
taška *handbag*
u taški (**k** does not change to **c** here)
policijska stanica *police station*
krasti, ukrasti *to steal*
(kradem, ukradem; krao, ukrao:
  followed by dat. meaning *from me*)

novčanik *wallet, purse*
pasoš *passport*
putnički čekovi *travellers' cheques*
A koje je boje..? *And what
  colour is..?*
policajac *policeman*

---

1 Što je gospođa Turner izgubila?
  (*a*) Izgubila je tašku.
  (*b*) Izgubila je doručak.
  (*c*) Izgubila je ključ od sobe.

2 Koga je gospođa Turner pitala?
  (*a*) Pitala je policajca.
  (*b*) Pitala je konobara.
  (*c*) Pitala je konobaricu.

3 Gjde je našla svoju tašku?
  (*a*) U restoranu.
  (*b*) U policijskoj stanici.
  (*c*) Na recepciji.

15

KAKO SE OSJEĆATE?
How do you feel?

In this unit you will learn how to

- refer to health, parts of the body and call a doctor
- express degrees of forbidding
- form comparative and superlative adjectives such as *good*, *better*, *best*

Dijalog

Jednog jutra Sandra i Mark su se probudili u svojoj hotelskoj sobi u Zagrebu. Vrijeme je postajalo hladnije i kiša je sve više padala. Mark se nije osjećao dobro.

Sandra Kako se osjećaš? Ne izgledaš dobro.
Mark To je istina. Uopće se ne osjećam dobro. Boli me glava. Nisam dobro spavao.
Sandra Zašto?
Mark Zato što nisam mogao spavati od kašlja.
Sandra Ništa nisam čula.

Mark   Otišao sam u kupaonicu dok nisam prestao kašljati. Nisam te htio probuditi.

Sandra   Ne brini se. To nije ništa opasno. Samo si prehlađen. To će proći.

Mark   Lako je tebi govoriti. Ne smijem biti u krevetu. Znaš da uskoro s Rudolfom putujem u Beograd.

Sandra   Ne trebaš kola za hitnu pomoć i ne moraš ići u bolnicu. Javit ću se recepciji. U hotelu moraju imati telefonski broj neke ambulante. Zamolit ću da liječnik dođe što prije.

hotelska soba *hotel room*	**prestati** (prestanem) *to stop*
postajati, postati (postajem, postanem) *to become*	**kašljati** (kašljem) *to cough*
	brinuti se (brinem se) *to worry*
sve više *all the more*	**opasan** *dangerous*
osjećati se, osjetiti se (dobro) *to feel* (well)	**biti prehlađen** *to have a cold*
	To će proći. *It will pass.*
izgledati (dobro) *to look* (well)	**Ne smijem.** *I must not.*
istina *truth*	**uskoro** *soon*
uopće ne... *not at all...*	**kola za hitnu pomoć** *ambulance*
boli me glava (boljeti) *I have a headache*. (Lit. *the head hurts me*).	**Ne moraš...** *You do not have to...*
	bolnica *hospital*
kašalj *cough, coughing*	**ambulanta** *clinic*
čuti (čujem) *to hear*	**liječnik** *doctor*
dok ne... *until...*	**što prije** *as soon as possible*

Kasnije netko kuca na vrata. Sandra ih otvara.

Liječnik   Dobar dan. Jeste li vi gospođa Bryant?

Sandra   Jesam. Izvolite, uđite. Moj muž je bolestan.

Liječnik   Dobar dan, gospodine. Kako se osjećate?

Mark   Osjećam se vrlo loše, doktore. Mnogo kašljem, slab sam, a i grlo me počinje boljeti.

Liječnik   Da vidimš Imate temperaturu. Molim vas, otvorite ustaş Imate i infekciju. Ukratko, prehlađeni ste, gospodine. Nije ništa opasno. Vi mlađi ljudi brže ozdravljate nego stariji ljudi. Uskoro ćete se osjećati bolje.

Mark   Najteže mi je ležati u krevetu. Moram se sutra vratiti na posao.

Liječnik   (Sandri) Gospođo, neka vaš muž ostane u krevetu najmanje tri dana. Dat ću vam najjači lijek protiv te infekcije. Posao će ga čekati.

kasnije *later*	**mlađi** *younger*
kucati na vrata *to knock at the door*	**brže** *quicker, more quickly*
bolestan *ill*	**ozdravljati, ozdraviti** *to recover, get better*
loš *bad*	**nego** *than*
slab *weak*	**stariji** *older*
grlo *throat*	**bolje** *better*
da vidim... *let me see...*	**najteže mi je** *most difficult for me is*
imati temperaturu *to have a temperature*	**neka... ostane** *let (him)... stay*
usta (neut. plural) *mouth*	**najmanje** *least, at least*
infekcija *infection*	**najjači** *strongest*
ukratko *in short, briefly*	**lijek** *medicine*
	protiv (with gen.) *against*

Istina ili neistina?

(a) Mark se nije osjećao dobro.
(b) Sandra je rekla da Mark mora ići u bolnicu.
(c) Liječnik je dao lijek protiv infekcije.

—————— **Objašnjenja i komentari** ——————

Doctor

In the event of illness any large hotel will be able to provide quick and easy access to a doctor. You may need to visit a doctor's surgery (**ordinacija**), a clinic (**poliklinika**) or a hospital (**bolnica**). To find medical help quickly look up in a telephone book **Dom zdravlja** where you will find the local clinics. When talking about doctors the word **liječnik** is used, but when talking to them the word **doktor** is commonly used. You may need to find a dentist (**zubar**) too. Although, you will hopefully not need any of this information.

Parts of the body

When visiting a doctor you may need to point out where the problem is. It may concern your hair (**kosa**), face (**lice**), eye (**oko**), ear (**uho**), nose (**nos**), lip (**usna**), chin (**brada**), neck (**vrat**), shoulder (**rame**), arm or hand (**ruka**), finger (**prst**), stomach (**stomak**), back (**leđa**) (neut. plural word like **vrata**), leg or foot (**noga**) or knee (**koljeno**).

Ključne fraze

How to:

- ask how people feel, say how you feel.

  Kako se osjećate?
  Osjećam se dobro.
  Ne osjećam se dobro.

- remark on how people look.

  Ne izgledate dobro.
  Dobro izgledate.

- comment on someone's health.

  Boli me glava.
  Grlo me počinje boljeti.
  Kašljati.
  Moj muž je bolestan.
  Ti si prehlađen.

- understand comments from a doctor.

  Imate temperaturu.
  Imate infekciju.
  Dat ću vam lijek protiv...
  Uskoro ćete ozdraviti.
  Uskoro ćete se bolje osjećati.

- express degrees of restriction.

  ne možeš
  ne moraš
  ne smiješ

- use phrases connected with comparative forms.

  što prije
  sve više

Jezični obrasci

1 Comparative forms

There is one basic way to form the comparative of an adjective, i.e. the difference between *old* (**star**) and *older* (**stariji**). There are also three subcategories which are a variation on this basic form and some adjectives which do not follow this pattern at all. Most comparative adjectives end in soft consonants and take the appropriate adjective endings.

(a) Basic Form

To form the comparative of an adjective add **-iji** to the adjective:

star	*old*	star + iji	stariji	*older*
slab	*weak*	slab + iji	slabiji	*weaker*
sretan	*happy*	sretan + iji	sretniji	*happier*
tužan	*sad*	tužan + iji	tužniji	*sadder*

(b) Subcategories

(i) With these adjectives you add **-ji** to the adjective. However, in the process of doing this the final consonant at the end of the adjective changes (d–đ, g–ž, h–š, k–č, s–š, t–ć, z–ž):

mlad	*young*	mlad + ji	mlađi	*younger*
blag	*gentle*	blag + ji	blaži	*gentler*
suh	*dry*	suh + ji	suši	*drier*
jak	*strong*	jak + ji	jači	*stronger*
ljut	*angry*	ljut + ji	ljući	*angrier*

(**ljut** and **ljući** also mean *spicy hot* referring to food.)

(ii) With adjectives which end in **-ak**, **-ek** or **-ok** remove these letters and then proceed in a similar way for (i) above:

težak	*difficult*	tež + ji	teži	*more difficult*
dalek	*far*	dal + ji	dalji	*further*
visok	*tall*	vis + ji	viši	*taller*

(iii) Some adjectives which end with **-b**, **-p**, **-m**, **-v** add **-lji**:

skup	*expensive*	skuplji	*more expensive*
kriv	*wrong*	krivlji	*more wrong*

(c) Irregular comparatives

dobar	*good*	bolji	*better*
loš	*bad*	gori	*worse*
mali	*small*	manji	*smaller*
lak	*easy*	lakši	*easier*
lijep	*beautiful*	ljepši	*more beautiful*
velik	*large*	veći	*larger*

2 Superlative form

To form the superlative (i.e. *best, tallest*, etc.) add **naj-** to the beginning of the comparative adjective:

najstariji	*oldest*
najmlađi	*youngest*
najteži	*most difficult* (also *heaviest*)
najskuplji	*most expensive*
najbolji	*best*

3 More and less

The words for *more* and *less* of something are followed by the genitive case:

više	*more*	**manje**	*less*

Rudolf je kupio mnogo knjiga, ali Mark je kupio više.	*Rudolf bought many books, but Mark bought more.*

These words can also be used to mean *more* or *less* with ordinary adjectives. In fact, **više** has to be used to form the comparative of adjectives which end in **-ski**:

više prijateljski	*more friendly*	**manje prijateljski**	*less friendly*

4 Comparative of adverbs

The comparative and superlative form of adverbs is, as for ordinary adjectives, the neuter singular form:

Jasna lijepo pjeva,
ali Sandra pjeva još ljepše.

Jasna sings beautifully, but Sandra sings even more beautifully.

Similarly:

Meni je teško,
ali znam da je tebi teže.

It is difficult for me, but I know that it is more difficult for you.

5 To say 'than'

There are two ways of saying *than*:

(*a*) Use **nego** with the same case endings before and after:

Njemu je teže nego tebi.

It is more difficult for him than for you.

Moja sestra je starija nego ja.
Hladnije je u Londonu nego u Zagrebu.

My sister is older than me.
It is colder in London than in Zagreb.

(*b*) Use the preposition **od** followed by the genitive case:

Moja sestra je starija od mene.
Ta knjiga je skuplja od ove.

My sister is older than me.
That book is more expensive than this one.

6 To say 'as ... as possible'

The phrase **što prije** means *as soon as possible*. Other similar phrases are formed by putting **što** in front of the comparative form of the adjective or adverb:

što teže
što lakše

as difficult as possible
as easily as possible

7 Other command forms

You have learnt how to tell someone to do something. There are other forms relating to other people:

To say *let him come* or *let them come* use **neka** with the appropriate part of the verb:

Neka liječnik dođe što prije.   *Let the doctor come as soon as possible.*

To say *let me see* or *let us see* use **da** with the appropriate part of the verb:

Da vidim vašeg muža.   *Let me see your husband.*

8 To say '...hurts'

The word **boljeti** is used in a slightly different way from the English expression:

Boli me grlo.   *My throat hurts (aches).*
Bole me leđa.   *My back hurts (aches).*

You are literally saying that *the throat hurts me*. The word **leđa** is one of those words like **kola** which is a neuter plural word, so it has to be used with the plural form of the verb **bole**.

9 To say 'until'

The word **dok** means *while*. When it is used with a negative verb it means *until*:

...dok nisam prestao kašljati.   *...until I stopped coughing.*

10 Subcategories of adjectives

There is another small group of adjectives like **bolestan** (*sick, ill*) which end in **-tan**, and lose both the **-t-** and the **-a-** when they change case ending:

Mark je bolestan.   *Mark is ill.*
Sandra je bolesna.   *Sandra is ill.*

11 Subcategories of nouns

A number of words which refer to parts of the body do not follow the standard patterns:

(a) **uho/oko**

The plural forms are feminine and follow a similar pattern:

nom.	uši (*ears*)	oči (*eyes*)
acc.	uši	oči
gen.	ušiju	očiju
dat.	ušima	očima
ins.	ušima	očima

(b) **ruka** (fem.)/**noga** (fem.)/**prst** (masc.)

These words follow the normal patterns except in the genitive plural. These forms are:

ruka	ruku
noga	nogu
prst	prstiju

The word **ruka** means both *hand* and *arm*.
The word **noga** means both *foot* and *leg*.
The word **prst** means both *finger* (**prst na ruci**) and *toe* (**prst na nozi**).

(c) **rame**

This word follows the same pattern as **vrijeme**:

nom.	rame
acc.	rame
gen.	ramena

It adds **-en** before the case endings.

Bole me ramena.   *My shoulders hurt (ache).*

(d) **usta/leđa**

These words are always in the plural and follow the pattern for neuter nouns:

Njegova usta su crvena.   *His mouth is red.*
Gledam njena leđa.   *I am watching her back.*

Vježbe

1   Fill in the missing parts of the dialogue:

Bolesnik je kod liječnika. Vi ste bolesnik.

Liječnik   Kako se osjećate, gospodine?
Bolesnik   (*I do not feel well.*)
Liječnik   Da li vas nešto boli?
Bolesnik   (*I have a headache / My head hurts.*)
Liječnik   Kad vas je počela boljeti glava?
Bolesnik   (*It began to ache / hurt yesterday.*)
Liječnik   Moram priznati da ne izgledate dobro, gospodine. Da li vas još nešto boli?
Bolesnik   (*I had a stomach-ache last week, but that has passed.*)
Liječnik   Dat ću vam lijek. Ostanite kod kuće dok ne ozdravite.

2   Name the parts of the body indicated in the illustration below:

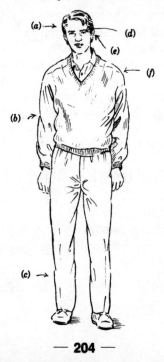

3 Change the adjectives in the sentences below into the required comparative forms with the correct case endings. They are given in brackets in the masculine nominative form.

(a) Sandra je (star) od Jasne.
(b) On je visok, ali je njegov brat (visok).
(c) Jučer je rekao (mlad) sestri da danas neće doći na večeru.
(d) Tko je (dobar), Mark ili Rudolf?
(e) Moj kaput je (skup) od vašeg.
(f) Bili smo zadovoljni (blag) klimom na Hvaru.
(g) Da li si vidio (veseo) čovjeka?
(h) Sjetila se njihove (velik) kuće u Varaždinu.

4 Give the superlative forms of the adjectives in brackets in the exercise above.

5 Change the adverbs in brackets in the sentences below into the correct comparative form:

(a) Jasna (lijepo) pjeva nego Sandra.
(b) (Toplo) je na Hvaru nego u Zagrebu.
(c) Zimi je (hladno) u Rusiji nego u Engleskoj.
(d) Meni je (lako) ići na odmor nego tebi.

6 Match the questions to the answers:

(a) Moram li ja ići na kolodvor s tobom?	(i) Još nije.
(b) Je li Rudolf pročitao tu knjigu?	(ii) Ne mogu dok ne završim ovaj posao.
(c) Kako je danas izgledala Jasna?	(iii) Ne moraš.
(d) Ideš li u kino večeras?	(iv) Loše je izgledala.

───── Dopunsko štivo 1 ─────

Informacije o hotelu

● Molimo da svoj odlazak prijavite recepciji do 12 sati i da napustite sobu do 14 sati, jer zadržavanje sobe poslije 14 sati uvjetuje plaćanje za još jedan dan.

● Ako odlazite iz hotela molimo Vas da sobu zaključate i ključ predate na recepciji.

● Za Vaš auto stoji Vam na raspolaganju naše parkiralište i garaža uz minimalnu naplatu.

● Prema Vašoj želji peremo, glačamo i kemijski čistimo Vaše rublje u najkraće vrijeme.

● Prema Vašoj želji uslužujemo jela i pića u sobi uz naplatu servisa od 20%.

moliti *to ask, beg*	**garaža** *garage*
prijaviti *to announce*	**uz minimalnu naplatu** *for a minimal fee*
napustiti *to leave*	
zadržavanje *keeping*	**prema Vašoj želji** *in accordance with your wishes*
uvjetovati *to cause, bring about*	
plaćanje *payment*	**prati** (perem) *to wash*
Vas/Vaš (these words usually spelt with a capital letter when meaning one person)	**glačati** *to iron*
	kemijski čistiti *to dry-clean*
	rublje *laundry*
zaključati *to lock*	**najkraće** *shortest*
predati *to hand over*	**usluživati** *to serve*
na raspolaganju *at* (your) *disposal*	**piće** *drink*
parkiralište *car park*	

Istina ili neistina?

(*a*) Morate prijaviti svoj odlazak recepciji do 14 sati.
(*b*) Parkiralište i garaža za auto ne koštaju mnogo.
(*c*) Ne možete dobiti jela i pića u hotelskoj sobi.

——— Dopunsko štivo 2 ———

Read the following passage and answer the questions that follow:

Kod liječnika

Rudolf se nije osjećao dobro. Imao je poslovni sastanak u gradu, ali je prije njega otišao k liječniku.

Liječnik Dobar dan, gospodine Šimuniću. Kako ste?
Rudolf Kad sam se jutros probudio, nisam se dobro osjećao. Ne znam što mi je. Sve me boli. Osjećam se sve gore kako dan prolazi.

Liječnik	Da li ste popili aspirin?
Rudolf	Nisam. Nisam znao što da radim. Rekao bih da sam inače zdrav čovjek.
Liječnik	U pravu ste, gospodine, jeste zdrav čovjek. Ali se možete razboljeti kao i svi drugi ljudi. Da pogledam vaše oči ... i sada da pogledam u usta... Da, ja bih rekao da ste uhvatili neku infekciju. Dat ću vam antibiotike. Morate se odmarati. Uskoro će proći.

---

poslovni sastanak *business meeting*
popiti aspirin *to take an aspirin*
Nisam znao što da radim. *I didn't know what to do.*
inače *otherwise*

razboljeti se *to fall ill*
kao i *like, as well as*
uhvatiti infekciju *to catch an infection*
antiobiotike *antibiotics*
odmarati se *to rest*

---

1 Kada je Rudolf išao k liječniku?
  (*a*) Prije poslovnog sastanka.
  (*b*) Poslije poslovnog sastanka.
  (*c*) Odmah poslije posla.

2 Što Rudolfa boli?
  (*a*) Bole ga oči.
  (*b*) Boli ga glava.
  (*c*) Sve ga boli.

3 Što će liječnik dati Rudolfu?
  (*a*) Dat će mu aspirin.
  (*b*) Dat će mu antibiotike.
  (*c*) Dat će mu infekciju.

16

POSLOVNI UGOVOR

Business contract

In this unit you will learn how to

- use words and expressions for a business meeting
- form complex sentences joined in the middle by *which*
- recognise some of the differences between the standard variants of the language as Mark and Rudolf go to Belgrade in Serbia (Do not worry if Mr Marković uses words that you recognise in the dialogue but with a slightly different spelling. That will be one of the differences.)

━━━━━━━━━ Dijalog ━━━━━━━━━

Mark i Rudolf su putovali u Beograd na poslovne pregovore sa gospodinom Markovićem. On je generalni direktor jedne beogradske firme. U vlaku, čitajući najnovije podatke o Markovićevoj firmi, Mark je slušao i sve što mu je Rudolf pričao o njoj. Pročitavši te podatke, Mark je počeo ispitivati Rudolfa detaljnije. Konačno su stigli u Beograd i odmah krenuli na sastanak. Ušli su u Markovićev ured.

Marković Dobar dan, gospodo, dobro došli. Želite li kafu?
Rudolf Ja bih. A ti, Mark?
Mark I ja bih isto, molim.

Čekaju kavu govoreći o svakodnevnim stvarima. Kava stiže a poslovni pregovori počinju.

pregovor (usu. used in plural) *negotiation*	**ispitivati, ispitati** (ispitujem, ispitam) *to question*
generalni direktor *general manager*	**detaljnije** *in more detail*
beogradski (adj.) *Belgrade, of Belgrade*	**konačno** *at last*
	kretati, krenuti (krećem, krenem) *to set off*
čitajući *reading*	**gospoda** *gentlemen*
podatak (usu. used in plural) *information*	**kafa** *coffee*
	govoreći *speaking, talking*
pročitavši *having read*	**svakodnevni** *everyday*

Marković Ovde, u našoj firmi, smatramo da možemo da prodamo vaše proizvode na našem tržištu.

Mark Zašto?

Marković Zato što sve zavisi od marketinga i znanja trendova koji se menjaju iz dana u dan. Imamo transportno odeljenje sa kamionima, imamo svoje radnje, imamo i svoje reklamno odeljenje.

Mark Vidim da imate razvijenu infrastrukturu. Tražite li pravo na uvoz, ili proizvođenje pod licencijom?

Marković Tražimo isključivo pravo na uvoz. To je naš kratkoročni plan za sledeću godinu dana. Posle toga, razmotrićemo situaciju i ako budemo imali uspeha, otvorićemo pregovore ponovo.

Mark Jeste li razmišljali kako ćete platiti za robu?

Marković Platićemo transferom preko banke.

Mark Poslat ću faks u London o našem razgovoru.

Marković Mogu da vam kažem da su svi naši uslovi napisani u ovom pismu. Možete da ga pošaljete u London.

smatrati *to consider*	**proizvođenje pod licencijom** *production under licence*
tržište *market*	**isključiv** *exclusive*
proizvod *product*	**kratkoročni plan** *short-term plan*
Zavisi od... (followed by gen.) *It depends on...*	**za sledeću godinu dana** *for the next year*
marketing *marketing*	**razmatrati, razmotriti** *to examine, discuss*
znanje *knowledge*	
trend *trend*	
koji *which*	**uspeh** *success*
menjati se, promeniti se *to change*	**otvarati, otvoriti** *to open*

iz dana u dan *from day to day*	**ponovo** *again*
transportno odeljenje *transport department*	**razmišljati, razmisliti** *to think about, consider*
kamion *lorry*	**roba** (sing. noun) *goods*
radnja *shop*	**transfer preko banke** *bank transfer*
reklamno odeljenje *advertising department*	**slati, poslati** (šaljem, pošaljem) *to send*
razvijen *developed*	**faks** *fax*
infrastruktura *infrastructure*	**uslov** *condition*
pravo na uvoz *right to import*	**napisan** *written*

Istina ili neistina?

(a) Gospodin Marković hoće prodati proizvode Markove firme.
(b) Gospodin Marković nema kamiona.
(c) Gospodin Marković će platiti za robu transferom preko banke.

—————— **Objašnjenja i komentari** ——————

Coffee

One of the first things you will be offered when visiting, either socially or on business, is coffee. The basic type of coffee is **turska kava** (*Turkish coffee*). Coffee made in this way is strong and served in small cups. It is also becoming increasingly popular to drink *espresso* coffee and instant coffee.

Economic affairs

For many years after the Second World War the state of Yugoslavia had a communist government and an economy in which there was little room for private enterprise. Companies were managed according to a system of self-managing socialism, somewhat similar in principle to the idea of workers' cooperatives. Following the division of the state into small countries, industry has largely been privatised and modern forms of information technology and commercial practice have been rapidly introduced.

Businessmen from Western Europe will find a common language with potential partners in the Serbo-Croat speaking area. Producing goods under licence is a fairly common practice whereby companies pay a fee to a foreign company to be allowed to manufacture those items in their own plants.

Information

Podatak means a piece of information. It is usually found in the plural **podaci**. If you want to find the information counter in a hotel or public building look for the sign **Informacije**.

Ključne fraze

How to:

- use words and expressions connected with business and commerce.

poslovni pregovori
proizvod
tržište
marketing
proizvođenje pod licencijom
kratkoročni plan
roba
transfer preko banke
faks

Jezični obrasci

1 Language differences

There are differences between the language as spoken in Serbia (eastern variant) and in Croatia (western variant). We have mentioned these differences before in the **Introduction**. Now that you have seen and, if you have the cassette, heard how Mr Marković speaks we can classify these differences in the following patterns:

(a) Differences in vocabulary: these differences may be variations in spelling or the use of completely different words (W = western variant; E = eastern variant).

kava (W)	kafa (E)	*coffee*
uvjet (W)	uslov (E)	*condition*
prodavaonica (W)	radnja (E)	*shop*

There are many other examples of this distinction:

kruh (W)	hleb (E)	*bread*
kolodvor (W)	stanica (E)	*station*
tisuća (W)	hiljada (E)	*thousand*

(b) Differences in vowels: in some words the vowel **e** in the eastern variant replaces **je** or **ije** in the western variant.

uspjeh (W)	uspeh (E)	*success*
mijenjati (W)	menjati (E)	*to change*
odjeljenje (W)	odeljenje (E)	*department*
poslije (W)	posle (E)	*after*
slijedeći (W)	sledeći (E)	*next*

(c) Future tense: this is written in different ways.

razmotrit ćemo (W)	razmotrićemo (E)	*we shall examine*
otvorit ćemo (W)	otvorićemo (E)	*we shall open*

In the eastern variant the future tense of verbs ending in **-ti** is formed as one word when the short form follows the infinitive, and the **-ti** is omitted from the infinitive.

(d) Infinitive patterns: in the eastern variant there is a strong tendency not to use the infinitive form, but to replace it with a pattern using the word **da** followed by the present tense. Mr Marković at one point says to Mark:

...mislimo da možemo da prodamo vaše proizvode.	...*we think that we can sell your products.*

This may be rewritten as:
...mislimo da možemo **prodati** veše proizvode.
as you have learnt with no difference in meaning.

(e) Alphabet: one of the striking differences immediately apparent to the visitor to Serbia is the use of the cyrillic alphabet. This script is similar to the one used in Russian. It is not, however, in sole use and you can find the latin alphabet in both personal and public use. Transliteration between the two alphabets presents no problem since there is one letter for each sound in both of them. (See p. 220.)

2 How to say 'which'

The word **koji** has two uses. It is used to join together two parts of a sentence and to ask questions.

(a) Joining together

Sve zavisi od marketinga i od znanja trendova. Oni se mijenjaju iz dana u dan.	*Everything depends on marketing and on knowledge of trends. They change from day to day.*

We can join these two sentences together:

Sve zavisi od marketinga i od znanja trendova koji se mijenjaju iz dana u dan.	*Everything depends on marketing and on knowlege of trends which change from day to day.*

The word **koji** is the equivalent of English *which* or *who*. It is an adjective and its ending depends on to what it refers from the first part of the sentence and how it is used in the second part of the sentence. In the example above **koji** refers to **marketing** and **znanje**. It refers to two things one of which is masculine and one of which is neuter, therefore it has to have a plural masculine ending. It is then used as the subject of the second part of the sentence and so has to be in the nominative case. It follows the same pattern of case endings as **moj**, so it has both **kojem/kojeg** and **kome/koga** forms. The long forms are used when referring to objects, and the short forms when referring to people.

Briefly, **koji** takes either singular or plural and masculine, feminine or neuter endings depending on to what it refers; while its case depends on how it is used. Look at the following example:

To je čovjek koga sam jučer vidio.	*That is the man whom I saw yesterday.*

In this example **koga** refers to **čovjek** and so is masculine singular. It is used as the object of the verb **vidio** and so it is accusative (i.e. it is the thing which is seen and not the person who sees).

To je pismo u kojem su napisani uvjeti.	*That is the letter in which the conditions are written.*

To je čovjek kome sam dao novac. *That is the person to whom I gave the money.*

(**kojem** is used as the word refers to an object, and **kome** is used because the word refers to a person)

The word for *which* after **to** (*that*) and **sve** (*everything*) is **što**:

Mark je slušao sve što je Rudolf govorio

Mark listened to everything which Rudolf was saying.

(*b*) Making questions
In questions **koji** means *which*:

Koju knjigu želite?	*Which book do you want?*
Koji je vaš stan?	*Which is your flat?*
Koja je žena uzela ključ?	*Which woman took the key?*
Kojoj ste ženi dali ključ?	*To which woman did you give the key?*

It means *which one* from a larger number of possible options.

3 Reading, having read, written, etc.

These patterns of a verb are not often found in the spoken language. They are examples of a formal or bookish style. However, you may come across them in newspapers or documents. They are easily formed:

(*a*) Čitajući (*reading*)
This is formed by adding **-ći** to the **oni** form of the verb.
It is the equivalent of the part of the verb which ends in *-ing* in English. It often means *while doing*, *by doing* or *in doing* as in the following examples:

Slušajući radio pisao je pismo.

While listening to the radio he was writing a letter.

Čitajući podatke slušao je i sve što mu je Rudolf pričao.

Reading the information he also listened to everything which Rudolf told him.

It is used when referring to two actions performed by the same subject which occur at the same time. It is formed only from imperfective verbs.

(b) Pročitavši (*Having read*)
This is formed by replacing **-o** at the end of the masculine past tense with **-vši**.

Pročitavši novine, počeo sam spremati večeru.	*Having read the newspaper I began to prepare dinner.*
Došavši u hotel Sandra je uzela ključ od sobe.	*Having arrived at the hotel Sandra took the key to the room.*

It is used when referring to two actions, the first being completed before the second takes place, performed by the same subject. It is formed only from perfective verbs.

(c) Napisan (*written*)
This is the equivalent in English of saying *something is done*. They are adjectives and agree with the noun to which they refer like any other adjective.

Uvjeti su napisani u pismu.	*The conditions are written in the letter.*
Pismo je napisano.	*The letter is written.*
Pismo je bilo napisano.	*The letter was written.*

It is formed from the infinitive:

(i) Infinitives which end in **-ati** replace **-ti** with **-n**:

napisati	napisan
čitati	čitan

(ii) Most infinitives which end in **-iti** and **-eti** (**-jeti**) replace **-iti** and **-eti** (**-jeti**) with **-jen**, and as the ending begins with **j** this may cause a preceding consonant to change as with comparative adjectives which take the **-ji** ending (see Unit 15):

vidjeti	viđen

(iii) Infinitives which end in **-nuti** replace **-ti** with **-t**:

okrenuti	okrenut

4 Subcategories of nouns

The plural forms of these three nouns do not follow the usual pattern:

gospodin	gospoda	*gentlemen*
brat	braća	*brothers*
dijete	djeca	*children*

Although they refer to more than one gentleman, brother and child these words are feminine singular nouns and they follow the regular pattern for feminine singular nouns which end in **-a** (hence, **gospodo** is the vocative form of **gospoda**). Adjectives which describe them also follow the regular pattern of feminine singular endings, while verbs are plural. Study the following examples:

Djeca su visoka.	*The children are tall.*
Imaju visoku djecu.	*They have tall children.*
Gospoda su govorila engleski.	*The gentlemen were speaking English.*

In the last example the verbal element from **biti** is plural, while the ending on **govorila** is feminine singular.

5 More about time

In the phrase **za slijedeću godinu dana** the word **dana** has no meaning. It is often found after the words **tjedan** (*week*), **mjesec** (*month*) and **godina** (*year*) without adding anything extra to the sense of the word.

6 More about cases

You have now reached a stage in Serbo-Croat when you can under-stand and produce for yourself sentences and phrases which are grammatically complicated. You have learnt all the basic forms of the verbs, case endings for adjectives (including comparative and superlative) and nouns. You have also learnt the basic meanings of those cases which often do away with the need for little words in English, such as *to*, *of*, *by*, etc. There is another example of the use of the instrumental case in this unit. Look at these examples:

Gospodin Marković će platiti robu transferom preko banke.	*Mr Marković will pay for the goods by a transfer through the bank.*
Mark će poslati pismo gospodina Markovića faksom.	*Mark will send Mister Marković's letter by fax.*

In both sentences the instrumental case is used to mean *by*. The case refers to the *instrument* by which an action is performed.

Vježbe

1. Mark has to inform his office in London about his conversation with Mr Marković. Follow the guidelines below in order to write a brief letter about the event as if you were Mark. Do not try to use complicated language, split the ideas up into separate sentences. Your intention is to convey the basic points of information.

   Say that you spoke with Mr Marković today.
   Say that he wants the exclusive right of import of our products from London.
   Say that you spoke about the conditions of the business contract with him.
   You are sending those conditions by fax.
   Say that you think the conditions are good. Mr Marković said that he would pay for the goods by bank transfer.

2. Put the correct form of **koji** into the sentences below:

   (a) To je ugovor (koji) sam jučer pročitao.
   (b) Govorio sam s gospodinom Markovićem, (koji) je generalni direktor te firme.
   (c) Moja sestra, (koji) živi u Engleskoj, radi u bolnici.
   (d) Ovo je najbolja knjiga (koji) imam.
   (e) Da li je to čovjek (koji) ste dali ključ od moje sobe?
   (f) To je škola u (koji) radim.

3. Put the correct form of **koji** into the questions below:

   (a) (Koji) faks šaljete u London?
   (b) Od (koji) konobar ste dobili čašu vode?
   (c) U (koji) sobi je gospodin Bryant?

(d) (Koji) žena je ušla u poštu?
(e) O (koji) ugovoru govorite?
(f) (Koji) sportom se bavite?

4 Make the bold parts of the following sentences plural:

(a) **Dijete je bilo** kod kuće.
(b) **Čovjek je ušao** u hotel.
(c) Vidjeli smo **gospodina** u uredu.
(d) **Gost je sjedio** u našoj dnevnoj sobi.
(e) Dobili su **čašu** vode.
(f) Dobila je pismo od **mlađeg brata**.
(g) **Kiosk je** ispred kolodvora.
(h) Nema **lijepog parka** u tom gradu.
(i) Nema **ga** kod kuće.
(j) Vidjeli su **njenog muža** u kavani.

5 Match the questions to the answers:

(a) Kamo šaljete faks?   (i) Vlakom.
(b) Kakvog čovjeka ste   (ii) Jesu.
    vidjeli tamo?
(c) Jesu li djeca bila u   (iii) U London.
    školi danas?
(d) Kako ćete putovati u   (iv) Visokoga.
    Zagreb?

Dopunsko štivo 1

Rudolf je napisao kratko pismo u kojem je rezervirao dvije sobe u jednom beogradskom hotelu.

Poštovani gospodine.
Želio bih rezervirati u Vašem hotelu dvije jednokrevetne sobe za osmi listopad. Ostali bismo tu jednu noć.
Srdačno Vas pozdravlja
Rudolf Šimunić.

The letter has a formal and polite tone, indicated by using the formula **Poštovani gospodine** (*Respected sir*) and the conditional forms of the verb. The end formula **Srdačno Vas pozdravlja Rudolf Šimunić** (Lit. *Cordially greets you Rudolf Šimunić*) is also polite. You shall learn more about letter writing in the last unit. If they were to stay for four days in Belgrade Rudolf would have reserved the rooms **od osmog do dvanaestog listopada**.

Istina ili neistina?

(a) Rudolf je rezervirao jednu sobu u Beogradu.
(b) Rudolf je rezervirao jednokrevetne sobe u Beogradu.
(c) Rudolf i Mark su ostali jednu noć u Beogradu.

——— Dopunsko štivo 2 ———

Read the passage below and answer the following questions:

Odmah poslije sastanka Mark je napisao kratku poruku koju je htio poslati faksom svom šefu u London. Kao svi veći hoteli u Zagrebu i Beogradu, i njihov hotel ima faks.

Poštovani gospodine
Danas sam razgovarao sa gospodinom Markovićem. Razgovor je bio vrlo koristan. Šaljem Vam njegovo pismo zajedno sa ovim pismom. Preporučujem da pažljivo proučite njegove uvjete za ugovor. Mislim da možemo s njim surađivati. Naš kolega iz Zagreba, gospodin Šimunić, smatra da u Beogradu nećemo dobiti bolju ponudu.
Srdačno Vas pozdravlja
Mark Bryant

šef	*boss*	**proučiti**	*to study*
koristan	*useful*	**surađivati**	*to cooperate*
pažljivo	*carefully*	**ponuda**	*offer*

1 Odakle Mark šalje svoj faks?
   (a) Iz ureda gospodina Markovića.
   (b) Iz njihovog beogradskog hotela.
   (c) Sa glavne pošte.

2 Što preporučuje Mark svom šefu?
   (a) Da pažljivo prouči Markovićeve uvjete?
   (b) Da pažljivo pročita svoju poruku.
   (c) Da dođe u Beograd.

3 Što smatra Rudolf?
   (a) Da neće dobiti ništa više od gospodina Markovića.
   (b) Da neće dobiti bolju ponudu u Beogradu.
   (c) Da je bolje da i Markov šef dođe u Beograd.

Cyrillic alphabet

Visitors to Belgrade and other towns where the cyrillic alphabet
(**ćirilica**) is used will soon get used to it. For each letter of the latin
alphabet (**latinica**) there is a corresponding cyrillic letter so it is not
difficult to find out what signs and other notices are saying. These
are the printed forms of the cyrillic alphabet (upper and lower case)
with their corresponding letter from the latin alphabet in brackets.
As you can see, the order of letters is different but with a little effort
you can get used to them:

А	а	(a)	Н	н	(n)
Б	б	(b)	Љ	љ	(nj)
В	в	(v)	О	о	(o)
Г	г	(g)	П	п	(p)
Д	д	(d)	Р	р	(r)
Ђ	ђ	(đ)	С	с	(s)
Е	е	(e)	Т	т	(t)
Ж	ж	(ž)	Ћ	ћ	(ć)
З	з	(z)	У	у	(u)
И	и	(i)	Ф	ф	(f)
Ј	ј	(j)	Х	х	(h)
К	к	(k)	Ц	ц	(c)
Л	л	(l)	Ч	ч	(č)
Љ	љ	(lj)	Џ	џ	(dž)
М	м	(m)	Ш	ш	(š)

17

U BEOGRADU
In Belgrade

In this unit you will learn how to

- say more numbers
- ask questions with *whose?*
- use reflexive verbs
- spot differences in the language
- talk about changing money
- make general enquiries at hotel reception (Units 17 and 18 also include revision exercises.)

Dijalog

Poslije sastanka Rudolf i Mark su izašli na ulicu. Mark je morao promijeniti novac. Zaustavili su se ispred banke i ušli. Mark je čekao u redu. U banci je bilo četvoro ljudi.

Mark   Kako danas stoji kurs?
Službenik Za koju valutu?

Mark	Za engleske funte.
Službenik	Danas je funta 100 dinara.
Mark	Želim promijeniti euročekove. Do koliko dinara se može ispuniti euroček?
Službenik	Do petnaest hiljada dinara. Potpišite ovde i ovde, i dajte mi, molim vas, pasoš.

---

zaustavljati se, zaustaviti se *to stop*
banka *bank*
četvoro ljudi *four people*
Kako danas stoji kurs? *What is the exchange rate today?*
službenik *desk clerk, counter clerk*
valuta *currency*
funta *pound*

euroček *Eurocheque*
Do koliko dinara se može ispuniti... *To what amount may one fill out...*
hiljada (E) *thousand*
potpisivati, potpisati (potpisujem, potpišem) *to sign*
pasoš *passport*

Poslije banke nastavili su put do hotela. Rudolf je prišao recepciji. Na recepciji su radila dvojica.

Rudolf	Dobar večer. Rezervirao sam dvije jednokrevetne sobe.
Recepcija	Dobro veče. Na čije ime, gospodine?
Rudolf	Na ime Šimunić.
Recepcija	Samo trenutak, gospodine, da vas nađem u knjizi... Da, tu ste. Rezervisali ste dve sobe za jednu noć.
Rudolf	Točno.
Recepcija	Daću vam ključeve od soba, koje se nalaze na petom spratu.
Rudolf	Naš vlak za Zagreb polazi rano ujutro. Želio bih sada platiti račun.
Recepcija	Naravno, gospodine. Kako želite da platite? U gotovom novcu ili na karticu?
Rudolf	Koje kartice primate?
Recepcija	Primamo American Express, Visa-karticu i Mastercard.
Rudolf	Platit ću na karticu. A htio bih naručiti i telefonsko buđenje u šest sati i naručiti taksi za kolodvor.
Recepcija	U redu. U koliko sati vam treba taksi?
Rudolf	Od koliko sati se služi doručak?
Recepcija	Od šest do devet sati u restoranu.
Rudolf	Onda, naručite, molim vas, taksi za petnaest do sedam.

nastavljati, nastaviti *to continue*	**Kako želite da platite?** (E) *How*
dvojica *two* (men)	*would you like to pay?*
Na čije ime? *In whose name?*	**gotov novac** *cash*
samo trenutak *just a moment*	**na karticu** *by credit card*
nalaziti, naći (nalazim, nađem;	**telefonsko buđenje** *alarm call*
nalazio, našao) *to find*	(telephone)
točno *exactly, right*	**naručivati, naručiti** (naručujem,
sprat (E) *floor, storey*	naručim) *to order*
polaziti, poći (polazim, pođem;	**...vam treba taksi?** (E) *...do you*
polazio, pošao) *to set off*	*need the taxi?*
Želio bih platiti račun. *I would like*	**služiti se, poslužiti se** *to be served*
to pay the bill.	

Istina ili neistina?

(*a*) Mark želi promijeniti novac u hotelu.
(*b*) Može se ispuniti Euroček do petnaest tisuća dinara.
(*c*) Rudolf će platiti račun na karticu.

--------- **Objašnjenja i komentari** ---------

Changing money

Money can be changed in a bank, bureau de change (**mjenjačnica**) and in the larger hotels. Cash, travellers' cheques and Eurocheques are all accepted. Hotels often charge a higher fee for changing money than do the banks. Hotels and larger shops also accept major credit cards. Recent high levels of inflation mean that it is not possible to give a realistic indication of currency exchange rates in the early 1990s.

--------- **Ključne fraze** ---------

How to:

● find somewhere to change money. **u banci**
u mjenjačnici

- ask for the rate of exchange, and in the currency.

  Kako danas stoji kurs? za engleske funte

- ask in whose name a booking is, and to reply.

  Na čije ime? Na ime...

- pay the bill.

  Želio bih platiti.

- be asked *how do you want to pay?*

  Kako želite da platite? (Kako želite platiti?)

- pay the bill.

  u gotovom novcu na karticu

- order an alarm call.

  naručiti telefonsko buđenje

- book a taxi.

  naručiti taksi

- ask when breakfast is served.

  Od koliko sati se služi doručak?

Jezični obrasci

1 More about numbers

In addition to the ones which you have already learnt there are two further sets of numbers. The first one refers to groups of children or to groups in which there are both men and women. The second refers to groups of men.

(a) Children/mixed groups
These are as follows:

dvoje	petoro
troje	šestoro
četvoro	sedmoro

Higher numbers follow the same pattern, i.e. they add **-oro** to the number. However, they are not so frequently used when referring to groups of more than ten. They are usually used alone (**dvoje** means *two children* or more often *a man and a woman*), or in combinations with the genitive case:

Vidio sam dvoje djece.	*I saw two children.*
Petoro ljudi je došlo.	*Five people came.*
	(adults with children perhaps)

When you use these numbers as a subject the verb is singular with the neuter gender in the past tense.

(*b*) **Groups of men**
These are as follows:

dvojica	petorica
trojica	šestorica
četvorica	sedmorica

Higher numbers follow the same pattern, i.e. they add **-orica** to the number. However, they are rarely used when referring to groups of more than ten. They are usually used alone (**dvojica** can only mean *two men*) or in combinations with the genitive case:

Imam dvojicu braće.	*I have two brothers.*
Njih trojica su došla.	*The three of them came.*

These are feminine nouns and they follow the regular pattern of case endings for feminine nouns. When you use these numbers as a subject the verb is plural with the feminine singular ending in the past tense (like **djeca**, etc).

It is often possible to avoid using these numbers. You can say **dva djeteta** or **dva brata**, but the other forms with **dvoje** and **dvojica** are in common usage.

2 Numbers as the subject

Subjects with **jedan**:

Jedan stol je u sobi.	*One table is in the room.*
Jedan stol je stajao u sobi.	*One table was standing in the room.*
Jedna stolica je stajala u sobi.	*One chair was standing in the room.*

With **jedan** you use a singular verb and the gender of the past tense is determined logically. The same also goes for compound numbers with **jedan**:

Trideset jedno dijete je stajalo na ulici.   *Thirty-one children were standing on the street.*

(compound numbers are those above 20, numbers 11–20 are not compound, they are one word, e.g. **jedanaest**)

Subjects with **dva/dvije**:

Dva službenika su radila u hotelu.   *Two desk clerks were working in the hotel.*

Dvije žene su plivale u moru.   *Two women were swimming in the sea.*

With **dva** and **dvije** you use a plural verb and with the past tense use **-a** with **dva** (masc. and neut. nouns) and **-e** with **dvije** (fem. nouns). The numbers **tri** and **četiri** follow the same pattern. The same also goes for compound numbers.

Dvadeset četiri konobara su radila u hotelskom restoranu.   *Twenty-four waiters worked in the hotel restaurant.*

Subjects with **pet**, **šest**, etc:

Pet kreveta je stajalo u sobi.   *Five beds stood in the room.*
Dvanaest sati je prošlo.   *Twelve hours passed.*

With all other numbers you use a singular verb and the gender of the past tense is neuter. The same also goes for compound numbers:

Četrdeset osam sati je prošlo.   *Forty-eight hours passed.*

3 To say 'whose'

The word for *whose* is **čiji**. It is an adjective and follows the usual pattern for soft adjectives. It always adds endings to **čij-**:

Na čije ime?   *In whose name?*
Čija je to žena?   *Whose wife is that?*
U čijem stanu sjedimo?   *In whose flat are we sitting?*
Ispred čije kuće ste parkirali auto?   *In front of whose house did you park the car?*

4 More about reflexive verbs

Some verbs can be used either with or without the reflexive pronoun **se**. Compare the following sentences:

Zaustavili su se ispred banke.   *They stopped in front of the bank.*

Zaustavili su auto.	*They stopped the car.*
Školski dan se završava u četiri.	*The school day finishes at four.*
Rudolf je završio posao.	*Rudolf finished the job.*

The first sentence in each example uses **se**. The second sentence does not use **se** and it answers the question *what* (*What did they stop?* and *What did Rudolf finish?*). When you have an object in such sentences you do not use **se**. Other examples are:

One se mijenja.	*He is changing.* (e.g. in personality)
Mark mijenja novac.	*Mark is changing money.*
Vratili smo se sa Hvara.	*We returned from Hvar.*
Vratili smo ključ recepciji.	*We returned the key to reception.*

5 More about variants in Serbo-Croat

The Serbian desk clerks in the bank and at hotel reception use some different words from those you have learnt.

Vowel Differences:

ovdje (W)	ovde (E)
dvije (W)	dve (E)

Different Spellings or Words:

dobar večer (W)	dobro veče (E)
rezervirati (W)	rezervisati, rezervišem (E)
kat (W)	sprat (E)

Different Language Pattern:

U koliko sati trebate taksi? (W)	*At what time do you need a taxi?*
U koliko sati vam treba taksi? (E)	*At what time do you need a taxi?*

The eastern variant tends to use the form **treba** which never changes, but the subject is put into the dative case. It is rather like saying *At what time is the taxi needed for you?*

Vježbe

1   Tko ste vi?

Ja sam Mark Bryant. Ja sam Englez. Radim u Zagrebu. Imam trideset sedam godina. Oženjen sam.

Make up similar sentences for:

	Name	Nationality	City	Age	Married
(a)	Branka	Serbian	Belgrade	23	no
(b)	Vjeko	Croatian	Split	48	yes
(c)	Margaret	English	Leeds	31	yes
(d)	Eva	German	Berlin	34	no

2   You are in the spot marked **X**. You ask a passer-by: **Molim vas, gospodine/gospođo kako mogu doći do**

(a)   kazališta?
(b)   pošte?
(c)   crkve?
(d)   glavnog trga?

Give the directions in Serbo-Croat.

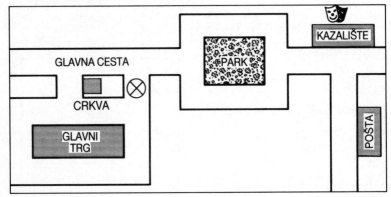

3   You walk into a restaurant and sit down for dinner. Complete the following dialogue between yourself and the waiter:

Dobar večer.
(*Good evening. Do you have the menu, please?*)
Da, izvolite, gospodine. Što biste željeli?
(*I would like soup, fish and salad.*)
Želite li nešto popiti, gospodine/gospođo?
(*What would you recommend?*)
Imamo vrlo dobro bijelo vino.
(*Then, I would like white wine, please.*)
A želite li nešto poslije?
(*May I have a coffee please?*)
Naravno. Hvala.

4 You are looking at the railway timetable in Zagreb. At what times do the following trains leave and at what times do they arrive at their destinations?

U koliko sati polazi vlak?
Vlak polazi u _____ iz Zagreba, i stiže u _____ u Beograd.

Zagreb			
(a)	8.00	12.10	Beograd
(b)	11.35	14.20	Rijeka
(c)	12.00	17.55	Split
(d)	14.45	21.45	Sarajevo

5 Kakav stan imate?

Look at the diagrams below and describe in Serbo-Croat the number and types of rooms:

(*a*)   (*b*)

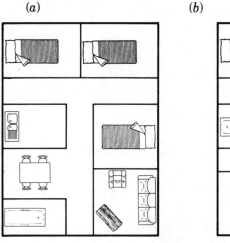 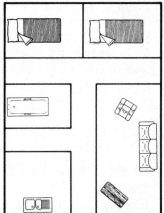

6 Fill in the date either in the nominative or the genitive as required:

(*a*) Igram tenis s Markom u srijedu   (*24 March*)

(*b*) Idem u Split početkom slijedećeg mjeseca   (*1 June*)

(*c*) Danas je   (*3 August*)

(*d*) Rudolf misli da će doći u London   (*18 November*)

Dopunsko štivo 1

Here is a recipe for the **zagrebački odrezak** which the friends ordered when they went to a restaurant in Unit Five.

6 velikih tankih telećih odrezaka
sol i papar po ukusu
6 malih ploški kuhane šunke
6 malih ploški sira
brašno
2 jaja stučena s malo mlijeka
mrvice
3 velike žlice ulja
3 velike žlice maslaca

Stavite sol i papar na teleće odreske.
Stavite na polovicu odreska plošku šunke i na nju plošku sira.
Stavite jednu polovicu odreska na drugu.
Dobro pritisnite krajeve mesa.
Stavite odreske prvo u brašno, zatim u jaje i na kraju u mrvice.
Dobro zagrijte maslac i ulje i pržite odreske na umjerenoj vatri dok ne budu svijetlosmeđi s obje strane.
Odreske poslužite s miješanom salatom, kriškama limuna i pireom od krumpira.

tanak *thin*	**polovica** *half*
teleći *veal* (adj.)	**pritisnuti** *to pinch* (together)
sol (fem.) *salt*	**kraj** *edge, end*
papar *pepper*	**zatim** *then, next*
po ukusu *according to taste*	**na kraju** *in the end, finally*
ploška kuhane šunke *slice of cooked ham*	**zagrijati** *to heat, warm up*
	pržiti *to fry*
ploška sira *slice of cheese*	**na umjerenoj vatri** *on a medium heat*
brašno *flour*	
jaje stučeno s malo mlijeka *egg beaten with a little milk*	**svijetlosmeđi** *light brown*
	s obje strane *on both sides*
mrvice *bread crumbs*	**miješana salata** *mixed salad*
ulje *oil*	**kriška limuna** *wedge of lemon*
maslac *butter*	**pire od krumpira** *mashed potato*

Now check your comprehension of the recipe with the translation on p. 231.

6 large thin veal cutlets (buy thick steaks and beat them)
salt and pepper according to taste
6 small slices of cooked ham
6 small slices of cheese (e.g. cheddar)
flour
2 eggs beaten with a little milk
bread crumbs
3 large spoons of oil
3 large spoons of butter

Put salt and pepper on the veal cutlets.
Put a slice of ham on one half of the cutlet and a slice of cheese
on top of that.
Put one half of the cutlet over the other half.
Pinch the edges of the meat firmly together.
Put the cutlets first into flour, then into the egg, and at the end
into the bread crumbs.
Heat the butter and oil and fry the cutlets on a medium heat
until light brown on both sides.
Serve the cutlets with a mixed salad, wedges of lemon and
mashed potato.

—— Dopunsko štivo 2 ——

Read the following **mali oglasi** (*small advertisements*) and answer
the questions below:

IZDAJEM trosoban komforan stan u centru Zagreba. Centralno grijanje, telefon. Plaćanje po dogovoru. Šifra 'Stan 1'.

IZDAJEM dvokrevetne sobe u vili na Braču. Blizu plaže i svih turističkih objekata. Posebni ulazi. Javite se na tel. 223 456 (Split).

IZDAJEM apartman u Dubrovniku. Dvije spavaće sobe, kupaonica i kuhinja. Balkon ima pogled na more. Tel. 155 677.

PRODAJEM poslovnu prostoriju u zgradi u centru Zagreba. Prodavaonica u prizemlju i ured na prvom katu. Šifra 'Posao'.

TRAŽIMO trosoban stan u centru Zagreba sa centralnim grijanjem i telefonom. Šifra 'Englezi'.

trosoban *three-roomed*	vila *villa*
komforan *comfortable*	objekt *facility*
grijanje *heating*	poseban ulaz *separate entry*
po dogovoru *by agreement*	prostorija *space*
šifra *box number*	prizemlje *ground floor*

Istina ili neistina?

(*a*) Stan u Zagrebu ima centralno grijanje.
(*b*) Nema posebnih ulaza u sobe na Braču.
(*c*) Netko u Zagrebu prodaje prodavaonicu u prizemlju.

18

TRI PISMA
Three letters

In this unit you will learn more about

● writing letters and short messages for people both in a social and in a business context

Poštovani...

Mark je dobio poslovno pismo iz Beograda od gospodina Markovića.

3. X. 1992.

Poštovani gospodine Brajante,

Šaljem Vam kopiju pisma koje sam dobio iz Londona. Možemo da sklopimo ugovor prema uslovima koji su dogovoreni. Čestitam Vam na uspehu u ovim našim pregovorima. Predložio bih Vam da još jednom dođete u Beograd na razgovor o mogućnosti uvoza i izvoza, a ja bih posetio London tek posle tog našeg sastanka.

Radujem se našoj budućoj saradnji.
Srdačno Vas pozdravlja

Marko Marković

kopija *copy*	**izvoz** *export*
sklopiti ugovor *sign a contract*	**posećivati, posetiti** (E) (posećujem,
dogovoren *agreed*	posetim) *to visit*
čestitati (followed by dat.)	**tek posle** (E) *only after*
to congratulate (someone)	**budući** *future*
predlagati, predložiti (predlažem,	**saradnja** (E) *co-operation*
predložim) *to suggest*	

Sandra je dobila kratko pismo od Jasne.

5. X. 1992.

Draga Sandra,

Morala sam ti odmah pisati. Ne možeš zamisliti što se sinoć desilo! Rudolf me je zaprosio. Udat ću se za njega. Nije više pitao da li bih ja htjela da se vjenčamo. Nestalo je to kolebanje. Vodili smo ozbiljan razgovor o našim osjećajima i o praktičnim stvarima. Previše sam uzbuđena da bih nastavila pisati. Javi se što prije!

Voli Te

Jasna

zamisliti *to imagine*	**voditi razgovor** *have a*
zaprositi *ask for a girl's hand*	*conversation*
in marriage	**praktičan** *practical*
nestajati, nestati (nestajem,	**uzbuđen** *excited*
nestanem) *to disappear*	**nastavljati, nastaviti** *to continue*
kolebanje *hesitation*	

Sandra piše pismo mami i tati.

10. X. 1992.

Dragi mama i tata,

Ispričavam se što dugo nisam pisala. Otkad smo se vratili s odmora život je postao burniji. Rudolf i Jasna će se vjenčati. Još se ne zna kada će to biti, ali mislim da ćemo imati svadbu tokom ove zime!

Druga stvar je još važnija. Mark je ovdje počeo otvarati tržište za svoju londonsku firmu. Njegovi šefovi su, očito, jako zadovoljni njime. Ponudili su mu da ostane u Zagrebu, i da postane glavni predstavnik u cijelom ovom kraju Evrope! Naravno, mi smo dugo razgovarali o ponudi, i došli smo do zaključka da bismo ovdje mogli lijepo živjeti. Odgovara nam grad, našli smo prijatelje a nismo daleko od Londona (samo dva sata avionom!). Mark je ovih dana imao mnogo posla u gradu, dok sam ja tražila stan. Pravi stan!

Pored toga, pisala sam svojoj školi da dajem ostavku. Jasna i moje prijateljice su me ohrabrile da ću naći posao kao nastavnica engleskog jezika. Pravo da vam kažem, već sam dobila posao u jednoj privatnoj školi za strane jezike.

Dolazimo u London za Božić. Pričat ćemo i tada o našem boravku u Zagrebu i u drugim mjestima, ne samo u prošlosti nego i u budućnosti.

Vole vas

Sandra i Mark

---

ispričavati se, ispričati se *to apologise*
otkad *from when, since*
buran *stormy*
Još se ne zna. *It is still not known.*
svadba *wedding*
tokom ove zime *during this winter*
važan *important*
očito *evidently, obviously*
nuditi, ponuditi *to offer*
doći do zaključka *to come to the conclusion*
odgovarati (with dat.) *to suit, correspond*

pravi *real*
ostavka *resignation*
ohrabrivati, ohrabriti (ohrabrujem, ohrabrim) *to encourage, cheer up*
nastavnica *teacher*
pravo da vam kažem *to tell you the truth*
privatna škola *private school*
strani jezik *foreign language*
Božić *Christmas*
tada *then*
ne samo… nego i… *not only… but also…*

Istina ili neistina?

(*a*) Gospodin Marković je pozvao Marka u Beograd.
(*b*) Rudolf i Jasna će se vjenčati.
(*c*) Sandra je tražila stan za sebe i za Marka.

Ključne fraze

Idiomatic and other phrases:

- sign a contract   **sklopiti ugovor**
- congratulations on your success   **čestitam Vam na usp(j)ehu**
- to have a conversation   **voditi razgovor**
- it is not yet known   **još se ne zna**
- to come to a conclusion   **doći do zaključka**
- to hand in one's resignation   **dati ostavku**
- to tell you the truth   **pravo da vam kažem**
- not only... but also ...   **ne samo... nego i...**

Jezični obrasci

1 Writing letters

There are a variety of formal and informal conventions used in writing letters.

(a) Formal
Beginning with:

Poštovani gospodine...	*Dear sir / Dear Mr...*
Poštovana gospođo...	*Dear madam / Dear Mrs...*

As you are addressing someone directly the vocative case is used. An alternative beginning is:

Poštovani kolega
Poštovana koleginice

The tone here is not quite so formal. The words **kolega** (masc. although ending in **-a**) and **koleginica** mean *colleague* but are more frequently used to refer to people with whom you work.

Such letters may end with:

Srdačno Vas pozdravlja...	*Yours sincerely...*

(*b*) Informal
Beginning with:

Dragi...	*Dear...* (to a man)
Draga...	*Dear...* (to a woman)

An alternative beginning is:

Zdravo...!	*Hi...!* (to a man or woman)

But in both instances you again use the vocative case for the name of the person to whom you are writing.

Such letters may end with:

Voli Te...	*Love...* (when signed by one person)
Vole Te...	*Love...* (when signed by more than one person)

An alternative ending is the less intimate:

Tvoj	*Yours* (signed by a man)
Tvoja	*Yours* (signed by a woman)

Another thing to bear in mind when writing letters is that there is a convention to spell **Vi/Vas**, etc. with a capital letter when addressing one person.

2 How to say 'from'

When saying from a place use **iz** and when saying from a person use **od**. When you would normally use **na** with a noun to mean *being there* or *going there*, then you use **s/sa** to mean *from there*. Look at the following examples:

Izašli smo iz sobe.	*We have come out of the room.*
Dobio je pismo iz Zagreba.	*He received a letter from Zagreb.*
Dobio je pismo od svog šefa.	*He received a letter from his boss.*
Idemo na odmor.	*We are going on holiday.*
Bili smo na odmoru.	*We were on holiday.*
Vratili smo se s odmora.	*We have returned from holiday.*

3 How to say 'then'

You have learnt two words for *then*:

onda (*then next*)

Stigli smo u Split, onda
smo kupili karte za brod.

*We arrived in Split, then
we bought tickets for the boat.*

tada (*at that time*)

Išli smo na Hvar na odmor.
Tada sam bio još dijete.

We went to Hvar on holiday.
I was still a child then.

4 Variants in Serbo-Croat

Another difference between the western and eastern variants of Serbo-Croat is in the spelling of foreign names and cities. In the western variant the original spellings are kept:

Mark Bryant radi u Zagrebu.
Idemo u Manchester.

In the Eastern variant the spelling is altered to a spelling which most approximates the pronunciation of the word in Serbo-Croat.

Mark Brajant radi u Zagrebu.
Idemo u Mančester.

5 Ispričavam se što

You usually use the word **da** to mean *that* in sentences like:

Rekao mi je da...
Mislio sam da...

He told me that...
I thought that...

However, in certain expressions the word **što** is used. These are in sentences in which you are about to give a reason for something. Look at the following examples:

Ispričavam se što...

I am sorry that...
(meaning *I apologise for not
having done something* after
which you can expect an
explanation)

Sretan sam što...   *I am happy that...*
                          (meaning *I am happy because*
                          of the following reasons)

Vježbe

1   You are in the tourist office in Zagreb. You want to know how much a particular journey costs and how long it takes. Make up the questions and answers as indicated in the example.

Example:

autobus, Rijeka, 350 dinars, 6 hours

Koliko košta autobusna karta za Rijeku?
Trista pedeset dinara.

Koliko dugo traje put autobusom do Rijeke?
Šest sati.

(*a*)   avion, Dubrovnik, 4 000 dinars, 45 minutes
(*b*)   vlak, Beograd, 980 dinars, 4 hours 10 minutes
(*c*)   autobus, Split, 435 dinars, 5 hours 30 minutes
(*d*)   vlak, Sarajevo, 830 dinars, 7 hours

2   Look at the weather forecasts for the following towns and answer the questions below:

Zagreb: Ujutro kratkotrajna magla, kasnije sunčano.
Pula: Vjetar slab. Dnevna temperatura od 22°C do 25°C.
Zadar: Ujutro oblačno. Dnevna temperatura od 20°C do 22°C.
Šibenik: Ujutro moguća kiša. Po podne slab vjetar.
Split: Jutarnja temperatura od 14°C do 18°C. Dnevna od 25°C do 29°C.
Hvar: Cijeli dan sunčano i slab vjetar.
Dubrovnik: Ujutro sumaglica. Danju sunčano.

(*a*)   U kojem gradu je moguća kiša?
(*b*)   Koji grad ima dnevnu temperaturu od 20°C do 22°C.
(*c*)   U kojem gradu je sunčano cijeli dan?
(*d*)   Koji grad ima kratkotrajnu maglu?

3 Answer the following questions:

   (a) Kako se kaže na srpskohrvatskom 'I have a headache'?
   (b) Kako se kaže na srpskohrvatskom 'I am going to the doctor's'?
   (c) Što znači riječ 'razglednica' na engleskom?
   (d) Što znači 'zubna pasta' na engleskom?

4 You want to reserve a room at a hotel. Write a short letter stating that you want a double room from 14 to 20 July.

5 You arrive at your hotel and you have some enquiries to make at reception. Fill in your part of the dialogue:

(*Good evening.*)
Dobar večer, gospodine/gospođo.
(*I would like an alarm call at 7.15 in the morning, please.*)
U redu, gospodine/gospođo. Odlazite li sutra?
(*Yes, I have to go to London as soon as possible. I have a business meeting there. I want to book a taxi for the airport, please.*)
U koliko sati trebate taksi?
(*At 8.00, please. Where is breakfast served?*)
U restoranu gospodine/gospođo.
(*And I shall pay the bill now.*)
U redu, gospodine/gospođo. Nadam se da ste zadovoljni našim hotelom?
(*Very pleased, thank you.*)

6 What do you say to people when:

   (a) meeting them for the first time?
   (b) greeting them in the morning?
   (c) saying goodbye?
   (d) saying good night?

Dopunsko štivo

Sandra je poslala pismo roditeljima. Tjedan dana kasnije javili su joj se njeni roditelji iz Londona. Imali su samo jednu poruku za Sandru i Marka 'Čestitamo vam!'

KEY TO THE EXERCISES

Unit 1

Dialogue True (T), False (F) (*a*) T (*b*) T (*c*) F
Exercises 1 (*a*) prijateljica (*b*) dobar večer (*c*) oprostite **2** (*a*) Ja sam Jasna. Ja sam Hrvatica. Govorim hrvatski. (*b*) Ja sam Rudolf. Ja sam Hrvat. Govorim hrvatski. (*c*) Ja sam Sandra. Ja sam Engleskinja. Govorim engleski. **3** (*a*) Ja sam Hans. Ja sam Nijemac. Govorite li njemački? Da, govorim njemački. (*b*) Ja sam Pierre. Ja sam Francuz. Govorite li francuski? Da, govorim francuski. (*c*) Ja sam Ivan. Ja sam Rus. Govorite li ruski? Da, govorim ruski. **4** (*a*) Govorite li engleski? (*b*) Govorite li francuski? (*c*) Govorite li hrvatski? (*d*) Govorite li srpski? **5** (*a*) dobro jutro (*b*) dobar dan (*c*) dobar večer (*d*) do viđenja **6** Dobar večer. Kako ste?/Drago mi je. Ja sam.../ Laku noć. **7** (*a*) Da vas upoznam. Ovo je Mark. Mark je moj muž. (*b*) Da vas upoznam. Ovo je Sandra. Sandra je moja žena.
Comprehension (*a*) F (*b*) T (*c*) T.

Unit 2

Dialogue (*a*) F (*b*) F (*c*) T.
Exercises 1 (*a*) Volim. Ne volim. (*b*) Govorim. Ne govorim. (*c*) Jesam. Nisam. (*d*) Volim. Ne volim. (*e*) Želim. Ne želim. (*f*) Želim ići. Ne želim ići. (*g*) Volim ići. Ne volim ići. (*h*) Idem. Ne idem. **2** (*a*) Voliš li kavu? (*b*) Govoriš li engleski? (*c*) Jesi li ti Englez? (*d*) Voliš li London? (*e*) Želiš li živjeti u Londonu? (*f*) Želiš li ići u grad? (*g*) Voliš li ići na posao? (*h*) Ideš li na kavu? **3** (*a*) ja sam/učim (*b*) ti želiš/ideš (*c*) mi razumijemo/učimo (*d*) vi ste/učite. **4** (*a*) grad (*b*) kavanu (*c*) školu (*d*) Zagreb (*e*) posao (*f*) kavu (*g*) gradu (*h*) Londonu (*i*) školi (*j*) poslu (*k*) kavani (*l*) predgrađu. **5** (*a*) želimo/Londonu (*b*) želim/Zagrebu (*c*) ideš/kavu (*d*) živim/gradu (*e*) živimo/predgrađu (*f*)

volite/poslu. **6** (*a*) ii, (*b*) iv, (*c*) i, (*d*) iii. **7** (*a*) dobar (*b*) žedna (*c*) naše (*d*) vaš (*e*) moja/dobra (*f*) tvoja (*g*) gladan.
Comprehension (*a*) T (*b*) F (*c*) F.

Unit 3

Dialogue (*a*) F (*b*) T (*c*) T.
Exercises 1 (*a*) Ja moram/mogu (*b*) ti govoriš/razumiješ (*c*) on dolazi/radi (*d*) mi vidimo/idemo (*e*) vi ste/govorite (*f*) oni idu/rade. **2** (*a*) parku (*b*) kavane (*c*) trgu (*d*) drveta (*e*) grad (*f*) poštu. **3** (*a*) Jasnu (*b*) spomenik (*c*) kavu/sok (*d*) vino (*e*) školu (*f*) gospodina. **4** (*a*) njen (*b*) njegovo (*c*) njena (*d*) njihov (*e*) njihovo (*f*) njihov. **5** (*a*) On je na lijevo ispred koldvora. Nije daleko od pošte. (*b*) Gdje mogu kupiti marke i koverte? Gdje je pošta? (*c*) Kamo Rudolf ide? Gdje radi? (*d*) Da, gleda Sandru. Sandra je blizu zgrade. **6** (*a*) ona (*b*) on (*c*) oni (*d*) ona (*e*) one (*f*) ono (*g*) oni (*h*) on.
Comprehension (*a*) T (*b*) F (*c*) T. **1** (*a*) **2** (*c*) **3** (*b*)

Unit 4

Dialogue (*a*) F (*b*) F (*c*) F.
Exercises 1 (*a*) pet dinara (*b*) jedanaest dinara (*c*) četiri dinara (dvadeset dinara). **2** (*b*) Sandra hoće razglednicu. Koliko košta razglednica? Razglednica košta osam dinara. (*c*) Mark hoće pivo. Koliko košta pivo? Pivo košta dvadeset dinara. (*d*) Jasna hoće šampon. Koliko košta šampon? Šampon košta sedamnaest dinara. (*e*) Zvonko hoće marku. Koliko košta marka? Marka košta dvanaest dinara. (*f*) Velimir hoće marku za Englesku. Koliko košta marka za Englesku? Marka za Englesku košta šestnaest dinara. **3** (*a*) marke/razglednice (*b*) parkove/spomenici (*c*) hoteli (*d*) ljudi (*e*) zgrade (*f*) koverte.

4 Dobar dan. Imate li razglednice? / Mogu li vidjeti velike razglednice? / Koliko košta jedna velika razglednica? / Dajte mi tri, molim vas. / Hvala. Do viđenja. **5** (*a*) Mark daje kavu Rudolfu. (*b*) Čovjek daje marku Jasni. (*c*) Mi dajemo sapun mami. (*d*) Žena daje pivo Velimiru. (*e*) Oni daju novac čovjeku. (*f*) Konobar daje vino Branki. **6** (*a*) ii, (*b*) iv, (*c*) i, (*d*) iii. **7** (*a*) mogu (*b*) govorite (*c*) žive (*d*) jeste (*e*) idu (*f*) volim. **Comprehension** (*a*) T (*b*) T (*c*) F. **1** (*b*) **2** (*c*) **3** (*c*).

Unit 5

Dialogue (*a*) T (*b*) F (*c*) F.
Exercises 1 (*a*) mu (*b*) nam (*c*) vam (*d*) joj (*e*) im (*f*) mi (*g*) ti (*h*) joj (*i*) mi (*j*) nam. **2** (*a*) Jasni (*b*) konobarima (*c*) čovjeka (*d*) zgradu (*e*) kavu (*f*) prijateljima (*g*) stolom/Jasnom (*h*) konobare (*i*) cigarete/novine (*j*) jezike. **3** Konobaru! Dobar dan. Da li imate jelovnik? / Hvala / Što mi preporučujete? / Više volim meso. Ja bih meso i salatu, molim vas. / Više volim crno, i mogu li dobiti čašu vode? **4** (*a*) iii (*b*) i (*c*) ii (*d*) iv. **5** (*a*) Imate li jelovnik? (*b*) Imate li ribu i salatu? (*c*) Dva piva, molim vas. (*d*) Mogu li dobiti čašu vode? **6** Dubrovnik. **7** (*a*) Volite li pivo? (*b*) Volite li pivo? (*c*) Kamo idete sutra? (*d*) Želite li piti bijelo vino? (*e*) Volite li ići u grad? (*f*) Mogu li dobiti čašu vode? **8** (*a*) kruha (*b*) parkova (*c*) salate (*d*) čovjeka (*e*) prijatelja (*f*) vina (*g*) ljudi (*h*) Engleza (*i*) kave (*j*) razglednica. **Comprehension** (*a*) F (*b*) F (*c*) F. **1** (*c*) **2** (*c*) **3** (*b*).

Unit 6

Dialogue (*a*) T (*b*) F (*c*) F.
Exercises 1 (*a*) pij (*b*) popijte (*c*) dođi (*d*) uzmite. **2** (*a*) sići (*b*) piti (*c*) doći (*d*) dati. **3** (*a*) Marka/Sandre (*b*) centru (*c*) centar (*d*) centru (*e*) trga (*f*) trgu (*g*) hotela/restorana (*h*) večeru (*i*) kolodvora (*j*) drveta/parku/stanice. **4** (*a*) Jasni/salatu (*b*) autobusom (*c*) Londona (*d*) Konobaru (*e*) Marku. **5** (*a*) Idite ravno i skrenite u drugu ulicu desno. (*b*) Idite do glavne ceste, skrenite lijevo onda

skrenite u prvu ulicu lijevo. (*c*) Idite do glavne ceste, skrenite desno onda skrenite u prvu ulicu desno. (*d*) Idite ravno i trg je na lijevo. **6** Hoću vas pozvati k meni danas. / Žao mi je. Možete li doći sutra? / U osam sati. / Uzmite autobus četrnaest ili tramvaj šest preko puta parka i siđite na sedmoj stanici. Moj stan je u bloku preko puta kazališta. / Moja adresa je ... Moj telefonski broj je ... **7** (*a*) Idemo k njemu. (*b*) Konobar joj je daje. (*c*) Gledamo ih na ulici. (*d*) Idite do njega. (*e*) Moram ih kupiti. (*f*) Oni im moraju pisati. (*g*) Rudolf stanuje blizu njega. (*h*) Oni je piju. **Comprehension** (*a*) F (*b*) F (*c*) T. **1** (*b*) **2** (*b*) **3** (*a*).

Unit 7

Dialogue (*a*) F (*b*) T (*c*) F.
Exercises 1 (*a*) star (*b*) vruć (*c*) svježa (*d*) odlično (*e*) žedna (*f*) skupa (*g*) bijelo (*h*) velika. **2** (*a*) lijepom (*b*) velike (*c*) skupe (*d*) treću (*e*) starog (*f*) velike (*g*) glavni (*h*) dobru/gradskoj. **3** (*a*) Pierre je Francuz. Živi u Francuskoj. Radi u uredu. (*b*) Vjekoslav je Hrvat. Živi u Hrvatskoj. Radi u restoranu. (*c*) Branka je Srpkinja. Živi u Srbiji. Radi u hotelu. (*d*) Maša je Ruskinja. Živi u Rusiji. Radi u školi. **4** (*a*) Brankinom (*b*) Markove (*c*) Sandrinu (*d*) Markov, (*e*) Rudolfov (*f*) Velimirovu. **5** Jeste li oženjeni, Rudolf? / Je li Jasna udata? **6** (*a*) ii (*b*) iv (*c*) iii (*d*) i. **7** dvadeset dva, četrdeset sedam, šezdeset četiri, dvadeset devet, sedamnaest, jedanaest, četrdeset tri, trideset osam, sedamdeset sedam, pedeset osam, devedeset, šezdeset jedan. **Comprehension** (*a*) F (*b*) T (*c*) T. **1** (*a*) **2** (*a*) **3** (*a*).

Unit 8

Dialogue (*a*) T (*b*) F (*c*) F
Exercises 1 (*a*) glavne (*b*) njegovom (*c*) crno (*d*) velikih (*e*) tvoju (*f*) udobnim. **2** (*a*) poslije (*b*) do (*c*) na (*d*) kroz (*e*) kod (*f*) iz. **3** (*a*) U dnevnoj sobi imam tri naslonjača, jedan stolić i televizor u uglu. (*b*) U kuhinji imam frižider, zamrzivač i ormare. (*c*) Imam tamo radni stol i dvije

police s knjigama. (*d*) Imam veliki stol i šest stolica za goste. **4** (*a*) iv (*b*) i (*c*) ii (*d*) iii. **5** (*a*) u osam i trideset (u pola devet) (*b*) petnaest do četiri (*c*) sedam i deset (*d*) deset do sedam (*e*) od devet sati do pet i petnaest. **6** (*a*) prije podne (*b*) večeras (*c*) noću (*d*) sutra.
Comprehension (*a*) T (*b*) T (*c*) T. **1** (*b*) **2** (*c*) **3** (*b*)

Unit 9

Dialogue (*a*) T (*b*) F (*c*) F.
Exercises 1 (*a*) Sviđaju im se ove knjige. (*b*) Sviđa mi se nogomet. (*c*) Da li vam se sviđa plivanje? (Sviđa li vam se plivanje?) (*d*) Rudolfu se sviđa košarka. (*e*) Sandri i Jasni se sviđa badminton. **2** (*a*) Čovjek mu ih daje. (*b*) Da li joj žena daje novac? (*c*) Vidim ga blizu spomenika. (*d*) Ljudi je piju u kavani. (*e*) Mark je gleda. (*f*) Pišemo joj. (*g*) Dajem im ih. (*h*) Sjeća se u Londonu. **3** Da li vam se sviđa plivanje? / Bavite li se sportom? / I ja volim igrati rukomet. Gdje je rukometno igralište? / Da li imaju zatvoren bazen? / U koliko sati radi? / Kada vi idete u sportski centar? **4** (*a*) svaki dan (*b*) svake subote (*c*) u srijedu (*d*) zimi (*e*) od svibnja do rujna (*f*) petkom (*g*) u proljeće (h) u nedjelju, (i) u. ožujku, (j) u subotu
Comprehension (*a*) F (*b*) T (*c*) T. **1** (*b*) **2** (*b*) **3** (*a*).

Unit 10

Dialogue (*a*) F (*b*) T (*c*) T.
Exercises 1 (*a*) njima (*b*) joj (*c*) nama (*d*) mnome (*e*) ih (*f*) njime (*g*) me (*h*) vama (*i*) me (*j*) tobom. **2** (*a*) Da li vam je teško? (*b*) Je li joj lako? (Da li joj je lako?) (*c*) Da li im je jasno? (*d*) Je li vam jasno? **3** (*a*) Da, teško mi je. Ne, nije mi teško. (*b*) Da, jasno im je. Ne, nije im jasno. (*c*) Da, jasno mu je. Ne, nije mu jasno. (*d*) Da, lako mi je. Ne, nije mi lako. **4** (*a*) kako (*b*) koliko (*c*) kakav (*d*) kamo (*e*) kada (*f*) tko (*g*) gdje (*h*) što. **5** (*a*) iii (*b*) ii (*c*) iv (*d*) i **6** (*a*) po Rudolfovom mišljenju (*b*) po njenom mišljenju (*c*) po mom mišljenju (*d*) po njihovom mišljenju. **7** (*a*) A je na jugu (*b*) B je na sjeveru. (*c*) C je na zapadu. (*d*) D je na istoku.

Comprehension (*a*) T (*b*) T (*c*) T. **1** (*c*) **2** (*a*) **3** (*b*)

Unit 11

Dialogue (*a*) T (*b*) F (*c*) T.
Exercises 1 (*a*) u putničku agenciju (*b*) avionske karte (*c*) povratne karte (*d*) u deset i petnaest (*e*) tri tisuće dinara (*f*) karte za brod (*g*) dva tjedna kasnije (*h*) te večeri (*i*) prije tri godine (*j*) Rudolfov kolega na poslu. **2** (*a*) Što ste pili svaki dan? (*b*) Što ste napisali? (*c*) Tko vam je dao knjigu? (*d*) Jeste li bili na Hvaru? (*e*) Jeste li bili u Dubrovniku? (*f*) Gdje su rezervirali karte? (*g*) Kad su otišli na odmor? (*h*) Kad ste bili u Dubrovniku? (*i*) Koliko košta povratna karta za Split? (*j*) Je li Rudolf radio u toj zgradi? **3** (*a*) pisao (*b*) dao (*c*) uzeli (*d*) popio. **4** (*a*) Nismo išli na Hvar prije tri godine. (*b*) Konobar mi nije dao salatu. (*c*) Konobar mi je nije dao. (*d*) Nisu kupili avionske karte u putničkoj agenciji. (*e*) Nisu ih kupili u putničkoj agenciji. (*f*) Nisam se jučer vratila iz Dubrovnika. (*g*) Nije čitao novine. (*h*) Nije ih čitao. **5** Dobar dan. Želim kupiti avionsku kartu za Dubrovnik. / U jednom smjeru, molim. Koliko košta karta? / U koliko sati ide iz Zagreba avion ponedjeljkom? / Želim kartu u ponedjeljak navečer, molim. / Imam privatnu sobu u Dubrovniku. / Hvala. Do viđenja. **6** (*a*) Koliko dugo traje put avionom od Zagreba do Splita? Četrdeset minuta. (*b*) Koliko dugo traje put autobusom od Zagreba do Rijeke? Šest sati. (*c*) Koliko dugo traje put avionom od Zagreba do Londona? Dva sata. (*d*) Koliko dugo traje put vlakom od Zagreba do Sarajeva? Sedam sati i dvadeset minuta.
Comprehension (*a*) F (*b*) T (*c*) T. **1** (*c*) **2** (*a*) **3** (*c*)

Unit 12

Dialogue (*a*) T (*b*) T (*c*) F.
Exercises 1 (*a*) Ići ćemo u dobar restoran. (*b*) Javit ću joj se. (*c*) Naći ćemo stolicu u blagavaonici. (*d*) Tko će stići? (*e*) Što ćete raditi na odmoru? (*f*) Da li ćeš mu dati ključ? (*g*) Neće doći k nama. (*h*) Neću biti na Hvaru. **2** Rekao/Rekla je (*a*) da

možemo kupiti novine tamo kod lifta. (*b*) da je zaboravio naše avionske karte. (*c*) da ćemo ih sutra dobiti. (*d*) da će nam sutra dati novac. (*e*) da prodaju razglednice, koverte i marke u hotelu. (*f*) da to nije naše pismo. (*g*) da će danas biti lijepo vrijeme. (*h*) da nisu izgubili ključ od naše sobe. (*i*) da nas je netko tražio u hotelu. (*j*) da ne zna odakle je bio. **3** Pitao/Pitala sam (*a*) da li je zaboravio gdje stanujemo. (*b*) da li će danas biti lijepo vrijeme. (*c*) da li je gospođa Bilčić kod kuće. (*d*) da li zna gdje mi je ključ. (*e*) da li će Rudolf doći u London. (*f*) da li je bio/bila u Engleskoj. (*g*) da li je bila u Engleskoj. (*h*) da li mogu dobiti čašu vode. (*i*) da li mogu doći sutra. (*j*) da li idemo k njegovom bratu sutra. **4** (*a*) netko (*b*) ništa (*c*) negdje (*d*) nikad (*e*) nešto (*f*) nigdje. **5** (*a*) iv (*b*) i (*c*) iii (*d*) ii. **6** Dobar dan. Je li gospodin Šimunić na poslu? / Molim vas, dajte mi njegov lokal. / Halo. Ja sam… / Zaboravio sam vašu adresu. Možete li mi reći gdje radite? / Mogu li danas doći k vama? / Hvala. Do viđenja. **Comprehension** (*a*) T (*b*) F (*c*) T. **1** (*b*) **2** (*b*) **3** (*a*).

Unit 13

Dialogue (*a*) T (*b*) F (*c*) F.
Exercises 1 petsto šezdeset sedam, dvjesta trideset devet, osamsto sedam, trista jedan, tisuća petsto, tri tisuće sedamsto devedeset. **2** (*a*) četrnaesti ožujak (*b*) prvi lipanj (*c*) osmi kolovoz (*d*) trećeg rujna (*e*) dvadeset petog lipnja (*f*) dvadeset sedmog prosinca (*g*) tisuću devetsto pedesete godine (*h*) tisuću devetsto šezdeset druge godine (*i*) dvadeset petog svibnja/ tisuću devetsto sedamdeset prve godine (*j*) jedanaestog siječnja/tisuću devetsto trideset pete godine. **3** (*a*) budućnosti (*b*) godinama (*c*) još (*d*) vremena (*e*) prošlosti (*f*) cijeli (*g*) čim. **4** (*a*) hoćete (*b*) hoću (*c*) hoće (*d*) htjela. **5** (*a*) tužno (*b*) veselo (*c*) iskreno (*d*) prijateljski. **6** (*a*) iii (*b*) iv (*c*) i (*d*) ii. **7** (*a*) Pije mi se čaj. (*b*) Danas nam se ide u grad. (*c*) Kupa joj se. (*d*) Danas mi se ide na plažu. **8** Tužan/Tužna sam. / Zato što mi se ne vraća kući. / Imam namjeru

da se vratim. / Ne ljutim se na vas. Radujem se povratku. **9** (*a*) sebe (*b*) sobom (*c*) sebe (*d*) sebi. **Comprehension** (*a*) T (*b*) F (*c*) F. **1** (*c*) **2** (*a*) **3** (*b*)

Unit 14

Dialogue (*a*) F (*b*) T (*c*) T.
Exercises 1 (*a*) Da (*b*) Ako (*c*) Da (*d*) Da (*e*) Ako/Kad (*f*) Ako (*g*) Ako (*h*) Da (*i*) Da (*j*) Ako/Kad. **2** Probudio sam se rano jutros. / Odlučio sam otići na plažu prije doručka. / Ako se vratim u devet sati, možemo ići zajedno na doručak. / Ako se ne vratim u devet, nemoj me čekati. / Idi na doručak. Kupit ću nešto na plaži. / Vidjet ću te u deset sati u našoj sobi. **3** (*a*) prešli (*b*) idete (*c*) izašla (*d*) doći (*e*) zalazi (*f*) prolazimo. **4** (*a*) kroz (*b*) na (*c*) po (*d*) iz (*e*) na (*f*) za (*g*) s (*h*) kod. **5** (*a*) kome (*b*) čime (*c*) nikoga (*d*) čega (*e*) ničega (*f*) koga (*g*) kome (*h*) nekome. **6** (*a*) iii (*b*) iv (*c*) i (*d*) ii. **Comprehension** (*a*) T (*b*) F (*c*) T. **1** (*a*) **2** (*b*) **3** (*c*).

Unit 15

Dialogue (*a*) T (*b*) F (*c*) T.
Exercises 1 Ne osjećam se dobro. / Boli me glava. / Jučer me je počela boljeti. / Bolio me je stomak prošlog tjedna, ali je to prošlo. / **2** (*a*) glava (*b*) ruka (*c*) noga (*d*) oko (*e*) uho (*f*) usta. **3** (*a*) starija (*b*) viši (*c*) mlađi (*d*) bolji (*e*) skuplji (*f*) blažom (*g*) veselijeg (*h*) veće. **4** najstarija/ najviši/ najmlađoj/ najbolji/ najskuplji/ najblažom/ najveselijeg/ najveće. **5** (*a*) ljepše (*b*) toplije (*c*) hladnije (*d*) lakše. **6** (*a*) iii (*b*) i (*c*) iv (*d*) ii. **Comprehension** (*a*) F (*b*) T (*c*) F. **1** (*a*) **2** (*c*) **3** (*b*).

Unit 16

Dialogue (*a*) T (*b*) F (*c*) T.
Exercises 1 Danas sam razgovarao s gosodinom Markovićem./ Želi isključivo pravo na uvoz naših proizvoda iz Londona./ Pričao sam s njim o uvjetima poslovnog ugovora./ Šaljem te uvjete ovim faksom./ Mislim da su uvjeti dobri./

Gospodin Marković je rekao da će platiti za robu transferom preko banke./ **2** (*a*) koji (*b*) koji (*c*) koja (*d*) koju (*e*) kome (*f*) kojoj. **3** (*a*) koji (*b*) kog (*c*) kojoj (*d*) koja (*e*) kojem (*f*) kojim. **4** (*a*) deca su bila (*b*) ljudi su ušli (*c*) gospodu (*d*) gosti su sjedjeli (*e*) čaše (*f*) mlađe braće (*g*) kiosci su (*h*) lijepih parkova (*i*) ih (*j*) njihove muževe. **5** (*a*) iii (*b*) iv (*c*) ii (*d*) i.
Comprehension (*a*) F (*b*) T (*c*) T. **1** (*b*) **2** (*a*) **3** (*b*)

Unit 17

Dialogue (*a*) F (*b*) T (*c*) T.
Exercises 1 (*a*) Ja sam Branka. Ja sam Srpkinja. Radim u Beogradu. Imam dvadeset tri godine. Nisam udata. (*b*) Ja sam Vjeko. Ja sam Hrvat. Radim u Splitu. Imam četrdeset osam godina. Oženjen sam. (*c*) Ja sam Margaret. Ja sam Engleskinja. Radim u Leedsu. Imam trideset jednu godinu. Udata sam. (*d*) Ja sam Eva. Ja sam Njemica. Radim u Berlinu. Imam trideset četiri godine. Nisam udata. **2** (*a*) Idite do glavne ceste, skrenite lijevo, idite kroz park, kazalište se nalazi na lijevo. (*b*) Idite do glavne ceste, skrenite desno, idite kroz park, skrenite desno kod kazališta, idite ravno i pošta se nalazi na lijevo. (*c*) Idite do glavne ceste, skrenite lijevo, idite ravno i skrenite u prvu ulicu desno (*d*) Idite ravno, ne prema glavnoj cesti, glavni trg se nalazi na desno. **3** Dobar večer. Imate li jelovnik, molim vas? / Ja bih juhu, ribu i salatu. / Što biste preporučili? / Onda, ja bih bijelo vino, molim. / Mogu li dobiti kavu, molim vas? **4** (*a*) Vlak polazi u osam sati iz Zagreba, i stiže u dvanaest i deset u Beograd. (*b*) Vlak polazi u dvadeset pet do dvanaest iz Zagreba, i stiže u dva i dvadeset po podne na Rijeku. (*c*) Vlak polazi u dvanaest sati iz Zagreba, i stiže u pet do šest po podne u Split. (*d*) Vlak polazi u petnaest do tri iz Zagreba, i stiže u petnaest do deset navečer u Sarajevo. **5** (*a*) dvije spavaće sobe, dnevna soba, kupaonica i kuhinja. (*b*) tri spavaće sobe, blagovaonica, dnevna soba, kuhinja i kupaonica. **6** (*a*) dvadeset četvrtog ožujka (*b*) prvog lipnja (*c*) treći kolovoz, osamnaestog studenog.

Comprehension (*a*) T (*b*) F (*c*) T.

Unit 18

Dialogue (*a*) T (*b*) T (*c*) T.
Exercises 1 (*a*) Koliko košta avionska karta za Dubrovnik? Četiri tisuće dinara. Koliko dugo traje put avionom do Dubrovnika? Četrdeset pet minuta. (*b*) Koliko košta vozna karta za Beograd? Devetsto osamdeset dinara. Koliko dugo traje put vlakom do Beograda? Četiri sata i deset minuta. (*c*) Koliko košta autobusna karta za Split? Četiristo trideset pet dinara. Koliko dugo traje put autobusom do Splita? Pet sati i trideset minuta. (*d*) Koliko košta vozna karta za Sarajevo? Osamsto trideset dinara. Koliko dugo traje put vlakom do Sarajeva? Sedam sati. **2** (*a*) U Šibeniku (*b*) Zadar (*c*) U Hvaru (*d*) Zagreb. **3** (*a*) Boli me glava. (*b*) Idem k liječniku. (*c*) postcard (*d*) toothpaste. **4** Poštovani gospodine, Želio bih rezervirati u Vašem hotelu jednu dvokrevetnu sobu od četrnaestog do dvadesetog srpnja. Srdačno Vas pozdravlja... **5** Dobar večer. / Želio/Željela bih telefonsko buđenje u sedam i petnaest ujutro, molim. / Da, moram ići u London što prije. Imam tamo poslovni sastanak. Želim naručiti taksi za aerodrom, molim. / U osam sati, molim vas. Gdje se služi doručak? / A ja ću sad platiti račun. / Vrlo zadovoljan/zadovoljna, hvala. **6** (*a*) drago mi je (*b*) dobro jutro (*c*) do viđenja (*d*) laku noć.

SUMMARY OF
—— LANGUAGE ——
PATTERNS

—————— General ——————

In this section you will find tables of the basic endings to nouns, adjectives and verbs which you have learnt in this course.

Remember that Serbo-Croat has some important spelling rules. Some consonants change when they occur before the vowel **i** in nouns: **k** changes to **c**, **g** changes to **z**, **h** changes to **s**. For example:

kiosk	kiosci
knjiga	u knjizi
orah (*walnut*)	orasi (*walnuts*)

There are some exceptions, such as personal names (e.g. **Branka** to **Branki**) and other isolated examples (e.g. **taška** to **u taški**).

Another spelling rule concerns consonants which occur before '**j**'. This is particularly important when forming the comparative of the adjectives (see Unit 15 for details).

Serbo-Croat is spelt as it is pronounced. This has the following consequences:

(*a*) it tends to avoid double consonants except in the superlative form of adjectives
e.g. jak, jači, najjači.

(b) when two consonants come into contact in a word because of losing the separating vowel the spelling of the word alters to match the pronunciation:

e.g. težak (masc.) teško (neut.)

Judge your spelling according to pronunciation.

Masculine and neuter nouns and adjectives are effected by soft consonants. They are c, č, ć, dž, đ, j, lj, nj, š and ž. The most important effect is the change of **o** to **e** after one of these consonants. Note that some neuter nouns ending in **e** do not necessarily follow one of these consonants. You will find examples of these below.

Beware that in some books, and other printed material, the letter **đ** appears as **dj**.

———— Nouns ————

Masculine

	singular	plural	singular	plural
nom.	grad	gradovi	prijatelj	prijatelji
voc.	grade	gradovi	prijatelju	prijatelji
acc.	grad	gradove	prijatelja	prijatelje
gen.	grada	gradova	prijatelja	prijatelja
dat.	gradu	gradovima	prijatelju	prijateljima
ins.	gradom	gradovima	prijateljem	prijateljima

In the singular of masculine nouns the accusative of inanimate objects is the same as the nominative, while the accusative of animate beings (human and animal) is the same as the genitive.

Sometimes there is a penultimate **a** which disappears when case endings are added. The **a** reappears in the genitive plural:

Nijemac (nom.) **Nijemca** (gen. singular) **Nijemaca** (gen. plural).

Similarly, in nouns which end in two or more consonants these letters are usually separated in the genitive plural by **a**, like the word for a *student*:

student (nom.) **studenta** (gen. singular) **studenata** (gen. plural).

Most masculine nouns of one syllable add **-ov-** before case endings (like **gradovi**) or **-ev-** after a soft consonant (like **muževi**).

Most masculine nouns end in a consonant. Some, however, end in **o** which converts to **l** when case endings are added:

posao (nom.)   **posla** (gen. singular).

Some masculine nouns end in **a**. They follow the pattern of the feminine nouns which end in **a** but all adjectives and verbs agree with them as if they were masculine: **Ovo je moj tata**.

Feminine				
	singular	plural	singular	plural
nom.	žena	žene	stvar	stvari
voc.	ženo	žene	stvar	stvari
acc.	ženu	žene	stvar	stvari
gen.	žene	žena	stvari	stvari
dat.	ženi	ženama	stvari	stvarima
ins.	ženom	ženama	stvari	stvarima

Feminine nouns which end in a consonant have an alternative instrumental singular form with **-ju** (e.g. **stvar** to **stvarju**).

In nouns which end in two or more consonants before **a** these letters are usually separated in the genitive plural by **a** (e.g. **marka** to **maraka**). Some also take the alternative ending **-i** (e.g. **torba** (*bag*) to **torbi**).

Neuter				
	singular	plural	singular	plural
nom.	selo	sela	more	mora
voc.	selo	sela	more	mora
acc.	selo	sela	more	mora
gen.	sela	sela	mora	mora
dat.	selu	selima	moru	morima
ins.	selom	selima	morem	morima

In nouns which end with two or more consonants before **o** or **e** these letters are usually separated by **a** in the genitive plural (e.g. **pismo** to **pisama**).

Some neuter nouns add **-en-** and others **-et** before adding the case endings:

vrijeme (nom.)   vremena (gen. singular)
dijete (nom.)   djeteta (gen. singular).

Adjectives

Masculine

	singular	singular (adjective ending in soft consonant)
nom.	star/stari	vruć/vrući
voc.	stari	vrući
acc.	(as nom. or gen.)	(as nom. or gen.)
gen.	starog(a)	vrućeg(a)
dat.	starom(e) (u)	vrućem(u)
ins.	starim	vrućim

Feminine

	singular	singular (adjective ending in soft consonant)
nom.	stara	vruća
voc.	stara	vruća
acc.	staru	vruću
gen.	stare	vruće
dat.	staroj	vrućoj
ins.	starom	vrućom

Neuter

	singular	singular (adjective ending in soft consonant)
nom.	staro	vruće
voc.	staro	vruće
acc.	staro	vruće
gen.	starog(a)	vrućeg(a)
dat.	starom(e) (u)	vrućem(u)
ins.	starim	vrućim

Plural

	Masc.	Fem.	Neut.
nom.	stari	stare	stara
voc.	stari	stare	stara
acc.	stare	stare	stara
gen.	starih	starih	starih
dat.	starim(a)	starim(a)	starim(a)
ins.	starim(a)	starim(a)	starim(a)

The additional vowels are usually added when the adjective is used without a noun.

In some adjectives the penultimate 'a' disappears when you add case endings. This sometimes has consequences for spelling:

bolestan (masc.)	bolesna (fem.)
dobar (masc.)	dobra (fem.)
kakav (masc.)	kakva (fem.)
težak (masc.)	teška (fem.)

Here is the pattern of changes for **koji** which is similar to **moj**, **tvoj** and **svoj** in having a shorter form without **-je-** in the middle:

	singular Masc.	Fem.	Neut.	plural Masc.	Fem.	Neut.
nom.	koji	koja	koje	koji	koje	koja
acc.	nom/gen	koju	koje	koje	koje	koja
gen.	kog(a) kojeg(a)	koje	kog(a) kojeg(a)	kojih	kojih	kojih
dat.	kom(e) kojem(u)	kojoj	kom(e) kojem(u)	kojim(a)	kojim(a)	kojim(a)
ins.	kojim	kojom	kojim	kojim(a)	kojim(a)	kojim(a)

Personal Pronouns

Singular

nom.	ja	ti	on	ona	ono
acc.	mene	tebe	njega	nju	njega
	me	te	ga	ju, je	ga
gen.	mene	tebe	njega	nje	njega
	me	te	ga	je	ga
dat.	meni	tebi	njemu	njoj	njemu
	mi	ti	mu	joj	mu
ins.	mnom(e)	tobom	njim(e)	njom(e)	njim(e)

Plural

nom.	mi	vi	oni	one	ona
acc.	nas	vas	njih	njih	njih
	nas	vas	ih	ih	ih
gen.	nas	vas	njih	njih	njih
	nas	vas	ih	ih	ih
dat.	nama	vama	njima	njima	njima
	nam	vam	im	im	im
ins.	nama	vama	njima	njima	njima

Verbs

There are three basic categories of verbs distinguished by the vowel which occurs before the ending:

- **a** category

ja	čitam	mi	čitamo
ti	čitaš	vi	čitate
on/a/o	čita	oni/e/a	čitaju

- **e** category

ja	idem	mi	idemo
ti	ideš	vi	idete
on/a/o	ide	oni/e/a	idu

- **i** category

ja	radim	mi	radimo
ti	radiš	vi	radite
on/a/o	radi	oni/e/a	rade

There is not always an obvious link between the infinitive and the present tense. However, if you know the **ja** form of the present tense you will be able to make all the other forms as almost all verbs follow one of these patterns. Important exceptions are **biti** and **moći** (see Unit 3) and **htjeti** (see Unit 4).

For how to make commands see Unit 6.

For how to form the past tense see Unit 11.

For how to form the future tense see Unit 12.

For how to form the conditional and use *if* see Unit 14.

SERBO-CROAT–ENGLISH
VOCABULARY

The following vocabulary consists of words used in the **Dialogues** and **Comprehension** passages of this course. Take note:
(a) the gender of nouns is indicated by **m** (masculine), **f** (feminine) or **n** (neuter) and by **pl** (plural) if it is a noun usually used in the plural;
(b) adjectives are given in the masculine singular nominative ending without **-i** when possible, followed by the endings for feminine and neuter nominative singular indicating when the penultimate **-a-** disappears (e.g. dobar, -bra, -bro);
(c) verbs are given in pairs with the imperfect form first, where there is only one verb it either functions as both imperfect and perfect or is the form which you have learnt to use in the language patterns explained in this course;
(d) the cases which follow prepositions are given;
(e) words characteristic of the eastern variant are marked with (E).

a *and, but*
adresa (f) *address*
aerodrom (m) *airport*
agencija (f) *agency*
ako *if*
ali *but*
ambulanta (f) *clinic*
Amerika (f) *America*
antibiotike (f pl) *antibiotics*
apartman (m) *holiday flatlet*
aperitif (m) *aperitif*
aspirin (m) *aspirin*
atletski, -a, -o *athletic*
auto (m) *car*
autobus (m) *bus*
autobusni, -a, -o *bus*
autoput (m) *motorway*
avion (m) *airplane*
avionski, -a, -o *airplane*
balkon (m) *balcony*
banka (f) *bank*
bar (m) *bar*
baš *quite*
baviti se *to take part in, to be occupied with*
bazen (m) *swimming-pool*
benzin (m) *petrol*

benzinska pumpa (f) *petrol pump, petrol station*
bez *without* (with gen. case)
bijel, -a, -o *white*
biti *to be*
blag, -a, -o *gentle*
blagajna (f) *checkout*
blagajnica (f) *checkout operator*
blagovaonica (f) *dining room*
blizina (f) *vicinity*
blizu *near* (with gen. case)
blok (m) *block of flats*
Bog (m) *God*
boja (f) *colour*
bolestan, -sna, -sno *ill*
bolnica (f) *hospital*
boljeti *to hurt, to ache*
bolji, -a, -e *better*
boraviti *to stay*
Božić (m) *Christmas*
brada (f) *chin*
brak (m) *marriage*
brašno (n) *flour*
brat (m) *brother*
brinuti se *to worry*
brod (m) *boat, ship*
broj (m) *number*

brz, -a, -o *quick, fast*
buditi se, probuditi se *to wake up*
budući, -a, -e *future*
budućnost (f) *future*
buran, -rna, -rno *stormy*

centar (m) *centre*
cesta (f) *road*
cigareta (f) *cigarette*
cijei, -a, -o *whole*
cipele (f pl) *shoes*
cjenovnik (m) *price list*
crkva (f) *church*
crn, -a, -o *black*
crno vino (n) *red wine*
crven, -a, -o *red*

čaj (m) *tea*
čamac (m) *boat*
čarapa (f) *sock*
čaša (f) *glass*
ček (m) *cheque*
čekati *to wait*
čestitati *to congratulate*
četvrtak (m) *Thursday*
čiji, -a, -e *whose*
čim *as soon as*
činiti se *to seem*
čitati, pročitati *to read*
čovjek (m) *person, man*
čuti *to hear*

da *yes, that*
dalek, -a, -o *far, distant*
daleko od *far from* (with gen. case)
Dalmacija (f) *Dalmatia*
dan (m) *day*
Danska *Denmark*
davati, dati *to give*
desno *right*
dešavati se, desiti se *to happen*
detaljan, -ljna, -ljno *detailed*
dijete (n) *child*
dinar (m) *dinar*
direktno *directly*
divan, -vna, -vno *wonderful*
dječji, -a, -e *children's*
djevojka (f) *girl, young lady*
dnevni, -a, -o *day, daily*
do *up to, as far as* (with gen. case)
do viđenja *goodbye*
dobar, -bra, -bro *good, fine*
dobiti *to get, to receive*
dogovor (m) *agreement*
dogovoren, -a, -o *agreed*

dok *while*
doktor (m) *doctor*
dolaziti, doći *to come*
donje rublje (n) *underwear*
doručak (m) *breakfast*
dosta *enough, much* (with gen. case)
drago mi je *pleased to meet you*
drugi, -a, -o *other, another, second*
društvo (n) *company, society*
drvo (n) *tree*
dva, dvije *two*

džem (m) *jam*
džep (m) *pocket*

ekran *screen*
Engleska *England*
  engleski, -a, -o *English*
  Englez (m) *Englishman*
  Engleskinja (f) *Englishwoman*
euroček (m) *eurocheque*
evo *here is* (with gen. case)

faks (m) *fax*
fasada (f) *facade*
firma (f) *firm, company*
Francuska *France*
  francuski, -a, -o *French*
  Francuz (m) *Frenchman*
  Francuskinja (f) *Frenchwoman*
frizerski salon (m) *hairdressing salon*
frižider (m) *fridge*
funta (f) *pound*

garaža (f) *garage*
gazdarica (f) *landlady*
gdje *where*
generalni direktor (m) *general manager*
glačati *to iron*
gladan, -dna, -dno *hungry*
glavan, -vna, -vno *main*
gledati, pogledati *to look at*
godina (f) *year*
gori, -a, -e *worse*
gospodin (m) *Mr, gentleman*
gospođa (f) *Mrs, madame*
gospođica (f) *Miss, young lady*
gost (m) *guest*
gotov novac (m) *cash*
govoriti *to speak*
grad (m) *town*
gradski, -a, -o *urban*
grijanje (n) *heating*
grlo (n) *throat*
gubiti, izgubiti *to lose*

halo *hello* (on telephone)
haljina (f) *dress*
hiljada (f) (E) *thousand*
hlače (f pl) *trousers*
hladan, -dna, -dno *cold*
hleb (m) (E) *bread*
hokej (m) *hockey*
hotel (m) *hotel*
Hrvatska *Croatia*
  hrvatski, -a, -o *Croatian*
  Hrvat (m) *Croat* (man)
  Hrvatica (f) *Croat* (woman)
htjeti *to want*
hvala *thank you*

i *and*
ići *to go*
igralište (n) *pitch, court, playing area*
igranje (n) *game, playing*
igrati *to play*
ili *or*
imati *to have*
ime (n) *name*
inače *otherwise*
industrijski, -a, -o *industrial*
infekcija (f) *infection*
informacije (f pl) *information*
infrastruktura (f) *infrastructure*
Irska *Ireland*
isključiv, -a, -o *exclusive*
iskreno *sincerely*
ispitivati, ispitati *to question*
ispod *under* (with gen. case)
ispred *in front of* (with gen. case)
ispričavati se, ispričati se *to apologise*
ispuniti *to fill out* (cheque, form)
isti, -a, -o *same*
istina (f) *truth*
istok (m) *east*
Istra (f) *Istria*
Italija (f) *Italy*
izdavati *to let out, to rent*
izgledati (dobro) *to look* (well)
izlaz (m) *exit*
izlaziti, izaći *to go out*
iznajmljivati, iznajmiti *to rent*
izvan *outside* (with gen. case)
izvolite *here you are*
izvoz (m) *export*

ja *I*
jaje (n) *egg*
jak, -a, -o *strong*
jakna (f) *jacket*

jasno *clear, understood*
javljati se, javiti se *to be in touch, to contact*
jedan, -dna, -dno *one*
jelo (n) *dish, meal*
jelovnik (m) *menu*
jer *for, since*
jesti *to eat*
jezik (m) *language, tongue*
još *else, more*
još uvijek *still*
jug (m) *south*
juha (f) *soup*
jutarnji, -a, -e *morning*
jutro (n) *morning*

k *towards* (with dat. case)
kabina (f) *booth*
kada *when*
kafa (f) (E) *coffee*
kakav -kva, -kvo *what kind of*
kako *how*
  kako da ne *of course*
  kako to? *how come?*
kamion (m) *lorry*
kamo *where to*
kao *as, like*
kaput (m) *coat*
karta (f) *ticket, map*
  karta u jednom smjeru *one-way ticket*
  povratna karta *return ticket*
  karta prvog razreda *first-class ticket*
  karta drugog razreda *second-class ticket*
kartica (f) *credit card*
kasnije *later*
kašalj (m) *cough*
kašljati *to cough*
kat (m) *floor, storey*
kauč (m) *couch*
kava (f) *coffee*
kavana (f) *café*
kazalište (n) *theatre*
kazati *to say, tell*
kćerka (f) *daughter*
kemijski čistiti *to dry-clean*
kino (n) *cinema*
kiosk (m) *kiosk*
kiša (f) *rain*
kišobran (m) *umbrella*
klima (f) *climate*
klizanje (n) *skating*
ključ (m) *key*

knjiga (f) *book*
kod *at the house of* (with gen. case)
koji, -a, -e *who, which*
kola (n pl) *car*
kola za hitnu pomoć *ambulance*
kolač (m) *cake*
kolebanje (n) *hesitation*
kolega (m) *colleague, person at work*
koliko *how much, how many*
kolodvor (m) *station*
koljeno (n) *knee*
komforan, -rna, -rno *comfortable*
kompjutor (m) *computer*
kompjutorski, -a, -o *computer*
konačno *at last*
konobar (m) *waiter*
konobarica (f) *waitress*
kopija (f) *copy*
koristan, -sna, -sno *useful*
koristiti *to use*
kosa (f) *hair*
košarka (f) *basketball*
koštati *to cost*
košulja (f) *shirt*
koverta (f) *envelope*
kraj (m) *area, end*
kraj *next to* (with gen. case)
krasti, ukrasti *to steal*
kratak, -tka, -tko *short*
kratkoročan, -čna, -čno *short-term*
kratkotrajan, -jna, -jno *short-lived*
kretati, krenuti *to set off*
krevet (m) *bed*
kriška (f) *wedge, piece*
kriv, -a, -o *wrong, guilty, at fault*
kroz *through* (with acc. case)
kruh (m) *bread*
kucati *to knock*
kuća (f) *house*
kuglana (f) *bowling alley*
kuhati *to cook*
kuhinja (f) *kitchen*
kulturan, -rna, -rno *cultural*
kupaći kostim (m) *swimming costume*
kupaonica (f) *bathroom*
kupati se *to bathe*
kupiti *to buy*
kurs (m) *exchange rate*

lagan, -a, -o *light*
lak, -a, -o *easy, light*
laku noć *good-night*
led (m) *ice*

leđa (n pl) *back*
lice (n) *face*
lift (m) *lift*
lignje (f pl) *squid*
lignje na ribarski način *squid 'fisherman style'*
liječnica (f) *doctor* (woman)
liječnik (m) *doctor* (man)
lijep, -a, -o *beautiful, nice*
lijevo *left*
limun (m) *lemon*
lipanj (m) *June*
listopad (m) *October*
lokal (m) *extension* (telephone)
loš, -a, -e *bad*
lozovača (f) *grape brandy*
luka (f) *harbour*

ljeti *in summer*
ljeto (n) *summer*
ljubazan, -zna, -zno *kind*
ljudi (m pl) *people, men*
ljut, -a, -o *angry*
ljutiti se *to be angry*

magla (f) *fog*
majica (f) *T-shirt*
majka (f) *mother*
Makedonija (f) *Macedonia*
makedonski, -a, -o *Macedonian*
Makedonac (m) *Macedonian man*
Makedonka (f) *Macedonian woman*
mali, -a, -o *small*
malo *a little*
Mama (f) *Mum*
marka (f) *stamp*
marketing (m) *marketing*
maslac (m) *butter*
medecina (f) *medicine*
mediteranski, -a, -o *Mediterranean*
međutim *however*
mehaničar (m) *mechanic*
menjati, promeniti (E) *change*
meso (n) *meat*
mi *we*
mijenjati se, promijeniti se *to change*
miješan, -šna, –šno *mixed*
milijun (m) *million*
miran, -rna, -rno *peaceful*
misliti *to think*
mišljenje (n) *opinion*
mjenjačnica (f) *exchange office, bureau de change*
mjesec (m) *month*

mjesto (n) *place*
mlad, -a, -o *young*
mlijeko (n) *milk*
mlijeko za sunčanje *suntan lotion*
mnogo *many, much, a lot of* (with gen. case)
moći *to be able, can*
mogući, -a, -e *possible*
mogućnost (f) *possibility*
moj, -a, -e *my*
molim *please*
moliti, zamoliti *to ask for, to beg*
morati *to have to, must*
more (n) *sea*
morski, -a, -o *sea*
možda *perhaps*
mraz (m) *frost*
mrvice (f pl) *breadcrumbs*
muž (m) *husband*

na *on* (with dat. case)
na *to* (with acc. case)
na žalost *unfortunately*
nacionalni specijalitet (m) *national dish*
nadati se *to hope*
nalaziti, naći *to find*
nalaziti se *to be situated*
namjera (f) *intention*
namještaj (m) *furniture*
naplata (f) *fee*
napuštati, napustiti *to leave*
naravno *of course*
naručivati, naručiti *to order*
naselje (n) *housing estate*
naslonjač (m) *armchair*
nastavljati, nastaviti *to continue*
nastavnica (f) *teacher*
nastavnik (m) *teacher*
naš, -a, -e *our*
natrag *backwards, back*
navečer *in the evening*
ne *no, not*
nebo (n) *sky*
nedjelja (f) *Sunday*
negdje *somewhere*
nego *than*
neki, -a, -o *some, a few*
nema na čemu *don't mention it*
nestajati, nestati *to disappear*
nešto *something*
netko *someone*
ništa *nothing*
nitko *no-one*

noć (f) *night*
noćenje (n) *overnight stay*
noćni klub (m) *night club*
noga (f) *leg, foot*
nogomet (m) *football*
nos (m) *nose*
nov, -a, -o *new*
novac (m) *money*
novčanik (m) *wallet, purse*
novine (f pl) *newspaper*
nož (m) *knife*
nuditi, ponuditi *to offer*

njegov, -a, -o *his*
Njemačka *Germany*
njemački, -a, -o *German*
Nijemac (m) *German* (man)
Njemica (f) *German* (woman)
njen (njezin), -a, -o *her*
njihov, -a, -o *their*

o *about* (with dat. case)
obala (f) *coast*
obalan, -lna, -lno *coastal*
obično *usually*
obitelj (f) *family*
objekat (m) *facility, object*
oblačan, -čna, -čno *cloudy*
oblak (m) *cloud*
obrok (m) *meal*
očito *evidently, obviously*
od *from* (with gen. case)
odakle *where from*
odgovarati *to suit, to correspond*
odijelo (n) *suit*
odlazati, otići *to go away*
odličan, -čna, -čno *excellent*
odlučivati, odlučiti *to decide*
odmah *immediately*
odmarati se, odmoriti se *to rest, to take a holiday*
odmor (m) *rest, holiday*
oglas (m) *advertisement*
ohrabrivati, ohrabriti *to encourage, to cheer up*
oko (n) *eye*
oko *around* (with gen. case)
okolina (f) *neighbourhood, vicinity*
okrenuti broj *to dial the number*
on *he*
ona *she*
onaj, ona, ono *that*
onda *then, next*
oni, one *they*

opasan, -sna, -sno *dangerous*
opet *again*
oprema (f) *equipment*
oprostite *excuse me*
ordinacija (f) *doctor's surgery*
ormar (m) *cupboard*
osim *except* (with gen. case)
osjećaj (m) *feeling, emotion*
osjećati se, osjetiti se *to feel*
osoba (f) *person*
ostajati, ostati *to stay, to remain*
ostavka (f) *resignation*
ostavljati, ostaviti *to leave*
otac (m) *father*
otkad *from when, since*
otok (m) *island*
otvarati, otvoriti *to open*
otvoren, -a, -o *open*
ovaj, ova, ovo *this*
ovdje *here*
ozdravljati, ozdraviti *to recover, to get better*
oženiti se *to get married* (of a man)
oženjen *married* (of a man)

padati *to fall*
pakovati, spakovati *to pack*
palačinka (f) *pancake*
papar (m) *pepper*
park (m) *park*
parkiralište (n) *car park*
parkirati *to park*
pasoš (m) *passport*
pauza (f) *pause, break*
pažljiv, -a, -o *careful*
pero (n) *pen*
pesimist (m) *pessimist*
piće (n) *drink*
pire od krumpira (n) *mashed potato*
pisati, napisati *to write*
pismo (n) *letter*
pitati *to ask*
piti, popiti *to drink*
pivo (n) *beer*
pješice *on foot*
pjevati *to sing*
plaćanje (n) *payment*
plaćati, platiti *to pay*
plan (m) *plan*
planina (f) *mountain*
plav, -a, -o *blue, blonde*
plaža (f) *beach*
ples (m) *dance, dancing*

plivanje (n) *swimming*
plivati *to swim*
ploška (f) *slice*
po *around, through* (with dat. case)
početak (m) *beginning*
počinjati, početi *to begin*
podatak (m) *information*
podne (n) *noon*
podnositi *to tolerate*
područje (n) *region*
pogled (m) *view*
pogrešan, -šna, -šno *wrong*
pokazivati, pokazati *to show*
poklon (m) *present*
polaziti, poći *to set off*
polica (f) *shelf*
policajac (m) *policeman*
policajska stanica (f) *police station*
poliklinika (f) *clinic*
polovica (f) *half*
polupansion (m) *half-board*
polje (n) *field*
Poljska *Poland*
ponašanje (n) *behaviour*
ponedjeljak (m) *Monday*
ponekad *sometimes*
ponovo *again*
ponuda (f) *offer*
pored *next to* (with gen. case)
poruka (f) *message*
posao (m) *work*
poseban, -bna, -bno *special, separate*
posjećivati, posjetiti *to visit*
poslije *after* (with gen. case)
poslovni sastanak (m) *business meeting*
postajati, postati *to become*
postojati *to exist*
pošta (f) *post office*
poštovan, -vna, -vno *respected*
poštovanje (n) *respect*
potpisivati, potpisati *to sign*
povratak (m) *return*
poziv (m) *invitation*
pozivati, pozvati *to invite*
pozivni broj (m) *code number* (telephone)
praktičan, -čna, -čno *practical*
prati, oprati *to wash*
pravac (m) *direction*
praviti, napraviti *to make*
pravo (n) *right*
predavati, predati *to hand over*
predgrađe (n) *suburb*
predjelo (n) *first course*

predlagati, predložiti *to suggest*
predstavnik (m) *representative*
pregovor (m) *negotiation*
prehlađen, -a, -o *cold* (to have a cold)
preko *across* (with gen. case)
prelaziti, preći *to cross*
prema *towards* (with dat. case)
preporučivati, preporučiti *to recommend*
prestati *to stop*
pretpostavljati *to suppose*
previše *too much*
pričati *to talk, to tell*
prihvaćati *to accept*
prijatelj (m) *friend*
prijateljica (f) *friend*
prijateljski, -a, -o *friendly*
prijavljati, prijaviti *to announce*
prije *before* (with gen. case)
prijedlog (m) *suggestion*
prijevoz (m) *transport*
prilaziti, prići *to approach, to go up to*
primorje (n) *coastal region, seashore*
priroda (f) *nature, countryside*
pristanište (n) *quay*
pritisnuti *to pinch together*
privatan, -tna, -tno *private*
privredan, -dna, -dno *economic*
prizemlje (n) *ground floor*
priznati *to confess, to admit*
probati *to try*
problem (m) *problem*
prodavač (m) *salesman*
prodavačica (f) *saleswoman*
prodavaonica (f) *shop*
prodavati, prodati *to sell*
proizvod (m) *product*
proizvođenje (n) *production*
proizvođenje pod licencijom *production under licence*
prostorija (f) *space*
prošlost (f) *past*
protiv *against* (with gen. case)
provoditi, provesti *to spend* (time)
prozor (m) *window*
prst (m) *finger*
prtljaga (f) *luggage*
prvi, -a, -o *first*
pržiti *to fry*
puni pansion (m) *full board*
put (m) *way, road, journey*
putnički, -a, -o *traveller's, travel*
putnik (m) *traveller*
putovati *to travel*

račun (m) *bill*
računovođa (m) *accountant*
raditi *to do, to work*
radni, -a, -o *working*
radnja (f) (E) *shop*
rado *gladly*
radovati se *to look forward to*
rakija (f) *brandy*
rame (n) *shoulder*
rano *early*
raspolaganje (n) *disposal*
raspoložen, -a, -o *disposed*
ravno *straight on*
razboljeti se *to fall ill*
razglednica (f) *postcard*
razgovarati *to chat*
razgovor *conversation*
razmatrati, razmotriti *to examine, to discuss*
razmišljati *to consider*
razumjeti *to understand*
razvijen, -a, -o *developed*
recepcija (f) *reception*
reci/recite *say, tell* (imperative of reći)
reći *to say, to tell*
reklamno odeljenje (n) (E) *advertising department*
restoran (m) *restaurant*
rezervirati *to reserve*
rezervisati (E) *to reserve*
riba (f) *fish*
ribarski, -a, -o *fishing*
riječ (f) *word*
rijeka (f) *river*
riva (f) *promenade* (by the sea)
roba (f) *goods*
roditelj (m) *parent*
rođen, -a, -o *born*
roštilj (m) *grill, barbecue*
rublje (n) *laundry*
ručak (m) *lunch*
ručati *to have lunch*
ručnik (m) *towel*
rujan (m) *September*
ruka (f) *arm, hand*
rukava (f) *sleeve*
rukomet (m) *handball*
rukometno igralište (n) *handball pitch*
Rusija *Russia*
ruski, -a, -o *Russian*
Rus (m) *Russian* (man)
Ruskinja (f) *Russian* (woman)

s *with* (with ins. case)
s *from, off* (with gen. case)
sada *now*
sadržaj (m) *facility, content*
sala (f) *hall*
sala za konferenciju *conference hall*
salata (f) *salad*
salon (m) *salon*
salon za masažu *massage salon*
sam, -a, -o *alone*
samac (m) *batchelor*
samo *only*
samoposluga (f) *self-service shop*
samostan (m) *monastery*
sandale (f pl) *sandals*
sanjati *to dream*
sapun (m) *soap*
saradnja (f) (E) *cooperation*
sastanak (m) *meeting*
sat (m) *clock, o'clock, class*
sav, sva, sve *all*
savjetovati *to advise*
saznati *to get to know, to find out*
sebe *oneself*
sekretarica (f) *secretary*
selo (n) *village*
sendvič (m) *sandwich*
sestra (f) *sister*
siguran, -rna, -rno *sure, certain*
sijati *to shine*
silaziti, sići *to get down, to get off*
sin (m) *son*
sir (m) *cheese*
sistem (m) *system*
siv, -a, -o *grey*
sjajan, -jna, -jno *wonderful, smashing*
sjećati se, sjetiti se *to remember*
sjediti *to be sitting*
sjesti *to sit down*
sjever (m) *north*
skijanje (n) *skiing*
skoro *almost*
skrenuti *to turn*
skup, -a, -o *expensive*
skupljati se *to gather together, to meet
  together*
slab, -a, -o *weak*
sladoled (m) *ice-cream*
slagati se *to agree*
slati, poslati *to send*
slatko (n) *sweet, dessert*
Slavonija (f) *Slavonia*
slijedeći, -a, -e *next, following*

slobodan, -dna, -dno *free*
Slovenija (f) *Slovenia*
slovenski, -a, -o *Slovenian*
Slovenac (m) *Slovenian man*
Slovenka (f) *Slovenian woman*
slučaj (m) *event, case*
slušati *to listen to*
službenik (m) *clerk, counter clerk*
služiti se, poslužiti se *to be served*
smatrati *to consider*
smještaj (m) *accommodation*
smješten, -a, -o *situated, sited*
snijeg (m) *snow*
soba (f) *room*
sok (m) *juice*
sol (f) *salt*
spajati *to link, to join*
spavaća soba (f) *bedroom*
spavati *to sleep*
spomenik (m) *monument*
sport (m) *sport*
sportsko-rekreacijski centar *sports
  centre*
sprat (m) (E) *floor, storey*
spreman, -mna, -mno *ready, prepared*
spremati *to prepare*
Srbija (f) *Serbia*
srpski, -a, -o *Serbian*
Srbin (m) *Serbian* (man)
Srpkinja (f) *Serbian* (woman)
srdačan, -čna, čno *cordial*
sredina (f) *middle*
središnji, -a, -e *middle, central*
sretan, -tna, -tno *happy*
srijeda (f) *Wednesday*
srpskohrvatski *Serbo-Croat*
stadion (m) *stadium*
stajati *to be standing*
stalno *continuously*
stan (m) *flat*
stanica (f) *stop*
stanovati *to live, to reside*
stanovnik (m) *inhabitant*
star, -a, -o *old*
stavljati, staviti *to put*
stizati, stići *to arrive*
stol (m) *table*
stolica (f) *chair*
stolić (m) *little table*
stolni tenis (m) *table-tennis*
stomak (m) *stomach*
stran, -a, -o *foreign*
strana (f) *side*

stric (m) *uncle*
strina (f) *aunt*
studirati *to study*
stvar (f) *thing*
stvarno *really*
subota (f) *Saturday*
suh, -a, -o *dry*
suknja (f) *skirt*
sumaglica (f) *mist*
sumrak (m) *dusk*
sunce (n) *sun*
sunčan, -a, -o *sunny*
sunčati se *to sunbathe*
suprug (m) *husband*
supruga (f) *wife*
surađivati *to cooperate*
sušiti se, osušiti se *to dry*
sutra *tomorrow*
suviše *too much*
svadba (f) *wedding*
svaki, -a, -o *each, every*
svakodnevni, -a, -o *everyday*
sveučilište (n) *university*
sviđati se *to like, to be pleasing*
svijetlosmeđi, -a, -e *light-brown*
svjež, -a, -e *fresh*
svoj, -a, -e *one's own*
svugdje *everywhere*

šalica (f) *cup*
šalter (m) *counter*
šampon (m) *shampoo*
šef (m) *boss*
šešir (m) *hat*
šifra (f) *box number*
škola (f) *school*
Škotska *Scotland*
šorc (m) *shorts*
što *what, that*
šuma (f) *forest*
šunka (f) *ham*

tada *then, at that time*
taj, ta, to *that*
tako *so*
također *also*
taksi (m) *taxi*
tanak, -nka, -nko *thin*
tamo *there*
tanjur (m) *plate*
taška (f) *bag, handbag*
tata (m) *Dad*

tava (f) *saucepan*
tečaj (m) *course*
teleći, -a, -e *veal*
telefon (m) *telephone*
telefonirati *to telephone*
telefonski broj (m) *telephone number*
telefonsko buđenje (n) *alarm call*
temperatura (f) *temperature*
tenis (m) *tennis*
tepih (m) *carpet*
terasa (f) *terrace*
teren (m) *pitch, court*
tetak (m) *uncle*
tetka (f) *aunt*
težak, -ška, -ško *difficult, heavy*
ti *you* (singular)
tih, -a, -o *quiet*
tipičan, -čna, -čno *typical*
tisuća (f) *thousand*
tjedan (m) *week*
tko *who*
točan, -čna, -čno *exact, precise*
tokom *during* (with gen. case)
topao, -pla, -plo *warm*
trajati *to last*
tramvaj (m) *tram*
transfer (m) *transfer*
transportno odeljenje (n) (E) *transport
   department*
trava (f) *grass*
travanj (m) *April*
tražiti *to look for*
trebati *to need, to require*
treći, -a, -e *third*
trend (m) *trend*
trenutak (m) *moment*
trg (m) *square*
tri *three*
trim kabinet (m) *exercise room*
tržište (n) *market*
turist (m) *tourist*
turistički, -a, -o *tourist*
turistkinja (f) *tourist*
tuš (m) *shower*
tuširati se, istuširati se *to shower, to
   have a shower*
tužan, -žna, -žno *sad*
tvoj, -a, -e *your* (singular)

u *in* (with dat. case)
u *to* (with acc. case)

u redu *ok, alright*
učenik (m) *pupil*
učitelj (m) *teacher*
učiteljica (f) *teacher*
učiti, naučiti *to learn*
udati se *to get married* (of female)
udoban, -bna, -bno *comfortable*
ugao (m) *corner*
ugovor (m) *contract*
uho (n) *ear*
ujak (m) *uncle*
ujna (f) *aunt*
ujutro *in the morning*
ukratko *in short, briefly*
ukus (m) *taste*
ulaz (m) *entry*
ulaziti, ući *to go in, to enter*
ulica (f) *street*
ulje (n) *oil*
ulje za sunčanje *suntain oil*
umoran, -rna, -rno *tired*
uopće ne *not at all*
upoznati *to introduce*
upravo *just now*
ured (m) *office*
uskoro *soon*
uslov (m) (E) *condition*
usluživati *to serve*
usna (f) *lip*
uspeh (m) (E) *success*
usta (n pl) *mouth*
ustajati, ustati *to get up*
uveček *in the evening*
uvijek *always*
uvjet (m) *condition*
uvjetovati *to cause, to bring about*
uvoz (m) *import*
uzbuđen, -a, -o *excited*
uzimati, uzeti *to take*

valuta (f) *currency*
vaš, -a, -e *your* (plural)
važan, -žna, -žno *important*
WC (m) (pronounced vetse) *toilet*
večer (m) (f) *evening*
večera (f) *dinner*
večerati *to have dinner*
već *already*
vedar, -dra, -dro *clear, bright*
velik, -a, -o *large, big*
veoma *very*

veseo, -sla, -slo *jolly, merry*
vi *you* (plural)
vidjeti *to see*
vilica (f) *fork*
vino (n) *wine*
visok, -a, -o *tall, high*
više *more*
vjenčati se *to get married*
vjerojatno *probably, likely*
vjetar (m) *wind*
vjetar puše *the wind is blowing*
vlak (m) *train*
vlastit, -a, -o *own*
voda (f) *water*
voditi *to lead*
voditi razgovor *to have a conversation*
vojnik (m) *soldier*
voljeti *to like, to love*
voziti *to drive*
vozni, -a, -o *train*
vraćati se, vratiti se *to return*
vrat (m) *neck*
vrata (n pl) *door*
vrijeme (n) *time, weather*
vrlo *very*
vrsta (f) *sort, kind*
vrt (m) *garden*
vruć, -a, -e *hot*

za *for* (with acc. case)
za *behind* (with ins. case)
zaboravljati, zaboraviti *to forget*
zadovoljan, -ljna, -ljno *pleased, satisfied*
zadržavanje (n) *keeping*
zagrebački odrezak (m) *Zagreb schnitzel*
zagrijati *to heat, to warm*
zaista *really*
zaključak (m) *conclusion*
zaključavati, zaključati *to lock*
zalaziti, zaći *to go behind*
zaljev (m) *bay*
zamišljati, zamisliti *to imagine*
zamrzivač (m) *freezer*
zapad (m) *west*
zapisivati, zapisati *to note down*
zaprositi *to ask for girl's hand in marriage*
zašto *why*
zatim *then, next*
zato što *because*
zatvoren, -a, -o *closed*

zaustavljati se, zaustaviti se *to stop*
zauzet, -a, -o *busy, engaged*
zavisi od *depends on* (with gen. case)
zavjesa (f) *curtain*
završavati, završiti *to finish*
zdravo *hello, goodbye* (colloquial)
zelen, -a, -o *green*
zgrada (f) *building*
zima (f) *winter*
zimi *in winter*
značiti *to mean*
znanje (n) *knowledge*
znati *to know*
zoološki vrt (m) *zoo*
zubar (m) *dentist*
zubna pasta (f) *toothpaste*
zvati, nazvati *to call*
zvati se *to be called*

žao mi je *I am sorry*
želja (f) *desire, wish*
žedan, -dna, -dno *thirsty*
željeti *to want, to desire*
žena (f) *woman, wife*
živjeti *to live*
život (m) *life*
žlica (f) *spoon*
žut, -a, -o *yellow*

— GRAMMATICAL INDEX —

The numbers below refer to units in the book.

BULGARIAN (mid-1993)

MICHAEL HOLMAN AND MIRA KOVATCHEVA

A complete course in spoken and written Bulgarian, *Teach Yourself Bulgarian* has twenty units containing dialogues, culture notes, grammar and exercises. The Bulgarian alphabet (cyrillic) is explained clearly as is its pronunciation. The book includes a Bulgarian–English vocabulary.

Based on the Council of Europe's Threshold guidelines on language learning, this course will enable you to deal confidently with a whole range of situations using Bulgarian. The course is also available as a pack including a 90-minute cassette specially recorded by native speakers.

HUNGARIAN

ZSUZSA PONTIFEX

If you have never learnt Hungarian before, or if your Hungarian needs brushing up, *Teach Yourself Hungarian* is for you. It is a 360-page book – also available with a 94-minute cassette. Zsuzsa Pontifex has created a practical course that is both fun and easy to work through. She explains everything clearly and gives you opportunities to practise what you learn.

There is a pronunciation guide and twenty-one graded units in two parts. The first part, of five units, gives you vocabulary and grammar to 'survive' in straightforward situations on a short holiday or business trip in Hungary. Part two builds on those language skills and teaches you what you need to deal with most everyday situations.

ROMANIAN

DENNIS DELETANT AND YVONNE ALEXANDRESCU

Based on the Council of Europe's Threshold guidelines on language learning, the course contains twenty carefully graded units of dialogues, notes on Romania and the Romanians, grammar and exercises. There is a step-by-step guide to Romanian pronunciation, an extensive grammar summary and Romanian–English and English–Romanian vocabularies.

The 256-page book is also available with a 74-minute cassette – specially recorded by native speakers. By the end of the course you'll be able to cope with a whole range of situations and participate fully and confidently in Romanian life.

RUSSIAN

DAPHNE M WEST

A holiday in the CIS or a business trip, an interest in world affairs or in the riches of Russian culture and history – there are many reasons for learning Russian, a language spoken by more than 285 million people (for about half of whom it is the mother tongue). Based on the Council of Europe's Threshold guidelines on language learning, the course is designed to teach specific uses of language and these are related to situations which visitors to Russian-speaking countries may encounter.

Daphne West clearly explains the cyrillic alphabet in both its printed and handwritten forms. The book contains dialogues, cultures notes, grammar and many exercises to help the learning process.